The Explore

The Explorer's Mindset

Lessons in Leadership in Applied Geoscience and the Energy Industry

Jonathan Rotzien

Interviews with geoscience and business leaders who explore new ways to solve energy challenges.

– Business – Science – Research – Technology – Academia – Government –

Learn what it takes to explore and succeed in the applied geosciences and energy industry. This book is a collection of interviews from leaders in the fields of business, technology, research and academia. Learn valuable lessons and perspectives from those who have blazed trails and those who are currently advancing energy markets. Geoscientists, engineers, managers, CEOs – from private to public companies – and from advisor to student, this book highlights what it takes to lead in the applied geosciences and energy industry.

- Interviews with leaders in geoscience who are shaping energy markets – past, present and future;
- Leadership principles applied in the broader energy industry can also be used in any profession;
- Perspectives on professional growth in the broad scope of the earth sciences;
- Diverse interviews with leaders who have worked on all oil-producing continents.

In the last four years, the broad field of the geosciences and the energy industry have undergone massive changes. Record high oil and gas output have been rivaled by growth in alternative forms of energy to meet global demand. The COVID-19 pandemic reduced oil and gas demand by less than 10% in a roughly $100T global economy, illustrating that oil and gas underpins the global economy and remains a necessity for a growing population. The pandemic also accelerated addition of alternative forms of energy in record time, with huge amounts of capital put to work in solar, wind, nuclear and the electrification of the world – from vehicles, to homes and other areas seeking to obviate classic energy sources. Whereas most students with a degree in earth science and an interest in drilling wells joined oil and gas companies three years ago, now they are joining mining companies to find elements required for batteries. Newly minted bachelors and masters in geoscience are also joining business units involved in carbon capture usage and sequestration (CCUS), geothermal exploration and production and in the decommissioning of oil and gas platforms. This fascinating period of the last four years (2019-2023) is documented in interviews with over 30 leaders in geoscience and the greater energy industry.

Acknowledgments

This volume is dedicated to past generations of leaders who inspired us with their vision, integrity and dedication to discovering new resources for civilization. Thank you to Susan Morrice and Charles Sternbach for their one-of-a-kind inspiration and comments on earlier versions of this work.

The Explorer's Mindset

Table of Contents

Preface..6
- I. Introduction to Key Principles in Leadership....................10
- II. The Pioneering Spirit..13
    - a. Eric and Sherry Muller...15
    - b. Lisa Goggin..27
    - c. Roger M. Slatt..38
    - d. Diane Woodruff...57
- III. The Explorer's Mindset..65
    - a. Cindy Yeilding...67
    - b. Richard Sears..79
    - c. Scott Tinker and Richard J. Chuchla..................113
    - d. Kurt W. Rudolph..142
- IV. Leadership in Applied Research...................................158
    - a. Sebastian Cardona...159
    - b. Anshuman Pradhan...166
    - c. Sumit Verma and Shuvajit Bhattacharya..............173
- V. Power of the Team..186
    - a. The Drifters Research Group.............................187
    - b. Paul Mann..206
    - c. F. Javier Hernández-Molina................................223
- VI. Entrepreneurship..233
    - a. Derek Adams..235
    - b. Per Avseth..248
    - c. Tom Fett..262
- VII. Business Success 286
    - a. Cheryl Collarini, Peter Lellis and Billy Quinn........288
    - b. Lori Fremin...301
    - c. Elijah White, Jr..313
    - d. Alex Cranberg...342
    - e. Benjamin Kirkland..349
    - f. Ryan Weber..356
- VIII. Closing Conversations..368

Preface

Why is leadership important in the geosciences, and in the broader energy industry? The world needs leaders. Even geoscientists who eventually graduate from a fully depreciated Carhartt outfit in the field to suit and tie in the skyscraper in downtown Houston. We still wear our field clothes, proudly, but our expertise is required to inform business decisions typically in office settings. On where to drill. How to drill. What acreage to buy. Where to develop the offshore wind farm. How many wells are needed to confirm a rare earth element mine final investment decision. The list goes on. Without geoscience leaders who are technically excellent in exploration and able to communicate information that makes sense to the needs of society, humanity will be at a loss on how to properly and efficiently find and use Earth's natural resources.

One of the main challenges today is how humans will find, develop and consume energy resources over the next year, 10 years, 100 years and beyond. Coal, oil and gas production are near all-time highs, yet investment in solar, wind, nuclear and other alternative forms of energy is increasing. Net-zero carbon goals are in place, yet every year without additional investment in alternative energy solutions makes those goals appear unrealistic and unattainable. Climate models can demonstrate climate change, but even if the human energy consumption landscape flips to only solar, wind and nuclear, can Earth avoid climate change that has been occurring since the end of the last glaciation? These are complex and difficult challenges and questions to answer, but the good thing is that society has good people working on those challenges. This book interviews some of those people that are making a positive difference.

While the technical content of the interviews covers many topics – from exploration leadership, to investment principles, to reservoir characterization, to deepwater boundary currents and seismic attributes – there are lessons in exploration and leadership described in this book that will withstand the test of time. These are timeless lessons that can be applied in the fields of geoscience and the energy industry no matter if it is 2023 or 3023.

This book captures the rapid changes taking place in the energy industry, academia and research at an important time in history when many energy resources are being evaluated on their merits and limitations to society. This book offers perspectives on technology, science, business, markets and entrepreneurship from over 30 of the world's estimable leaders: those who will shape the energy industry of the future, as well as those who came before, and those who are in the current midst of grappling with new and emerging science and technologies. It is the aim of this book to provide a broad spectrum of perspectives of how explorers think differently in the energy industry, with special attention to the oil and gas industry and its people.

Through the interviews, this book features the following principal areas: introduction to key leadership principles, how pioneers shape the energy landscape, the explorer's mindset, power of the team, excellence in applied research, entrepreneurship and how successful businesspeople are working assiduously on energy and geoscience challenges.

This book is intended to describe and explore leadership to serve these primary audiences: first and foremost university students who want to learn more about career paths and their plusses and pitfalls; second, mid-career scientists and business people who seek to take their careers to a whole new level, and; third, people at or near retirement ("onto new beginnings") who like to know where we've been as a community, and where the next generation is taking us.

While this book is primarily intended for students, recent graduates and early career geoscientists, all of the interviews in this book offer useful perspectives to inspire achievement and problem-solving. I wish I had a book like this when attending college and university. Working in the energy industry requires preparation. The corporate world is different, requires different skills, a different mindset, and because of that, top graduates are met with varying levels of success. When I was in graduate school, occasionally we received books in our student mailboxes at GeoCorner (Braun Hall). One was a book by Raymond Plank titled "A Small Difference" that described his success and life story in building Apache. The biography covered his pre-, early and mid-career. *The Explorer's Mindset: Lessons in Leadership in Applied Geoscience and Energy Industry* attempts to highlight a great range and diversity of leaders in the geosciences who continue to rise, in part because they have had great adversity in their careers – and learned how to turn those tough times into learning experiences and steppingstones along their path to success.

There are lots of books on leadership, but exceedingly few in the sciences and even less in the geosciences (this may be the first?). Why must science and leadership be kept apart? Further, many of the existing books are written by one or a few experts on the subject. I am not an expert in the field of leadership, but have always been enthused about leadership ever since I joined Boy Scouts as a teenager. The collective lessons on leadership described in these interviews with scientific and industry leaders – if taken to heart – can promote even the youngest leader far ahead in their career. These interviews are diverse, full of wisdom, and define the essence of many challenges when it comes to accomplishing tasks and achieving what seem to be insurmountable goals – which is where leadership and faith often come in. Being able to define what success looks like and striving towards it, often with a team.

Collectively, this book strives to show the diverse leadership traits that successful geoscientists and energy industry professionals exude. As Cheryl Collarini says, "It takes more than a village…to reach the finish line. It takes experts who understand costs and risks of drilling, completion, flow assurance, platforms, facilities, pipelines (or maybe FPSOs), oil and gas markets, contracts, politics, legalities, and more." Well, it takes at least a "village" of traits to explain how and why explorers succeed as they do in the energy industry.

We should talk about teams briefly. "Team" can be defined by a wide spectrum of size, or numbers. Some teams described in this book are just a few people; others include the largest universities and energy companies in the world. No matter the size, these teams are *winning teams*. Winning at starting a new company where none existed; winning at deploying teams to various assets to assess stratigraphic heterogeneity; winning at producing first oil from a discovery half a world away from company headquarters; winning at accurately characterizing the landscape of what energy means to humanity.

Geoscientists and energy industry professionals are explorers at heart. I hope you enjoy this book, learn new aspects on leadership in the geosciences and apply these successful concepts to improve the effectiveness of your leadership. I've certainly received immense joy from getting to know these individuals and their fascinating life experiences. It is an honor to call them friends, colleagues, mentors, teammates and associates.

Yours truly,
Jonathan Rotzien, Ph.D.

Introduction to Key Principles in Leadership

To frame leadership in the geosciences, you need to understand the current challenges and how technology, business savvy and personal achievement are being used to overcome those challenges. This first part is dedicated to forward thinking in the geosciences from academia, research, industry and government.

The importance of leadership is multifaceted, and herein are some of the key principles established in the interviews in this book. These are 22 pillars of geoscience leadership that can be applied more broadly to most professions in energy resource exploration and production:

1. There is no substitute for daily preparation. You need to prepare for success mentally, physically, emotionally and spiritually.
2. You need to understand where you want to end up before you start a project. Know how to develop goals, and be able to assess progress.
3. Be technically excellent. Proper geological characterization is required to inform good investment decisions. Know your skills and be aware of deficiencies.
4. Building a team gives you the opportunity to surround yourself with individuals who complement the project, which makes for a stronger team. Empower your teammates.
5. Some leadership is best described as a servant leadership.
6. One of the best ways to lead by example is by knowing how to do everything in a business to make it work. Be willing and able to do more than what you ask of your team members.
7. Identify unknown opportunities "off the beaten path" and go for them. You may find the next big discovery. Create a safe space to fail.
8. Have the ability to go boldly into exploration plays knowing that the tools might not be the most accurate for measuring the subsurface.
9. Salesmanship, or the ability to sell a prospect or work proposal – or sell the idea or new technology – is an important skill to master.

10. Work hard to build a foundation and a compendium of results that you may draw upon to build a positive track record for consistency.
11. Be nice. Work to build a diverse community of talented individuals.
12. Be a good steward to your environment and your work environment. Be supportive of your colleagues.
13. Focus on the right conversation. Be able to identify the correct problem, ask the right questions. Do not be distracted by noise, and stay tied to the facts and fundamentals.
14. Be curious about the unknown or things that appear not to fit the paradigm. This will help you continue to grow.
15. Having a close-knit community and strength in numbers are important.
16. Exercise discipline and patience; know which business cycle you're in. Be able to be decisive when required. Exercise good timing.
17. Draw on collective knowledge to determine the best avenue for success, for example, to determine resource in place.
18. Appreciate the greater business and stakeholders involved in your results or work. Know the team's goals.
19. Do due diligence to make sure your research is new and makes at least incremental improvements in the understanding of Earth. Keep multiple working hypotheses.
20. Don't be afraid of trying to balance life, extracurriculars and hobbies.
21. Scale matters. Know how to apply scale to the equation in business.
22. Be able to change your mind and be flexible with geological models when new evidence presents itself. Be aware of dogma and bias.

This book is based on interviews with leaders in the broad field of the geosciences and the energy industry – more specifically in the focus area of the oil and gas industry. Throughout the book, there are several themes that kept on coming up in conversations. At first, I didn't recognize the true significance. With time, I began to appreciate that these replies and aspects of the conversation were principles of leadership. There is a lot of wisdom captured in the interviews. There are principles to be learned, and methods and workflows and ways to be followed.

There are many key learnings outlined above, distilled into 22 principles of leadership in the geosciences. These are probably quite common in other disciplines' leadership values. I haven't gone so far as to check and research these principles' distribution in other leadership volumes. This is a first-of-its-kind book. Perhaps the second edition of this book will evaluate these principles more critically.

There are also six higher order, longer wavelength themes that naturally arose from the conversations included in this book: i) the pioneering spirit; ii) the explorer's mindset; iii) excellence in applied research; iv) power of the team; v) entrepreneurship and; vi) business success. While principles cross from theme to theme, and the conversations are not mutually exclusive to one theme or another, they highlight several principles associated with that theme.

The Pioneering Spirit

Geoscientists are explorers. They go where others haven't. They think creatively to solve problems. The first principle of leadership is to be able to go where others have not gone to make a discovery, to pave new ground, to forge new pathways for others. The four interviews in this section focus on those pioneers whose capabilities and charisma inspired a generation.

Eric and Sherry Muller describe a prominent 20th century geologist, Siemon W. Muller, who left a rich legacy to his students, research and applied geological engineering achievements with the US government. Pioneering leadership principles described in this interview originating from the mid-1900s are more relevant than ever in the current energy environment.

Dr. Lisa R. Goggin shows how to lead from the perspective of a geoscientist at a supermajor energy company. Lisa has led in many capacities, from building teams, to deploying new technology, to sharing her knowledge with the next generation of explorers in in-house training courses. Lisa's original research led to multiple patented technological breakthroughs.

Professor Roger M. Slatt was one of the most prolific and dynamic professors of modern geology. Roger's work aided in the characterization of both conventional deepwater and onshore tight rock and source rock plays with the Shale Revolution of the early 21st century. Slatt shares his insights on how to build a successful team and how to make new discoveries in known basins.

Dr. Diane Woodruff currently explores for oil and gas in the Gulf of Mexico. Her drilling success and effective team leadership have been transformational. Further, she co-led the development of the Houston Explorers Club, a new ~50-member organization that inspires and nurtures wildcatters.

These inspirational leaders harnessed powerful thinking as a way to overcome challenges – from understanding permafrost to help the U.S. and Allied Powers end WWII, to examining complex outcrops around the world to assist oil and gas production in the Gulf of Mexico's deepwater frontier, to building process-based models to better understand reservoir distribution in petroleum reservoirs and plan development drilling campaigns, to creating and cultivating a community of explorers with whom to share exploration success and failures to increase long-term drilling success in the energy industry. These leaders demonstrate the importance of creating new avenues where there was no path before.

Eric and Sherry Muller (September 2019)

"Our existence as advanced society depends on identifying, measuring and judiciously harvesting resources created by the geologic sequence of events. As a geologist, you need to be able to take all the proper measurements, interpret them carefully and use them properly." – Eric Muller

Eric and Sherry Muller sailing aboard their boat Dolphin in Alaska.

"Are you our graduate student?" asked Sherry. Eric looked at me intently. "Well, yes I am," I replied. That introduction led to a great friendship. I first met Eric and Sherry Muller at the Earth Sciences homecoming reception in October of 2011, about midway through my PhD program. We had a great conversation and found out we had many things in common. We exchanged stories for hours until the reception ended that night. Since then, we have kept in touch, mostly through the shared connection of geology, the energy industry and our alma mater. Sherry is a Stanford graduate, and Eric's father, Siemon, was one of the most beloved professors of geology to ever work at Stanford. His achievements were numerous and profound, and Professor Siemon "Si" Muller's legacy continues to be a foundation of the School of Earth. You can learn more about his life and contributions not only to sedimentary geology, but also to the engineering concepts pertaining to *permafrost*, the word Professor Muller coined in the 1940s and explained in the book "Frozen in Time: Permafrost and Engineering Problems" a first-of-its-kind book based on work he provided as a civilian for the Alaskan Division of the U.S. Air Transport Command under the command of Brigadier General Gaffney. Professor Muller had one of the most interesting life stories and careers in geoscience, summarized in one key obituary from the Stanford Department of Geological Sciences (the Memorial article written by Benjamin M. Page, Norman J. Silberling and A. Myra Keen in the Geological Society of America archives). To honor his father's contributions to the university and the global earth sciences community, Eric created an endowed fellowship bearing his father's name that is awarded to a PhD student studying sedimentary geology. To this day, I am grateful for holding this fellowship for my final two years of graduate school – for its funding it provided for me to do my research and complete my degree – but most of all for the opportunity to get to know these most wonderful people – Eric and Sherry Muller. They are two of the most fun, adventurous, indefatigable, intrepid and joyous people I have ever met. They are well known by the earth sciences community for their generosity, friendly nature and passion for educating future leaders in the geosciences, especially in energy resource exploration and development.

I interviewed Eric on two occasions in September and October 2019. Read Eric's interview below.

Jon Rotzien (JR): Eric and Sherry, I'm so thankful you had the time to visit today and share some of Professor Si Muller's achievements. It's important for my generation to understand the impact that earlier generations of stratigraphers had on our science and the industry applications. One of the main ways he is remembered today at Stanford is through the graduate fellowship that carries his name. What is the fellowship about, and why did you start the fellowship in his name? Could you share a bit on this?

Eric Muller (EM): We wanted to create an emphasis on basic scientific studies to advance historical geoscience topics, including student-led research pertaining to the flora, fauna, and overall depositional history of Earth that has led to the creation of natural resources.

One of the reasons we set up the Siemon W. Muller Graduate Fellowship was to have a legacy vehicle to honor my father and establish a trail to legends of the Stanford School of Earth. Some of these geologists include J. P. Smith, John Casper Branner, Eliot Blackwelder, Bailey Willis – these were the old timers and compatriots of my father. J. P. Smith was my father's mentor, and

Dad actually filled his job upon J. P.'s retirement. When I was a young boy, I remember conversations Dad had with Willis and Blackwelder on campus and in Palo Alto.

JR: The fellowship goes to a student studying sedimentary geology, with a focus toward applied aspects of geoscience. Why is the "applied" aspect of the geosciences so critical today?

EM: Our existence as advanced society depends on identifying, measuring and judiciously harvesting resources created by the geologic sequence of events. As a geologist, you need to be able to take all the proper measurements, interpret them carefully and use them properly.

JR: Si was particularly fortunate to arrive on U.S. soil shortly after the Russian Revolution began. Can you tell that story? As well as some of the challenges he faced during his research expeditions in the 1930s and 1950s in Europe following his duties with the U.S. Geological Survey?

EM: I refer you to the preface I wrote in *Frozen in Time*.

Quoted from Frozen in Time... "I would like to expand on some items in the biographical sketch of quite a remarkable man and his adventurous life. It started in Eastern Siberia, then an escape to China, passage from Shanghai to the United States by way of the steamship, "Golden State" of the Pacific Mail Steamship Line in the early 1920s. He followed his brother, Bill, to the University of Oregon where he entered as a sophomore based on an incredibly strong transcript from his high school in Vladivostok.

While doing field studies for his Stanford Doctoral Dissertation in 1928, he discovered a fossilized *Ichthyosaurus* in Central Nevada. This site subsequently yielded more than 40 of the largest remains of this creature ever found in North America, some over 50 feet in length.

His special interest in stratigraphy and paleontology led him to investigate the connections between North American geological formations with those of Europe. During a sabbatical in Germany in 1937-38, he started this research, but Hitler sent him home before he could complete it. During 1956-57, he returned to continue his research, but this time he was interrupted by the Hungarian Revolution and the call by the U.S. State Department to interview and help place academic refugees.

During World War Two, Dad served his country with the United States Geological Survey. First, he identified the location of strategic resources, and second, he completed a tour of duty as a Civilian Scientific Consultant assigned to the Alaska Division of the U.S. Air Transport Command under the command of Brigadier General Gaffney. Dad greatly appreciated the full support of the General and his staff during his work in Alaska.

JR: Most of Professor Muller's work evaluated, for the first time in American history, the paleontology of Mesozoic stratigraphic successions in the western US. What was it like to do fieldwork at this time? I have a picture of Si standing in knee-high snake boots looking over Walker Lake, Nevada (pg. 16). You almost never see those today. Field work at that time seemed to be much riskier.

EM: Yes, those historical pictures show the expeditions clad in ancient attire, in front of the field vehicles of the time. That picture specifically was from a field camp as a graduate student at Stanford in 1928. I know Dad went out and did a lot of legwork on his own establishing field camps throughout his career, working farther north of Walker Lake into Gabbs and Austin and other places. That's how he found the *Ichthyosaur* that no one ever knew existed in that part of the world, tramping through many miles in the backcountry.

Until the 1940s when aerial photographs started to emerge, the mapping had to be done manually using plane table, Brunton compasses (to do the triangulation), and extensive hand-written notes. There was no refrigeration, so Dad used a cold box to store items that needed to be kept from spoiling. Of course, they ate a lot of canned food since it would last. They would remain in the backcountry sometimes for a month to complete the geologic mapping and surveys.

JR: Sounds similar to the mapping techniques employed by Steineke's team in the discovery of Ghawar, told by Wallace Stegner in the book *Discovery!*

EM: Yes, and the boots you mention were hobnailed and as you say knee high as protection from rattlesnake strikes that could be lethal. One time he had student with him who had never seen a snake before. The student was mapping along and found a pit full of rattlesnakes, a hole in ground with a huge colony! Sights like these would make you wary of sleeping close to the ground, and the early mappers slept on cots. You might have to check your bunk for rattlers, and then in the morning check your boots. I remember being out in Nevada in 1943, where Dad was performing a mineral survey to confirm some of the early mapping. One of the key lessons he taught me was to always look before putting your hand on a rock as there might be a rattlesnake lurking.

JR: Sage advice, still. We have "safety moments" like those today while doing fieldwork around the world.

EM: You must keep in mind that prior to the middle of the 20th century, geology was mostly a mostly male profession. Dad was instrumental in getting the first women registered on summer geology camp in 1950s. As an interesting fact, when we were setting up the graduate fellowship at Stanford, we met with Judy Smith, who was one of the first women to participate in Stanford's field camps.

"Look at the whole picture, but think to scale and don't shortcut the details." – Eric Muller

JR: Si's academic work was briefly interrupted with the outbreak of WWII. He was soon enlisted by the US government to investigate the scientific and engineering problems in battle zones that have permanently frozen ground. These were really serious situations for the U.S. Armed Forces at the time. But in a few years Professor Muller's research and analysis produced solutions to most of the problems and were published in a book that became the manual for construction in a permafrost environment. Can you provide some insight into this particular achievement?

EM: The primary objective by the U.S. Military was to begin work in Alaska for a variety of reasons. The U.S. needed a road through Alaska to defend against foreign attacks on the Aleutians. There was no frame of reference in US-based scientific and engineering literature for how this could be done on permanently frozen ground. However, Russian scientists had done a lot of work in this area of frozen ground. My father sat down with the Russian literature, translated it and put down the necessary information for the war department to use. His first book, "Permafrost," published in 1943, became somewhat of a manual for construction of the Alcan the U.S. Army Corps of Engineers, and provided information critical to the Highway. This was instrumental in building the Alcan Highway. By finishing the highway, the U.S. had a more direct route to get supplies out to the Aleutians – now the U.S. wasn't limited to using only barges to ship supplies.

JR: That is a huge effort to translate Russian scientific literature. Now can you describe some of his next work assignment in Canada, too?

EM: I remember that Dad was called to duty in Edmonton, Alberta, where he assisted air transport command under the direction of Gaffney. My Dad, though he was a civilian, reported directly to the general – they were good friends. Dad's rank was probably closer to the equivalent of Major all else being equal. Set yourself in Edmonton at that time. You can imagine as they laid down the steel planks to form runways over the permafrost, with the hot midday sun shining on steel, the differential warming it caused. It was quite a challenge to maintain a stable runway in those conditions. To acknowledge Dad's contributions, the War Department awarded him the Medal of Freedom.

JR: That is amazing! What an incredible honor.

EM: The most important item in there is the book *Frozen in Time*, later published in 2008. Dad wanted to publish the book in the 1960s to update all materials previously sent to the military. An earlier version was actually published as a civilian book by the University of Michigan in Ann Arbor in 1947. That early version essentially turned out to be textbook on the topic of permafrost until Dad updated it in the 60s, which would turn out to be this book *Frozen in Time*. However, because this was the middle of the Cold War, the U.S. State Department wouldn't let him publish it. I recall it being a huge disappointment to Dad.

Siemon W. Muller surveying Walker Lake in Nevada as a PhD student at Stanford University (c. 1928). Photo courtesy of Eric and Sherry Muller.

JR: So, the information was kept under wraps for over 40 years?

EM: That's right. Fast forward to the 9th International Permafrost Meeting in 2008 in Fairbanks. How that manuscript was found since being buried in the 1960s is a story in itself.

The manuscript had been lost among a lot of paperwork that I had to look at and sort after Dad passed away. I recalled Dad had only one graduate student in permafrost who later became a professor at Arizona State in Tempe – his name was Troy Pewe. I knew he would be the only one who could use these boxes of research papers and manuscripts. When Pewe passed away, a fellow at University of Ottawa somehow became the custodian of these records. This professor at Ottawa was Hugh French. He had a librarian brain – never forgot anything because he'd mentally catalogued all of it. When he came across the manuscript he recognized the wording and writing but didn't find any identification on it. He remembered reading a review of a similar manuscript some years ago, and that reviewer, Pewe, had also passed away. However, after further investigation he was able to match the review with Dad's manuscript. Now how were they going to track down the origin and author of this manuscript!

JR: This manuscript has a certain amount of luck on its side.

EM: French eventually sent it to Frederick "Fritz" Nelson at the University of Delaware (would you believe they had a huge Arctic program in their geophysics department at the time), and Fritz said, "This is a major contribution to our knowledge of permafrost and we have to publish it." Well, they gave it the name, "Frozen in Time," and were about to publish it, but they still needed to know who "owned" this manuscript. So, for the next year they searched for Professor Muller's son. They contacted the Stanford Geology Department but whoever they talked to had never heard of me. As it happened we were just then setting up the Si Muller Fellowship. Finally, the American Society of Civil Engineers (ASCE) search party led by Bucky Tart found me. "Boy, have we been looking for you!" he exclaimed. I told him I remembered the manuscript, and how disappointed Dad had been. Bucky explained the situation and asked, "What do you want for it?" I said, "The only thing that matters is to get it published. That would close the whole circle, and would be the best honor Dad could have."

JR: Amazing Bucky finally found you. Kudos to his perseverance.

EM: Bucky could hardly wait to meet us, and it turned out he lived about 40 miles away from us. He asked that I write a preface for the book, then he came to the house, we signed the papers, and it was off to the printer. Delivery would be just in time for the conference in Fairbanks.

I'd like to acknowledge and thank the American Society of Civil Engineers and in particular, Bucky Tart, Western Representative for ASCE, as well as Dr. Hugh French, Dr. Fritz Nelson and Dr. Jerry Brown of the International Permafrost Group, for the work they all did to bring this manuscript to publication.

We were then on our boat in Sitka. So, we flew to Fairbanks and arrived just as the UPS boxes of the books were delivered to the conference building. I got the first copy, and all the key people responsible for putting it together got their own copy and signed mine. Fritz then announced, "This book would have saved 25 years of similar research had it been available when originally written."

JR: What a compliment. That puts our research today into perspective.

EM: Later in the evening one of the Russian scientists took me into a quiet corner and said, "Let me tell you why it didn't get published," he began. "When Stalin found out about the first book in the 1940s, he was furious about sharing critical scientific information." Dad had kept an extensive bibliography of all the literature he had translated into English directly from the Russian texts. The scientist continued, "The university department was immediately shut down and those scientists were sent off to the Gulag."

JR: So that is the rest of the story. Wow. Indeed, that is so fortunate the manuscript was finally released to the public.

I'm going to switch gears back to Stanford...one of the weekly events Professor Muller started. As you know graduate school is a very busy time with work around the clock. I understand Si encouraged collaboration throughout the Geology Department.One of his ideas was the Friday Beer Hour at GeoCorner, the southwest corner of the Quad. In fact, I remember during grad school that some young PhD

The Explorer's Mindset

students were appointed "Beer Czars" and were responsible for the beer delivery every Friday.

As you mention in your preface in "Frozen in Time" Professor Muller really enjoyed teaching his students – in the classroom and in the field – and this was one more way he encouraged and nurtured the Stanford Geology community to share ideas and collaborate. He wanted to encourage students to get out of their respective labs and to talk and discuss their area of science with others. The aim was more collaboration and cross pollination of scientific thinking. And this event continues today.

EM: Dad liked to meet with the graduate students he was mentoring. He enjoyed beer and encouraged Beer Friday for all the grad students. He would always join the group to exchange ideas and share experiences with the graduate community. If you overcome a problem, and if you can share that process with your colleagues, everyone benefits. Those afternoon get-togethers brought Beer Friday into prominence. When I was a boy I remember he really enjoyed meeting with the students to discuss their research and tackle new scientific challenges.

JR: Si had an important cadre of brilliant scientists with whom he worked – great geologists like J. P. Smith, Max Steineke and Bailey Willis, among others. And after the war there was "Lev" Levorsen who no doubt inspired many oil finders in later years. What do you think Si's message would be today for oil and gas explorers?

EM: I think that is best summed up in a letter to the Dean Pam Matson about ten years ago (*on next page*), from a former student of Si's who went on to become a very successful geologist and businessman, George McCleod '48.

I think Dad's message would be to look at the whole picture, but *think to scale* and don't shortcut the details.

JR: Thank you so much Eric and Sherry for sharing this fascinating story about one of Stanford Geology's most colorful professors.

The Explorer's Mindset

December 15, 2010

Dear Pam,

    I so enjoyed and appreciated the great Earth Scientist report earlier this fall. But more importantly to me was the review of the Professor Si Muller book "Frozen In Time" brought back and continues to bring back to this day my memories of Professor Si and his huge impact on my life.

    He was my graduate student coach and leader as I did the field work for my thesis, The Geology of Bitterwater Creek. Among other graduate students I took a course in Field Geology from Si in winter quarter 1947 or 1948. I know Bob Compton was in the course ,I think Larry Funkhouser and maybe five or six others. He gave us a group assignment for the Quarter to do a Geologic Report on the geology of the Mission Peak quadrangle across the bay above Milpitas.

    As a group we went at it hammer and tongs with all the enthusiasm of youth and were working over there every weekend as well as several days or half days during the week. After six or seven weeks of the quarter and this intense effort and work it became obvious to us that we could not possibly complete the job during this quarter. And that we had to select a committee to meet with Professor Si and complain and tell him we could not complete his assignment.

    I remember Professor Si and his bright twinkling eyes and smile as he listened to our complaining as if the meeting was yesterday. He heard us out with almost a joyous expression on his face. Finally he responded.

    "I sent you over there on this assignment to teach you something that you must learn. Before you start a new job look at the job and the amount of time you have available to complete it and THEN make your work plan. You must learn to THINK TO SCALE. You only have four more weeks. Now review how much time you have before the end of the Quarter and what you can accomplish in that time. Then I want you to go back over there and bring me a report."

    From that day on the concept of Thinking To Scale has been a huge, huge assist to me and has been a factor in every single project I have tackled over the past sixty years. How big is the job, how important is it, how much time do I have, and then how to go about it.

    Way to Go Professor Si Muller!

    Pam, you and your associates have a great job. You can really accomplish something significant with all those bright young men and women you have and send them out to meet the successes and failures and disappointments, sad nesses, and joys all with the skills of Thinking To Scale!

Cordially and Good Vibes

George, '43, '48

The Explorer's Mindset

Above: Pershing Mine northeast of Lovelock, Nevada (c. 1943), from Professor Siemon W. Muller's archives. Professor Muller's research in Nevada began in the late 1920s in Triassic-Jurassic stratigraphy under the guidance of J. P. Smith. Photo courtesy of Eric & Sherry Muller.

Lisa R. Goggin (July 2022)

"Successful explorers in our industry have several things in common: a sound foundation in the entire system of oil and gas (source, maturation, migration, reservoir, and seal), acumen in the critical tools of the trade (including interpretation, geophysics, risk, and economics) an ability to see opportunity in both an abundance of and a lack of data and a willingness to embrace alternative perspectives. Most failures I have observed have been tied to a desire to "protect" a favorite concept or reinforce an earlier decision. The idea that there "cannot be reservoir in a slope environment" has kept many an explorer from even looking in that space for resource. To me that is an opportunity! I once told a boss I was working for who refused to fund my drilling projects the following: "I can guarantee that I will never find oil, if you never let me get a rig on location." If we don't look, we won't find. It is that simple."
– Dr. Lisa R. Goggin

Dr. Lisa R. Goggin is currently with Chevron Corporation in Houston, Texas. She joined the company 25 years ago after completing her Ph.D. in geology at Indiana University. Her technical responsibilities have included the planning and completion of exploration and development wells in both deepwater and deltaic environments, lease sale evaluations in the Gulf of Mexico and Africa, instructing deep and shallow water field and digital technology schools, and patenting new research and development concepts. She is currently part of a digital team on assignment as a digital product owner managing the transition of Chevron's geologic interpretation tools into cloud-based systems. She is an advocate of volumetric interpretation and 3D visualization and her most recent research focuses on the application of artificial intelligence to seismic shale analysis and the use of clastic computational stratigraphy to enhance exploration and development outcomes in clastic fields. She is actively serving on AAPG convention organizing committees, is a former AAPG Distinguished Lecturer (2019-2020) and a former Board Member of the National Cave and Karst Research Institute.

What sets Dr. Goggin apart is her incredibly focused work ethic, positivity and ability to lead in nearly every situation – whether it's finding oil, building reservoir models, teaching courses and training the next generation, collaborating across the value chain, growing teams, research and much more. I've never met someone who has such a convincing "can do" attitude. Behind her charismatic smile is one of the most determined minds in the industry. Perhaps that's why she holds multiple patents – a very difficult achievement in such a technologically advanced industry. Before I had a chance to get to collaborate with Dr. Goggin, I had admired her work for years. I found out she was named AAPG Distinguished Lecturer for 2020 and tuned in for her presentation. After listening to her clear, concise and powerful work on subsurface modeling, I thought we absolutely needed her input for the book *Deepwater Sedimentary Systems*. I was very fortunate to get to work with her on developing Chapter 8: *Deepwater Depositional Environments*. She took that chapter to a whole new level, bringing in a supermajor's industry leading capabilities in process stratigraphic modeling, a very useful style of modeling to predict where high-quality petroleum reservoirs will be found in submarine fan environments. Dr. Goggin is highly engaging, upbeat and is always the first person to make you feel so welcome. She is a leader who can bring people together from all over the world (and she does this on a daily basis in her current role) to effectively deliver a high-quality project.

I interviewed Dr. Lisa Goggin in July 2022. Read her interview below.

Jon Rotzien (JR): Lisa, I'm so thankful you had the time to visit today. Could you share your background and how you became a geoscientist?

Lisa Goggin (LG): As an undergraduate studying to become a chemist, I had an advisor who insisted that I take a geology course. I fought this concept until the first semester of my junior year, then gave in and took Historical Geology. After this first course, I recognized the wisdom of his advice and had to sheepishly apologize to him when I changed my major to geology in the second semester of my junior year! I have never regretted that decision or his advice. He understood my passion for the outdoors and my love of science would be a perfect match in the earth sciences. This was an early lesson in listening to and accepting the advice of others and learning to adapt my plans to incorporate divergent ideas. It was the best advice I ever received as an aspiring scientist.

Both of my undergraduate geology instructors had worked in the oil industry. They gave me a rigorous foundation in earth science theory and application. I even spent one summer "sitting" (mud logging) an exploratory well for them in the Illinois Basin. This early industry exposure was fascinating and led me to consider a career in the oil and gas industry.

JR: You obviously enjoy being a geoscientist. How did you develop your specialty in geology?

LG: My early well-sitting experience and the advice of my early professors gave me a desire to pursue a career as an oil and gas geologist. These professors helped me understand that to attain this goal I would need advanced degree(s) and a strong foundation in critical thinking. I followed their advice and completed both an M.S. and Ph.D. at Indiana University. My M.S. was focused on the provenance and process sedimentology of the deepwater turbidites of the McCall Ridge Formation of the Wrangellia Terrane in south-central Alaska. For my Ph.D., I leveraged my undergraduate chemistry background to design and complete a study of the chemostratigraphy of the Borden siltstones (distal deltaic rocks) in southern Indiana.

My focus on clastic sedimentology and stratigraphy were a product of my experiences at IU's field camp, the advice and supervision of skilled professors in these fields and the rigor of the geology program at IU. Demonstrating an ability to conduct research and apply critical thinking to solve problems and IU's industry recruiting programs were crucial to helping me get four internships with different companies in the last few years of my Ph.D. Internships allowed me to evaluate the working conditions and opportunities provided by the oil and gas industry and convinced me that a career in this field would be very rewarding.

JR: Now you hold multiple patents. What was it like to get awarded your first patent? Your most recent?

LG: Since joining Chevron in 1997, I have had the opportunity to work in many different roles. I am both a generalist and subject-matter expert (SME). For example, I have drilled exploration, appraisal, and development wells, served as a regional geologist and provided lease sale evaluations. I have conducted shallow hazard investigations for drilling, pipeline and facilities design and remediation. I have interpreted micro-image and wireline logs, described cores, taught numerous deep and shallow water clastic field schools, served as a corporate geologic software instructor, and worked in research and development. Most recently, I have become a product owner and manager of a team responsible for the deployment of all of Chevron's geologic interpretation tools into the new cloud-based environments that will help us realize some of my greatest dreams for geologic interpretation. Each of these assignments exposed me to the varied issues facing our business and the uncertainty impacting our ability to interpret the subsurface. This broad experiential background has given me the ability to apply geologic insight to a wide variety of technical challenges.

The first patent I co-invented: ID: 7363158, April, 2008; "Method for creating a stratigraphic model using pseudocores created from borehole images," was the culmination of a research project I worked on with four other experts at Chevron in 2005. At the time, we were a team tasked with interpreting OBMI (Oil-Based Micro Imaging) data from deepwater wells offshore West Africa. These were the early days of the development of what are now industry-standard micro-imaging tools and workflows. We realized that if we validated our images against whole core, we could interpret a great deal more from these imaging tools. In this case the patenting process required years of work and scientific collaboration with many people and vendors and significant support from our patent attorneys. We were very excited and pleased to receive our patent grant. I have this patent framed on my wall and whenever I look at it, I am reminded of the friendships I developed with my co-inventors. The greatest part of the patenting process is the shared dialog, collaborative research and camaraderie that develops as you work to apply ideas to solve problems.

The most recent patent I helped co-invent: ID: 10948618, March 2021; "System and method for automated seismic interpretation," is also the product of a team effort. It utilizes AVA concepts in seismic data and the power of machine learning algorithms to isolate and predict seismic geobodies. In this case, we are combining – in an unconventional way – numerous known concepts of seismic processing and interpretation with guided and un-guided machine learning capabilities to create predictive models of the subsurface.

As with all the patents and invention disclosures I have had the privilege to contribute to while working at Chevron, the technologies we create are designed to help accelerate and improve the consistency and accuracy of subsurface predictions. We routinely work in cross-functional groups of geologists, geophysicists, computer programmers, mathematicians and engineers. It has been both an honor and an exciting adventure to work in this industry as it has allowed me to continue to learn new things and make new friends every day!

JR: Before the patents, many colleagues and other leaders told you, "That'll never work." Many people probably shut down when they hear that about their idea. What did you do differently?

LG: I perceive a "rejection" of an idea as a challenge, not an end. When an inventor comes up with a new idea, their solution to a problem is based upon the culmination of all their experience. When I present an idea to others, I do not expect them to intuitively recognize or see the "end solution" that I am framing. I have had many ideas rejected, but I have persevered when I am convinced my idea has potential. The most important attitude to have is to be unafraid of rejection and to proactively pursue feedback from the individuals who do not think an idea has merit. They have experience you may need to understand and incorporate into your idea. By gathering the perspectives from experts within and beyond my discipline, I become more able to objectively assess whether my idea needs further development or may simply not make economic or applied sense. If I believe there is still merit, I put the idea back in the oven to bake. Some of my ideas have been "baking" for more than 25 years!

JR: Many people in the world probably don't even know what a company like yours does, or any of the supermajor integrated oil companies, recently termed "energy companies." Maybe just provide gasoline to put in our tanks at the local gas station.

LG: The oil industry is so much more than just a provider of oil and gas at a gas station! I personally think that burning our commodity in a car is a waste. This product we produce is a foundation of the world economy and is currently fundamental to keeping our quality of life viable. For example, transportation (by air, sea, rail or truck) is dependent upon just one of our products (fuel). Without fuel, transportation of people by car, train or plane would cease. Though electric cars are becoming economic, the electricity they consume is generated by power plants that primarily utilize either oil, gas or coal. So, our electric supply is still fuel dependent. Even more fundamentally dependent upon fuel is the world's supply chain. Without fuel, supplies (commodities) could not be transported to point of sale. What would you do if your local grocery store ran out of supplies? Beyond fuel, just one other product that comes from the petroleum industry is plastic. For better or worse, plastic is ingrained in our world economy and quality of life. Almost everything we touch today has some relationship or dependency on this product. For example, appliances like televisions and computers, cars, cell phones, many clothing items, most medical packaging, and food storage containers are often made using plastic. Electrical wires are wrapped in it, and water pipes are composed of it. A world without these items is now unimaginable to most of us. If the petroleum industry were to cease to exist tomorrow, everyone on the planet would soon experience catastrophic outcomes. I believe humans can and should wean ourselves from the wasteful use of products from the oil and gas industry, and I believe we can learn to properly recycle and dispose of our plastic waste. Even when we do accomplish these changes, I believe this industry will still be a necessary part of everyone's quality of life. This means there will continue to be a need for geologists who can find oil and gas, far into the future.

JR: How did you find yourself in the Chevron Digital Product Owner space?

LG: When Chevron decided to transform our computer systems from an "on-prem" environment to a cloud-based system, the company recruited subject-matter experts who had demonstrated experience with computer-based tools in their areas of expertise to help guide the transition. I spent 6 years teaching our global pool of interpreters how to use new computer-based interpretation software systems and then another four years in R&D helping to develop proprietary computer-based interpretation software and workflows. I have had 25 years to develop and nurture relationships with colleagues who are now dispersed across the globe. I assume my broad assignment background, experience with experimental interpretation software combined with my desire to help others and widespread network, made me an obvious candidate to be the geologic interpretation tool PO for this transition. It has been a tough, fast-paced and rewarding assignment that has given me insight into what the future could hold for our interpretation community. It allows me to influence the creation of the tools of tomorrow and has allowed me to test my leadership ability.

JR: What skills do you think are important for a career in the energy industry today?

LG: A successful geologist in our industry needs a strong foundation in geologic principles and should be able to demonstrate they are capable of critical and logical thinking. They should also demonstrate competency in the use of computer technologies, have business awareness, be able to communicate and write clearly, and have well-developed soft skills. The most successful geologists I have worked with at Chevron are effective influencers who deliver business-focused results. To work as a geologic interpreter for any a major company in the oil and gas industry, you must have either an M.S. or Ph.D. in geology. Since most major oil companies recruit from universities with which they maintain collaborations, it is extremely important that you ask prospective university geology departments which industry connections they maintain, and which of those companies interview at their departments.

There are many paths to a fulfilling career in this industry that do not require working for a major company, but I started and will finish my career with a major. The opportunities I've had by taking this route have been nearly limitless and the journey has been both exciting and enlightening. The opportunities this industry provides are not limited to oil and gas production, they include environmental geology, engineering geology, geophysics, and more recently geothermal endeavors. I urge students who are studying geology to investigate a career in this industry as we have moved beyond just oil and gas, we are now "Energy" companies. With this expansion of our focus, so to will the need for new and different skills expand.

JR: You have had a long and distinguished career at Chevron. Can you describe what it takes to grow within a company like have done at Chevron?

LG: Have patience and approach each assignment as an opportunity to learn something new about the business. A strong foundation in the principles of your expertise is crucial but only a starting point for success. Focus on the details of your work but never lose sight of the bigger picture of how your work relates to the success of the company. The technical leaders in our company have attained recognition of their mastery of their field from their peers and superiors. Those who aspire to leadership often demonstrate acumen in broader aspects of the business.

Maintain a willingness to see the opportunity in any assignment, even if it is outside of your field of expertise because those assignments that seem farthest from your specialty may be crucial for your growth as a leader later.

It is also extremely important to build networks of your peers. Earn their respect and trust by delivering and learn to rely on them for your growth. Learn to give and take freely the knowledge and advice offered to us by others. Embrace and give honest feedback.

JR: Your Ph.D. committee member had a memorable quote about your dissertation defense. What was the quote? What would be your message to students at universities interested in making a career in the energy industry?

LG: Dr. Basu took my parents aside after my defense and told them: "She has tenacity." That comment resonates because my philosophy about my studies, research, career, and life in general is to "never give up." This philosophy, perseverance and patience has allowed me to reach many goals in life. The unexpected leadership role I currently have gives me the opportunity to try to make some of my long-imagined interpretive goals come true. I am hopeful and looking forward to what comes next!

JR: What attracted you to leadership roles within Chevron?

LG: I believe true leaders are people who listen to and respect others, have a vision of what can be, have sufficient experience to chart a path forward to achieve what is possible, have earned the respect of their peers and have developed the wisdom and skills to bring others into the process that leads to success.

I have held many different positions in Chevron and with each new assignment, I have worked with and learned from many leaders. The opportunity to observe the impact these leaders have on the direction and success of our business inspired me to develop leadership skills and seek leadership assignments. I have tried to adopt the most effective leadership practices from those I work with and routinely seek feedback from my direct reports, peers and supervisors. I embrace this feedback and use it to modify my ineffective behaviors. As a result, I have been rewarded with the respect and support of my peers and superiors. Chevron is also focusing more on empowering all employees to be leaders by adopting a "bottom-up" project management process that gives individuals a voice in project execution. This change in process is increasing the diversity of perspectives and solutions we are using to succeed.

JR: What is the best part of your job?

LG: Working with a wide diverse group of people from all cultures, philosophies and perspectives. With every new person I work with, I learn new things and learn to see the world and our work with a new pair of eyes. Truly amazing!

JR: What is the worst part of your job?

LG: Dealing with the frustrations and occasional demands that come with unexpected problems. These create a short-lived stress that can be challenging. That is when a good network of peers who can and are willing to help is crucial.

JR: You've been around a lot of oil and gas explorers for decades...you've seen some succeed, and some fail. However, lessons can be learned from both of these experiences. What is your message for oil and gas explorers today?

LG: Successful explorers in our industry have several things in common: a sound foundation in the entire system of oil and gas (source, maturation, migration, reservoir and seal), acumen in the critical tools of the trade (including interpretation, geophysics, risk and economics) an ability to see opportunity in both an abundance of and a lack of data and a willingness to embrace alternative perspectives. Most failures I have observed have been tied to a desire to "protect" a favorite concept or reinforce an earlier decision. The idea that there "cannot be reservoir in a slope environment" has kept many an explorer from even looking in that space for resource. To me that is an opportunity! I once told a boss I was working for who refused to fund my drilling projects the following: "I can guarantee that I will never find oil, if you never let me get a rig on location." If we don't look, we won't find. It is that simple.

JR: What would you like the global community of geoscientists and energy professionals to know about Lisa Goggin?

LG: I am thrilled to be asked to share my perspectives with the community and our future oil and gas colleagues. I owe much of my success to so many others who helped shape my experiences, knowledge, career, and have helped me learn how to lead. Without all these people, and the support of my friends and family, none of what I have accomplished would have been possible. I wish to thank all of them for all they have done to help me succeed and thank them for the years of camaraderie and laughter we have shared along the way!

JR: Thank you so much Dr. Goggin.

The Explorer's Mindset

Above: Dr. Lisa Goggin (front row, left) and a team of geoscientists and engineers briefly pose for a photo while working the deepwater Carboniferous Jackfork Group in Arkansas, USA.

Roger M. Slatt (November 2019)

"When I saw the outcrops along Pukearuhe Beach, I said to myself, "My God, this is what they're drilling in the Gulf of Mexico. It'd be a great analog for relatively thin-bedded pay zones." At that beach, you've got it laid out like a picture book." – Professor Roger M. Slatt (5-Sept. 2019)

Professor Roger Slatt served as the Gungoll Family Chair Professor in Petroleum Geology and Geophysics at the University of Oklahoma and Director of the Institute of Reservoir Characterization in the Sarkeys Energy Center. Professor Slatt was one of the most dynamic professors of geology at University of Oklahoma, and his contributions continue to inspire the OU School of Geosciences to new heights. In this interview, you will learn more about his contributions to not only sedimentary geology in industry and academia, but also to the broad field of *applied petroleum geoscience*, one of the key subject areas required for success in the global energy industry.

I met Professor Roger Slatt in an elevator in Beijing in October 2018. We were both in China for about a week to give presentations and chair sessions at a conference on deepwater systems. I introduced myself and said, "It's nice to finally meet you." He asked, "So you were you the one working in Taranaki – did you find anything to prove us wrong?" I replied, "Well, we had more weeks to study there and collected a lot of data, but we found out you were right all along about the geology." He replied, "Oh good," and chuckled. That brief conversation set up a friendship that would last until Professor Slatt passed away in a few years later. We kept in touch, shared data and interpretations on our mutual field area in Taranaki, New Zealand. We had numerous projects in the works including a review paper on deepwater sedimentation that eventually turned into multiple textbook chapters in *Deepwater Sedimentary Systems* published in 2022. In 2019, he agreed to do an interview, and the interview lasted several hours. During that time, we were interrupted by several persistent phone calls by his students. I thought to myself, "These students won't give their professor a break!" Just the opposite – they were calling to check in to see how he was doing and to make sure he was ok. At that time, his age was catching up with him, and his students cared a great deal for his health. Roger Slatt wasn't just a renowned geologist and professor, but he was such a caring person to those in his life that inspired generosity of spirit and reflected kindness back toward him. Roger had a superb eye for talent, and when asked about his success, he would instead give credit to the team, saying, "I have great grad students." Roger is dearly missed by the world of geoscientists and people he inspired.

Roger was hardly skeptical of diving headfirst into projects. His thirst for new avenues in applied sedimentary geology research resulted in great success throughout his career. I finally had the chance to interview Professor Roger Slatt in November 2019 to learn about his contributions to stratigraphic reservoir characterization, sedimentology and the petroleum geology of mudrocks. One of the most creative minds in sedimentology and stratigraphy, Professor Slatt published over 150 articles and abstracts and was author/ co-author/ editor of six books on petroleum geoscience. From 1992-2000, he was Head of the Department of Geology and Geological Engineering at Colorado School of Mines. A distinguished lecturer for AAPG and SEG several times on multiple continents, he was also the recipient of the AAPG Distinguished Service Award. He was a graduate of San Francisco City college ('61), California State University San Jose ('65), and University of Alaska (M.S. '67 and Ph.D. '70) and graduated over 100 M.S. and Ph.D. students.

Read Roger's interview from November 2019.

Jon Rotzien (JR): Professor Slatt, I'm so thankful you had the time to visit today and share some of your research history. You've done countless other interviews, including a recent one with Dr. Susan Nash with AAPG for the Innovators in Geoscience Technology Series (23 January 2018) and with Amy Miller, also with AAPG, on the Unconventional Reservoir Characterization Summit held in January 2013 in Houston. It's important for my generation to understand the impact that your research and collaborations continue to have on stratigraphy and petroleum geology in the 21st century. First off, what drove you to study geology? Could you share more on this?

Roger Slatt (RS): In my recent book on Reservoir Characterization for stratigraphers, I spent a lot of time writing the preface on why geology was and is still important to me, and why I got in. I got into geology for the love of outdoors – I was always an outdoor person. When I went to junior college, I had a professor, like many people who cite a key professor in their development of the love for geology. His name was Professor "Old Doc" Crowell, who taught everything in geology at the junior college in San Francisco. He must have been 70 at that time, and taught mineralogy, physical geology, historical geology. He sparked my interest in geology, and coupled with my love for the outdoors – that's what initially got me into geology. Ever since then, it took off uphill. I've never regretted my profession. And that's what I tell my students now. There will be bumps in the road, but you can have a great career. It is particularly important to tell students this now, when they're having so much trouble securing jobs.

And you can refer to my 2018 AAPG Explorer interview, which shows how we're helping our students at OU and companies in their search for oil and gas.

JR: Much of your research is applied to the upstream oil and gas industry. Why was this such a focus of your research and publications?

RS: I'm a very applied person. When I took other geology courses as a student, I was never too much into granites and metamorphic studies or stuff like that. I was much more interested in studies that could be applied and also provided some sense of "forensic historical geology" (i.e., formation of rock layers, etc.). I credit my good instructors in sedimentology. When I go way back in my career, I've always been oriented that way. When I started my graduate degree in Alaska, I was working with more pure scientists. I researched glaciers for my dissertation, nine or ten of them to be exact. After that, I did a post-doc stint with the famous Swiss geologist (now deceased) Werner Bruckner. I then moved onto an Assistant Professorship at Arizona State. I met a fine fellow named Burr Silver, long retired now. He was the one lone departmental "soft rocker" among a faculty of hard rock petrologists and geochemists and meteorite scientists. Burr was a carbonate stratigrapher, and I became the clastics stratigrapher. It was a natural fit, and he was my first teammate. Burr also had an oil background, so I guess that rubbed off on me. It was in that partnership that I began to focus on the applied aspects of stratigraphy to oil and gas exploration. If I was going to have a profession in the geosciences, I wanted to make a difference. Not just study geology for the sake of studying it, like much basic science is done today. I've never been much of a pure scientist. Basic science, that's not me. I had the desire to satisfy myself with answers, along the road to helping others. I wanted to learn things that could be used by the oil and gas industry in their search for energy resources for the world. This noble endeavor, though discounted by many naïve individuals today, helps the planet (and eventually the solar system) with global economies and individuals who work in the industry.

JR: I understand while you were at Mines, you had to wear many hats, and that has only increased with time. What challenges did you face as a leader of a department as well as an active researcher?

RS: I took this step as a big honor at Mines. I still stayed in the loop with active research, and a lot of my research at that time was in deepwater depositional systems. I graduated a lot of students in deep water including outstanding, now well-established students like Dave Pyles. I always wanted to try to stay one step ahead of the profession – both academically and with the applied industry studies. It paid off really well to continue publishing peer-reviewed research while maintaining my role as an academic Head of Department. Because when I went from Mines to industry, I was accepted as someone who had a background in both.

JR: But I may have skipped a step – your industry experience.

RS: As for the petroleum industry, I served at both Arco (research) and City Services (research and research management) prior to joining Mines. Because I had a lengthy publication record and management experience, I fit right into the job I was hired to accomplish – and improved the petroleum program. I didn't have any trouble securing the job. Regarding your question, the challenge has always been the people that you work with. If you don't have good people, you simply can't accomplish what you set out to do. I've managed through the years to be able to identify what constitutes a good geologist I'd like to work with, and the same is true vice versa. I've often told my students, "I'm not some super scientist, but my forfeit is that I have a good eye for choosing good graduate students as well as faculty and other scientists." As my reputation has grown, more hardworking and talented students have joined our research group.

JR: Sounds like a positive feedback cycle. Good students, good reputation, more selective the application process becomes for your research group.

RS: By the way, I was hired at Mines by Bob Weimer and John Haun. They were exceptional petroleum geologists at Mines with worldwide reputations. Both of them did most of their careers there at Mines. But they were getting on in years, and the department and alumni sought to keep improving the School's reputation in the petroleum geoscience area. So, they went out looking for a replacement to specifically build the program up again. That's why they chose me. They knew I had administrative experience and scientific documentation and evidence in the form of my publications and abstracts. They chose me fairly easily to do that job. When I first started Mines, there was a dwindling interest in petroleum geology. I focused on bringing that back and was pretty successful. They didn't want me to leave Mines.

JR: Of course not, and that takes so much dedication and perseverance to revitalize a department.

RS: It reminds me of the going away party Mines threw for me upon leaving for my new position as Director of the School of Geology and Geophysics at OU. It was a comment by Mike Gardner that stuck in my mind – it resonated with me. Very important to me. He told me, "Look over the people assembled here today – you have everyone from the President of the University to the janitorial staff. We'll miss you." And he was right. It was the whole spectrum of people with whom I'd become acquainted and worked with during my six-year tenure at Mines. From the President to the janitor, and everyone in between. It was very moving. I consider it a reflection of my ability and versatility to bring diverse people together, including those representing academia and the oil and gas industry.

JR: What a kind gesture and nice celebration of your time and memories with Mines, to have such a diverse crowd to wish you farewell. I'd like to revisit some of your earlier times at Mines.....I believe you met Peter King and Greg Browne with GNS Science in New Zealand during this time, co-authors and mentors of mine as well. How did you meet them?

RS: That is an interesting story. It all began when I gave a lecture at a New Orleans industry luncheon, it was on the work we were doing investigating the value of deepwater outcrops. Peter and Greg's boss heard me present, and then invited me to come down there and give a multi-day seminar. I accepted the invitation and met Peter and Greg. They said, "Wow – we've got fantastic outcrops that no one has really looked at. While you're here in New Zealand, stick around an extra day to visit Pukearuhe Beach."

When I saw the outcrops along Pukearuhe Beach, I said to myself, "My God, this is what they're drilling in the GOM. It'd be a great analog for relatively thin-bedded pay zones." At that beach, you've got it laid out like a picture book. And you examined those outcrops of the Mount Messenger Formation in much more depth than I ever had the chance to.

JR: We had a good contingent from Stanford working those outcrops around 2007-2015. You'd be happy to know those beautiful outcrops along Pukearuhe Beach made the cover of AAPG Bulletin in September 2018.

RS: When I came back from my trip to New Zealand, I had the idea to work on additional projects in Taranaki. But of course, it was going to cost money to travel and set up a research program there. Back then, deepwater was a pretty hot topic, so I went about organizing a consortium. There was some initial head scratching by the management at these oil and gas companies I approached.

They would ask, "Why do you have to go to NZ if were drilling in the GOM?" The premise didn't make sense to managers, who couldn't fathom studying an analog halfway around the world! In the end, however, I convinced a large number of companies to join our consortium, perhaps 20 companies. The members kicked in $20,000 each to fund this research. One of the first things we did was lead a field trip to Pukearuhe, that beach was very popular with that consortium, and is still a popular field trip area. That's also not the first time I led a consortium. I had practice with generating research funded by industry.

JR: No? What was the first?

RS: When I first went to City Services Research Lab, they had formed a consortium on sandy shelf depositional systems. When I took the job, the manager at the time, Rod Tillman, asked me if I would be able to run it. The consortium lasted for several years. It was the first experience I had at managing a consortium, with a large number of different companies. Each company had different goals, different ideas – really a diverse bunch. I brought that experience to the Taranaki work in the Mt Messenger Formation, which I thought then and still do now, as world-class outcrops. You and Steve and Don understand this.

JR: We certainly enjoyed studying the Taranaki outcrops. Didn't you also have a Lewis Shale consortium?

RS: After my experience with the Mt Messenger, we had a Lewis Shale consortium – something like 23 member companies. A student of mine named Elizabeth Whitten published the first major research on the Lewis, the formation really had been neglected for years.

I first came across the Lewis on a field trip led by a geologist from Denver. It was organized by the Colorado Geological Society. One of the stops we made on the trip featured an outcrop of the Lewis, and the leader pronounced, "You're looking at a Bouma sequence here." Well, the outcrop was 30 ft at least in thickness. Yes, it was overall fining upward, and the beds thinned upward, but this was clearly not a single sedimentation unit! It was comprised of many beds, each consisting of partial or complete Bouma sequences. From my experience in the Mount Messenger, I recognized this outcrop had submarine fan to slope to deltaic deposits and represented several (overall decreasing water depth) changes in depositional environment.

This outcrop was also the one where one of my former students, Dave Pyles, coined the term "bashful outcrop" since it was a bit hidden and recessed, and not a dramatic or sheer cliff that immediately caught one's eye.

JR: What a great phrase.

RS: This outcrop was rubbly and poorly exposed. If you drove by it, and you easily could without stopping, you'd say, "That's a lump of rock." However, with some imagination and experience, you could recognize this for what it was. So, Whitten, my student, went out there, measured the first complete section. It had thick-bedded sandstone at the base that thinned and decreased in sandstone ratio to the top of the outcrop. If you knew anything about stratigraphy, you could see it was a complete upward shallowing interval. Pyles did a MS and measured a section there too. We also drilled a well behind outcrop, and that's why we need to revisit the Mount Messenger for a minute...

JR: Why the Mount Messenger?

RS: Well, you remember we drilled behind outcrop in the Mount Messenger, too.

JR: That's right! Your paper with Greg (Browne and Slatt, 2002) was one of the first that showed the 3D architecture of the Pukearuhe Beach portion of the Upper Mount Messenger Formation and even earlier – the paper from 1994 with Peter as lead author. You had behind-outcrop core – what was it like to make the decision to get this core? What was it like to drill one of the first behind-outcrop wells in deepwater outcrops? Please share that story.

RS: That was an ordeal in itself. While we had received lots of money from the consortium members, we still had no equipment for drilling wells behind outcrop. But we wanted to because we felt that a core/log behind this outcrop, that showed such superb, low dip angle stratigraphy could improve our understanding of limitations of core stratigraphic analysis. So, I teamed up with Bob Davis from Schlumberger. He was able to persuade Schlumberger to send a logging tool all the way from Malaysia to drill a 100-ft-deep behind-outcrop well at Pukearuhe.

JR: This would be known as Pukearuhe-1 in your 2002 paper with Greg.

RS: Yes, that's right. We had actually planned to drill three wells to get a 3D perspective of the stratigraphy from behind outcrop to tie to the outcrop, but we only completed two and then something broke on the rig and that was it for our coring campaign. However, the fact that Bob was able to persuade Schlumberger to do a research well – and bring the equipment all the way from Malaysia – that was a tremendous effort on his part. When all was said and done, Schlumberger used the core quite a bit in their stratigraphic modeling, all as a result of our drilling, coring and logging. Now if I jump forward again to the Lewis…

JR: Sure.

RS: This was an offshoot of drilling a well in the Mount Messenger. We drilled one well to core the entire stratigraphic interval of the Lewis we saw in outcrop. The goal was to identify features we observed in outcrop in three dimensions – is the bedding laterally continuous? Where are the major surfaces? We wanted to find criteria to differentiate which bedding was continuous and which bedding was discontinuous.

JR: Those data you gathered are valuable for populating reservoir models. On the Mount Messenger coring, did it all go smoothly?

RS: I recall we performed the coring at the top of the hill in order to drill through the thickest part of the Mount Messenger which dipped beneath the wellsite. We had to get the rig up that steep clay-rich and narrow little road, that went from bottom to the top of the ridge in a small truck. At the bottom there was a paved road, not a problem. That's where the Waikaramarama River entered to the beach. When the rig started going up that steep hill, it started to slide back, but I don't remember details. One of those interesting geological experiences that all field geologists have.

JR: Not a good thing to have the rig sliding downhill toward all the sunbathers along Pukearuhe Beach!

RS: One of the beauties about the West Coast of the North Island of New Zealand is that consists of lengthy, beautiful beaches, normally vacant, so not a great deal of sunbathers – just great geology. I've had recent correspondence with Greg, and we've talked about our research days in Taranaki. When I first visited, they warned me that the sun was intense and the air thin, to not wear shorts – because one could burn easily.

I thought to myself, "I'm from California, I don't need to listen to all that nonsense." Sure enough after the first day, I really was like a lobster. I could hardly walk, couldn't bend my knees. The sun had gotten me. We created some interesting experiences.

I also remember the whitebait fritters, with the little eyes looking back at you. And vegemite, boy, I fell in love with vegemite. Wrapped in cubes of butter, smear it on your toast. We stayed at the Awakino Motor Lodge. Heaven forbid we were staying there the same time the rugby team was in town, they raised all sorts of commotion. You might as well write off the night.

JR: We still stay at the Whitebait Inn – and enjoy those whitebait fritters. That Awakino Beach is one of the most underrated beaches (see the picture below).

RS: On that lower part of the stratigraphy of the upper Miocene, we never did too much with the Lower Mount Messenger or Mohakatino or Moki formations. We were working on the relatively thin-bedded facies, and that's why we focused on Pukearuhe. That is a towering section of rock, and formed the basis for the paper Greg and I wrote. We also wrote a few internal consortium reports based on those studies.

JR: We also worked Pukearuhe with Don, Steve, Peter and Greg and essentially confirmed your findings. What sort of connections do you see between the Jackfork and the Wai iti Group in New Zealand. Both have been published extensively, but I think you have more publications and abstracts on the Jackfork than anyone else, including your GPR studies. In the AAPG Memoir 72, Chapter 17, you make the case for "Why Outcrop Characterization of Turbidite Systems."

RS: The first GPR we did on the Jackfork, then on the Lewis. First of all, the reason we started using GPR was because of an OU professor named Roger Young, deceased now. He had a student doing basic backyard GPR, and I told him. I said, "Look Roger, we have these fantastic outcrops where we can use GPR to get three dimensionality." He was a pure scientist and at first, was a little reluctant. But I got him to give it a try. We went to Hollywood Quarry.

JR: Last time I saw those was not too long ago.

Above: View to the south along the Taranaki Coast near Awakino, with Mount Taranaki in the background. Photo taken January 2019.

"One of the things about me, I'm not a regional person. I find that boring, quite frankly. It's the details I like. You're either a lumper or splitter. If you're a lumper, you can make big maps of thick sections, but often they don't tell you as much as you would if you knew the details. These tell you about the deposition. Sometimes splitters get in trouble because the boss doesn't give them the time to split. We've done projects where I train my students to be splitters. I use several examples of the Barnett and Woodford. When you construct big, broad maps, they're more or less uniform across large areas. When you start splitting, you can observe changes in transport

direction, depositional style, TOC content, reservoir thickness, and the list goes on. These important details are completely lost in making big maps."
– Roger M. Slatt

RS: If you haven't been back, you need to go again! That quarry is what got us interested in GPR. Alan Whitten became the chief GPR guy in our group. He was a really fantastic scientist, also now deceased. At his funeral, I was able to state he was one of the greatest scientists I ever had the pleasure to work and to travel with. His focus was on ground penetrating radar. His was a life lost too soon.

That's when we went to the Lewis. At the time, we were trying to decide if the thin beds filled and represented sinuous channel forms behind outcrop. At that time, no one really knew. There was a lot of speculation – especially using the seismic data of the time. We chose the outcrop where we had measured the stratigraphy. Our GPR data confirmed an almost 90-degree bend in the channel behind outcrop! I published it in my 2007 first edition book on reservoir characterization. Then the research really took off for my students. A guy named Steffan Van Dyke, once he knew what we were looking at, measured 150 stratigraphic sections for his MS thesis. He described what the *outside* looked like on the *inside* of the outcrop, including that beautiful 90-degree bend in one of the sandstone bodies.

We therefore demonstrated what some of these 2D outcrops looked like in 3D. Since then, Exxon and ExxonMobil have all gone to the Brushy [Canyon Formation, West Texas] where those rocks also have 3D sinuosity, but to my knowledge, we were the first ones to document it.

JR: Awesome.

RS: Since those days, we've been back and have built our confidence. We returned specifically to Hollywood, did some neat work, but it was only published as oral publication at meetings. This research showed the internal stratigraphy of a sandstone body, on the east side of Hollywood Quarry. Some students, namely Richard

Brito and Oswoldo Davogustto, really did fine GPR work on the internal stratigraphy of another Jackfork channelized interval. Since that time, the quarry management has cut back that wall to expose what we'd found years earlier using GPR.

JR: Stunning really, and a great validation of the methods.

RS: This was followed by a GPR survey in the DeGray Spillway. We had measured walls in the spillway, yet we didn't understand how those beds connected, or if they even were continuous. So, we conducted GPR across the middle of the spillway to see how the two measured sections related, bed-by-bed essentially. One of our findings was that the beds alternate in thickness. Where you have one bed that's thick on one side, on the other side it's thin, and so on and so forth. This we attributed to compensation style deposition at a small scale.

JR: An excellent example of compensation stacking.

RS: Exactly. The depocenter for the flows shifted from place to place. While the axis of deposition remained relatively constant, the beds were always choosing the "low point" to deposit. We published this.

One of the things about me, I'm not a regional person. I find that boring, quite frankly. It's the details I like. You're either a lumper or splitter. If you're a lumper, you can make big maps of thick sections, but often they don't tell you as much as you would if you knew the details. These tell you about the deposition. Sometimes splitters get in trouble because the boss doesn't give them the time to split. We've done projects where I train my students to be splitters. I use several examples of the Barnett and Woodford. When you construct big, broad maps, they're more or less uniform across large areas. When you start splitting, you can observe changes in transport direction, depositional style, TOC content, reservoir thickness, and the list goes on. These important details are completely lost in making big maps.

JR: Those are critical details that inform business decisions, especially as you mention in mapping mudrock reservoirs. There are stories of companies with multi-billion dollar write-offs because the mapping wasn't done correctly.

Professor Slatt, your work in the Jackfork is indeed impressive. It was a privilege to be in the audience to see your presentation in Beijing on the Jackfork in 2019. You've mapped more of that outcrop belt than anyone. What is next in that episode? Surely there must be more work (there's always more)...

RS: For example, I had a PhD student, very bright, very dedicated, now working for Marathon. He took every measured section in the Jackfork (in the dead of winter by the way) under rough weather conditions, and assembled the stratigraphy into a basin-scale model. He then took classic Chinese deepwater outcrops and also published this for comparison in his dissertation.

I consider that research a very important part of any field trip to that area. The ability to place in basin scale the sequence of key stratigraphic surfaces and intervals. He also did a really nice piece in Baumgartner Quarry, in the Jackfork. I recall he was just learning modeling at that time. We had three dimensionality to the outcrops in this quarry, so he ultimately built a model and did a bunch of simulations to determine what degree of connectivity you need in these analog deepwater sandstone intervals to improve your production, and then applied it to the GOM. We published both of these works in AAPG Bulletin a few years ago.

What is rewarding is that our work in the Jackfork has basically withstood the test of time. That's good when that happens, rather than the alternative: you do something, build a model and someone shoots it down a year later.

JR: That's a huge accomplishment. So how did you know when the time was right to shift your research focus to unconventional source rock reservoirs? When did it become apparent to you to make that shift? And you've had the Woodford Resource Shale Research Group for at least 8 years running....your most recent work is on the Barnett and Woodford, including your AAPG Bulletin with N.R. O'Brien from 2011. This paper has 642 citations as of the date of this interview.

RS: If Neil knew that he'd be turning around his grave! I never dreamed it would have garnered that amount of citations. Let me tell you about that paper.

We wrote that for a specific reason. That was when people were starting to use SEM for 3D work on mudrock pores. We said, "That's great, but you still have issues pertaining to the uncertainty in the pores with those 3D realizations." Everyone went crazy for these beautiful block diagrams with pore space in between, and many people still do. A problem is the scale – it only captures a few millimeters. People were trying to upscale that and having real trouble because you'd end up with 30 ft diameter pores! We wrote that paper as a scientific rebuttal to keep that bandwagon from charging out of control. We have had some success as more papers are appearing that use the 'old school' approach, coupled with the more advanced SEM capabilities. But with the advanced imaging of today, people sometimes get lost in the imagery without thinking what they are imaging and at what scale. Two recent AAPG books provide good examples of SEM imagery.

JR: Well, that message is resonating loud and clear with the industry. But your earlier work hinted at that later research.

RS: Neil (now deceased) and I had written a book in the 90s on basic microtexture properties of mudrocks. Neil spent his whole life on the subject, working under his $5000 SEM. He examined thousands and thousands and thousands of mudrock intervals. Our book had a lot of material in 2D of SEM textures. My role was the mineralogy variations in the rocks. The book has been out of print for many years, but that was the start of our 2D examination into the pores of mudrocks. We wrote that book to encompass all of the basic geology of shale microtextures. We didn't have any fancy, expensive equipment.

When all these fancy new methods came along, it was like, "My God, look at all these issues with these techniques they're having." Four to five different papers came out to rebut the new techniques – these papers said we shouldn't abandon the plain old SEM techniques that allow for an examination of the textures, porosity and tortuosity, etc. There was still a lot to see with the standard old $5000 SEM.

Since published, I'm glad we can say, people started thinking a little bit more about using SEM in conjunction with high-resolution ion milling. Our paper – O'Brien and Slatt accomplished that. I'm happy to report today we're in a state now where more people have come to realize this, but much still remains to be done. Two AAPG SEM books later, we're the only paper in there that talks about the standard techniques. Everything in there is high-resolution, ion-milled 3D models of small cubes, and ours is the outlier. Professionals and academics alike need to be careful to not forget the surface textures – use those in conjunction with the 3D block diagrams. Somehow the problems still exist, industry is still trying to upscale, and there remain challenges with that.

In recent years, URTeC has featured 7-8 papers touting the standard technique of SEM analysis. But there were still critics saying, "Who needs that?" and "We've got this fancy stuff that makes block figures." I got tired of it. Finally, we got out of that research area.

As a final note, one of those SEM books published by AAPG featured on the cover one of our 2D images, rather than a 3D block. The editor who did that was earlier one of the staunchest disbelievers in our 2D work. We made progress, but it was a hard fight, so eventually we stopped doing porosity level work.

JR: While you may have exited the work, 642 citations say people are still using your research. Congratulations.

To continue onward: What do you think about the outcrop work done on tight sandstone reservoirs and source rock reservoirs. Is there a better way to understand geologic risk in those reservoirs?

RS: That reminds me of some of the work done by BP on the Eagle Ford, and to bring the conversation back around to drilling wells behind outcrop. While the Eagle Ford is a source rock reservoir, understanding it from an outcrop perspective as BP did under Art Donovan has brought geologic risking of those stratigraphic intervals into perspective.

JR: Art's contributions are legendary.

RS: I remember they kept getting held up on drilling behind outcrop there in West Texas. They finally got it together and drilled a well, and did fantastic work on it. One of our students did a lot of geochemistry on that core. I was one of the guys Art originally invited out to throw in any experience I might have had to make sure coring would go well

— as we've discussed today on the Jackfork, Lewis and Mt Messenger. I've had my hand in a lot of such projects through time.

JR: You read about Professor Si Muller's contribution to Beer Friday at GeoCorner at Stanford. I've met many of your students, mentored them during internships, observed them receiving awards at conferences (kudos, by the way), and they've contributed to our GCAGS (now *GeoGulf*) program in 2017-2019. All of your students seem to be really tuned in and passionate about their research. How were you able to create such a successful research group? What is your secret, if you can tell?

RS: That's a good question, and a very interesting end to this story, too. It boils down to loving what you do. Shales have always been my first love, going back to 1990 working with O'Brien. When I was at ARCO, they let me work on shales. Always had a love for them because they're so tough to work on.

At about the same time, when shales started to become popular as a resource, I wanted to jump in. At first I had a simple idea: we'll compare and contrast different shales around the US. I soon found out that wasn't going to work. Different universities were lining up to work in the shale plays nearest to them. There was no point in going to the Marcellus — those faculty would know more.

Jon Comer firmed up our Woodford studies many years ago. More recently one of our geochemists at OU, Paul Philp, has been taking our research forward. We focused on the Woodford. During that time, one scientist with the Oklahoma Survey tried to get me to work up a consortium on the Stanley. Thank God we didn't do that — the consortium would've died immediately! We were thankful we chose the Woodford. We had a great team with my contacts from industry and the university. We went out and attracted some great students for the projects. One amazing thing about those students was they were off working on the Woodford before we had finished talking to them! Very eager to complete their research.

Paul Philp was fortunate to have own group of geochemistry students — and he is widely considered a world expert in petroleum geochemistry. That's how our Woodford Consortium got started, and it was very successful.

You'll find this interesting. Through my years leading consortiums, I was amazed that many industry geoscientists don't even look at outcrops. I'm sure you know this! It was like trying to pull teeth to get people down to New Zealand to view the Mount Messenger. When it came to asking oil companies to send a business unit there, managers would say, "Oh my God, why are you sending people to New Zealand? Can't you go down the road in Houston and look at something easy?" Amoco was the only one to send a week-long field party. Mainly Greg and I worked with them when they went out in the field with us. Amoco brought their whole team – petrophysicists, seismic processors, geologists – the whole crew. It was because at the time they were having problems developing thin-bedded turbidite reservoirs offshore New Orleans.

For these offshore oil fields, they required a completely different model from what had been used in the past with 90%+ net:gross, thick-bedded, amalgamated turbidite intervals. Their work turned out to be very successful. They drilled a horizontal well after coming back from our New Zealand field trip – not *into* a channel – but into the *proximal levee facies* and they found high permeability, thin-bedded pay parallel to the channel axis. It turned out to be sufficiently high net pay, better than the channel-fill itself, and was an extremely successful recipe (even record breaking) that led to best production from a horizontal well in the GOM. This was to be called Ram Powell. They drilled 5-6 wells in the channelized facies, and it was all water wet there. It was a very interesting story, that history to the Ram Powell field.

Why do I tell you all this about the success of the consortiums? Because it comes down to having the best team in place. My best talent is being able to find best students. I can tell when I talk to them. A few principles I'll share with you: never take a student you've never met. I used to take them from their resume, and in the end, some would work out, others would not. By doing face-to-face interviews and drawing conclusions from that, that's how I was able to recruit excellent students. We've had 30 something theses just in Woodford, then we followed the money into the Sycamore and Meramac and Springer trends and some of the others – always with good, dedicated students.

JR: You've surrounded yourself with successful and brilliant scientists – that no doubt inspires collaboration and creative inquiry. What is your message to the upstream oil and gas industry today?

RS: Think a little past the next quarter. You're going to need people especially if you want to keep a standard of excellent exploration going. You have to ask your people how long they'll be willing to go back-and-forth in these up and down cycles before retiring. Companies are increasingly bottom line and monthly oriented. Companies are going to suffer in the end with that short term view. You can *hire and fire at will* is the mentality out there. People are considered more important as numbers instead of their skills sets they bring to exploration.

JR: Thank you so much Professor Slatt for sharing your fascinating story.

Diane Woodruff (December 2021)

"You can have the most talented people in the world, but you need the right mix. Team members need passion and humility, which is very important as I think back to Anadarko. These were the core values we had as a company. Trust and integrity are important. Work ethic is so important. It is summarized in servant leadership, which means everyone on your team has to be thinking about each other and what they can do for the greater good of the team. All the pieces of the puzzle are needed to make a good and complete team when it's assembled. You don't want a team with too many leaders, but a team with linked arms to move forward as one. Those are the components to make a great team." – Dr. Diane Woodruff

Diane Woodruff, Ph.D., delivering the Cindy A. Yeilding Honorary Lecture on Deepwater Exploration at GeoGulf in Houston Texas, on the 25th of April 2023.

Anyone who has met Dr. Woodruff or read her work understands her in-depth expertise in exploration, appraisal and development of energy resources. She is a wealth of knowledge and experience in exploration, appraisal and development of energy resources as well as the energy it takes to succeed in a fast-paced industry. She is currently a geologist at Occidental Petroleum Corporation. She started her career working both exploration and development projects in deepwater Gulf of Mexico with Anadarko Petroleum Corporation. Currently, she is working on the development team for eastern Gulf of Mexico assets at Occidental. She received a Ph.D. and Sc.M. in Geological Sciences from Brown University after studying the geochemistry of lunar and terrestrial basalts. She received a B.S. in Geological Engineering with an emphasis in Mineral and Petroleum Exploration and a minor in Public Affairs from Colorado School of Mines.

I first met Dr. Woodruff in a bustling neighborhood restaurant in Houston. We quickly covered the topics of petroleum geology, completing a Ph.D. program, running marathons and competing in triathlons. Diane has a very high energy level both on the job and out of the office. Her engaging and focused personality is part of what makes her an exceptional leader. You want to be on her team. Several years later, we connected again with a small group of explorers to form the Houston Explorers Club, a leadership club built for early career oil and gas exploration professionals. Since then, the Houston Explorers Club has hosted some of the most successful explorers from the early 21st century, focusing on discoveries in the US Gulf of Mexico, Guyana, Mexican Gulf of Mexico, North Slope of Alaska, onshore Gulf Coast, Belize, Middle East and the Permian Basin. The Houston Explorers Club now shares input and collaboration from nearly 50 companies – both large and small, and from domestic and international – at periodic meetings. Dr. Woodruff has been instrumental in building this group of leaders in the Houston area. In addition, she is an integral part of the Gulf Coast geological societies, often helping lead, organize and participate in society meetings and annual events. This year, she delivered the Cindy A. Yeilding Honorary Lecture in Deepwater Exploration at the 72nd Annual GeoGulf Convention in Houston.

I had the opportunity to work with Dr. Woodruff on the first chapter of the *Deepwater Sedimentary Systems* book during the pandemic. Not only does she have a consummate understanding of the upstream exploration and production business, she is also extremely talented at analyzing and interpreting new developments in the global energy industry. One of Diane's most important contributions to the book was the analysis of global markets and the new developments in carbon capture, use and storage (CCUS). In addition, she condensed the exploration and production business into a primer of incredibly useful pages and tables. This primer is informative for professionals across the value chain to understand business models and what data and decisions are required for various stage gates and investment decisions. She brought our team together by leading by example, part of the recipe for servant leadership that she describes in the interview, and that was quite a convincing and motivating way of getting our chapter done.

Read the interview with Dr. Diane Woodruff from December 2021 below.

Jon Rotzien (JR): Dr. Woodruff, I'm so thankful you had the time to visit today.
Congratulations on another successful year in the energy industry. Can you tell us more about your current roles?

Diane Woodruff (DW): I'm a senior geologist with Occidental Petroleum Corporation. I work in the Gulf of Mexico (GOM) Asset Development team, specifically on the Horn Mountain team within the Eastern GOM. It's one of our 10 GOM platforms. I'm in charge of the development wells already producing and responsible for bringing more online. The cool thing about the GOM team is we tend to run lean. This means we get to work a lot with the GOM Exploration team and look at exploration and appraisal wells within tieback distance.

JR: Did you know, while you were a PhD student at Brown studying *Abundance, Speciation, and Role of Volatiles in Planetary Basalts*, that you would be drilling successful development wells in the deepwater GOM a decade later? By the way, that is the best dissertation title.

DW: I knew going into the PhD that I wanted to get back into the oil and gas industry. I wanted it, but I didn't expect to still be in the GOM. I thought maybe I'd be doing onshore or international, but I've been able to work the GOM the last 7 years. It's been an exciting time to drill so many development wells.

JR: What are some of the current challenges facing the energy industry?

DW: Two things, which most in the industry know well. First, the slow change toward a different energy mix, as we move from fossil fuels to renewables and other energy forms. As an industry, we're continuing to think outside the box and put on our creative hats to find ways to provide energy that the world needs. Knowing there is going to be a change, geologists are still needed but our jobs will look a little different. Second, early career folks understand the impact of the bimodal distribution of ages in the industry. In the next few years, retirements will continue as the experienced group leave to enjoy the retirement they deserve. Younger and early career folks need to step into new roles and become mentors as new mentees join our industry. This shift will require early to mid-career folks to network more in order to leverage the expertise and knowledge of our peers as we move forward to be the best industry out there.

JR: The energy industry is known for periodic technical breakthroughs – that no one really sees coming. What are some of the developing technologies that may be mainstream in 5-10 years?

DW: That is a tough question. You have those breakthroughs yet you just don't know what will be next. Technologies to help implement carbon sequestration in deepwater will be required next. For example, ExxonMobil just picked up a bunch of leases for carbon sequestration in the GOM lease sale this week. Other companies like Talos Energy are also thinking about sequestration in the GOM. There is a lot of focus in the onshore world, but the next big thing is offshore and being able to effectively move that technology and concept to deepwater. This is definitely going to be a complex problem. Another I could foresee would be some new latest and greatest seismic reprocessing or acquisition. After ocean bottom node technology (OBN), what will be the next big thing in 10 years? Also just thinking about horizontal wells onshore, it will be challenging to apply the same technology and concept offshore. Thinking about drilling deeper and into higher pressure zones, we might use horizontal wells to tap in to secondary and tertiary reservoirs. These reservoirs may not be as good as the high porosity and permeability zones the GOM has been known for in the last 30 years, but may represent the next big technological push.

JR: You're an exploration and appraisal geoscientist by training, having worked at one of the best companies for deepwater exploration and production – Anadarko and now Oxy. Was it Van Mount who made the cover of an Anadarko annual report in the early 2000s with a title that read *Deepwater*? A legendary track record from the deepest wells in the Paleogene Trend of the GOM to offshore Africa – Anadarko had great success. What are some of the lessons learned that you can share about what it takes to be a successful oil finder?

DW: One of the main things I've learned is that you must rely on the greater team you have access to. As you do your due diligence and evaluate all aspects of prospects, leverage all experts in the company – other teams, peers, colleagues within different business units to get different perspectives and to make sure you haven't missed anything. You'll learn from these conversations the ways a prospect could work or fail. One of most important things is to leverage expertise of subject matter experts – experts like Van – early on in the evaluation and then again in a post drill analysis. All companies are always busy and move from one well to the next. However, there is value to understand what was predicted and what was found. With post drill analyses, you're able to apply these learnings to future wells. Mentors have told me, "Whatever you map, it will not be correct. There will always be a change in the map after you drill." When trying to find oil, you have to be humble and accept surprises that come your way. You need to take what you learn and apply it and integrate it into the next prospects.

JR: Many people say our generation isn't as savvy when it comes to building a successful network of peers in our chosen career. You've been able to create a new professional network – the Houston Explorers Club. What's next for the Houston Explorers Club?

DW: I think that as we go into next year and as Covid numbers go down, we need to focus our next year on meeting in person. We should be able to continue to strengthen new membership relationships and grow relationships within the Club. Hopefully we'll have some social events to build the network. After 20 months of feeling pretty isolated and only able to see each other on the screen, meeting face-to-face to build those relationships and continue to hear great talks from industry leaders will make for a great 2022 (our fourth year!).

JR: Leadership is an important theme, and has always been important in the geosciences and in the energy industry. How did your style of leadership develop? Did you gain insight from peers and mentors? You were captain of a few soccer teams, too, even your alma mater, Colorado School of Mines.

DW: Yes, I was captain for my soccer teams in high school, club soccer as well as Colorado School of Mines (CSM). Actually, our freshman year was the inaugural year for the CSM team, so I was captain for all four years. I feel truly blessed to have that opportunity. If I would think back about how I'd developed my leadership skills I guess I'd have to say I never saw myself as a leader. I know there are the leaders we see, and they're public, high-profile figures. What I've been told by mentors and coaches is that I have another leadership style: a type that focuses on one-on-one personal connection. We can lead in all different capacities. As I try to wrap my mind around my different leadership positions, I'm thankful for what others see in me, but I don't see in myself. I thank other leaders and coaches that have expanded my thinking, and especially thinking about now how I can help others. That's what I enjoy most as I move into more mentor roles in my current job. I've definitely been thinking back to how my coaches and mentors helped me. They took the time to sit down with me, develop soft skills, and encouraged me to build relationships with others. In that thinking, leaders can really help move a team forward in these different capacities.

JR: What are your perspectives on how to develop a great team?

DW: So, I think what you have to look for has to do with character. You can have the most talented people in the world, but you need the right mix. Team members need passion and humility, which is very important as I think back to Anadarko. These were the core values we had as a company. Trust and integrity are important. Work ethic is so important. It is summarized in *servant leadership*, which means everyone on your team has to be thinking about each other and what they can do for the greater good of the team. All the pieces of the puzzle are needed to make a good and complete team when it's assembled. You don't want a team with too many leaders, but a team with linked arms to move forward as one. Those are the components to make a great team.

JR: What is your message to students pursuing geoscience as an area of study, or a career?

DW: There's several different ways you could go with geoscience. As early as you can, seek out opportunities to talk to others in different roles and get internships early on. Schedules get full quickly, but if you can get many internships in, that was something that benefited me. Originally, I wanted to go more geotechnical, so I did a geotech engineering internship. It was fun, but learned it was not for me. I tried an oil and gas internship the next summer and absolutely loved it. Try to get a good range of courses under your belt as you try to prepare for all options you can have throughout your career.

JR: Glad you gave the oil and gas industry a try. One last question: we've talked about the energy industry, Houston Explorers Club, leadership, NCAA sports – you keep incredibly busy! How do you achieve balance?

DW: I think it's really important to communicate having a work and life balance. Life is short. Yes careers are fun, but it's also important to find a good fit and to find things that make you happy. This concept makes me appreciate most leaders I work under. They actually live out having that good work-life balance. It's so critical to continue to pursue your passions in order to have a long career as well as for health and the culture of your organization. Having the understanding as a leader that work isn't 100% of life is critical too. As a student so focused on writing a dissertation, you need to stop and remember there is a life outside of research, too.

JR: Thank you so much Dr. Woodruff.

Above: Dr. Diane Woodruff examining the complex Carboniferous stratigraphy of the Western Irish Namurian Basin, County Clare, Ireland. Long used as an analog for fine- to very fine-grained deepwater depositional systems, such as the Paleogene Trend and portions of the Miocene, US Gulf of Mexico, the Ross Formation in particular has shed new light on the ramifications of transitional flow deposits as high-quality petroleum reservoirs in basins worldwide.

The Explorer's Mindset

Part of positive leadership is having the right mindset. Here are stories of inspirational leaders that harnessed powerful thinking to make big discoveries and succeed through some of the energy industry's biggest challenges.

Cindy A. Yeilding coined the term, *The Explorer's Mindset*, in an AAPG Distinguished Lecture tour and went on to explain the key traits of a successful explorer at the inaugural Houston Explorers Club seminar in February 2019. One of the most influential explorers of all time, her interview shares the important role of creativity in finding new fields, such as Thunder Horse in the US deepwater Gulf of Mexico.

Richard Sears describes the importance of cultivating curiosity of the unknown in deepwater protraction areas. In his fascinating interview and must-read for anyone working in the energy business, Rich describes the "hey lookies" that sometimes turn out to be the next frontier play types in world-class deepwater basins.

Dr. Scott Tinker and Richard Chuchla explain the big picture and how exploration is critical to address global energy demand across the spectrum of energy resources. Through their leadership, these explorers have done more to inform the world about energy challenges than nearly anyone in our current generation.

Kurt Rudolph stresses that in order to properly execute the exploration business, portfolio analysis and benchmarking are required to assess and ultimately achieve greater success over years and decades. Arguably one of the most knowledgeable petroleum geologists in the world, Kurt's unique insight has empowered generations of geoscientists on a global scale.

In this section on The Explorer's Mindset, all of these geoscience leaders and executives explain how events in the applied geosciences and energy industry unfolded, and how the energy world is never moribund and constantly changing.

As these leaders explain, The Explorer's Mindset includes some aspects of thinking that would get you fired in some jobs. But in exploration, these traits are celebrated – to a point. Bill Armstrong, one of the most successful wildcatters of the modern era, described some of the detail concerning this rare trait after his team's Pikka discovery on the Alaskan North Slope: 10% of the oil and gas finders find 90% of the oil, yet nearly everyone has the same access to the data and interpretation tools. This suggests creativity in the mind of the geologist still plays a major role in finding oil. It is in the careful delivery of a prospect proposal that will govern its success or failure. Failure is also important to take into consideration in exploration of any type. Exploration is necessarily going where others haven't – and with new concepts and new ideas that haven't been tested. There will be failure if you choose to be an explorer. Or you can look at those failures as leaning opportunities as to what didn't work out. Rank wildcat wells find commercial oil and gas fields about about 10% of the time. Which means 90% of the time, you get a "kick in the gut" as Richard Chuchla explains in his interview.

Exploration is often glamorized. It shouldn't be. Success and failure rates can be calibrated, reviewed, analyzed and prescribed, in many ways like a sport is analyzed. However, the plays in baseball are well defined and repeatable. Exploration in highly variable geological conditions in new areas with less than ten wells in a basin does not bode well for statistical analysis, which still strongly favors the creative mind of a geoscientist. Upon receiving a lifetime achievement award at his alma mater, L. W. Funkhouser stated, "It takes the curiosity of the geological mind to set the stage for exploration." Enjoy this section on The Explorer's Mindset.

Cindy A. Yeilding (May 2021)

"As an explorer, your job is to see opportunities that others can't see, and this can often be contentious at first. You're annoying, you're a dreamer and there are a million reasons people think you should halt. Colleagues will point out that other great minds, often with more experience, have often seen the same data but not come to the same conclusion. You note that they are solving different problems and may miss opportunities or not have access to successful analogs that offer new insights... thus annoying your colleagues even more... or so it seems! If they're telling you to get back in your box, then you're probably doing your job." – Cindy A. Yeilding

Cindy A. Yeilding most recently served as Senior Vice President of Strategic Initiatives, BP America. Previous roles include VP Gulf of Mexico Exploration & Appraisal, VP of Basin Studies & Access and Global Geoscience Research & Technology Manager for BP. Cindy earned her MSc in Geology from University of North Carolina after receiving a BS in Geology from Southern Methodist University.

Cindy's specialties include Exploration and Technology, and she most recently chaired the study team for the U.S. National Petroleum Council report on Carbon Capture, Use and Storage (CCUS).

Cindy is Chair of the Offshore Technology Conference and served on the Board of Directors of BPX&P and the Greater Houston Partnership until end 2020. She was BP's Executive Sponsor for Princeton University and is a member of the U.T. Jackson School's Advisory Council. Cindy has served as an AAPG Distinguished Lecturer and was named a "Legend in Exploration" by AAPG. In 2021, Cindy joined the Board of Directors of Denbury Inc. and is a board member of the Center for Houston's Future.

Cindy has been recognized for her leadership in energy by numerous organizations, including the "Women in Energy Leadership" award from the *Houston Business Journal*, and has been recognized as one of Houston's Top 15 Businesswomen by the National Diversity Council, one of Houston's "50 Most Influential Women" by *Houston Woman magazine* and one of *Hart Energy's* "25 Influential Women in Energy." Cindy is active in promoting STEM and women's education and created the Offshore Technology Conference (OTC) High School Energy Challenge and Women in Industry (WISE) programs for OTC.

Cindy A. Yeilding's list of achievements, awards and accomplishments is long, distinguished, and in many cases, unparalleled by anyone else in the applied geosciences and energy industry. One of the many ways she stands out is her ability to relate to so many people and inspire future leaders.

For example, Dr. Yuqian (Philomena) Gan, geoscientist with Eriksfiord and global expert in deltaic sedimentary processes, describes what it means for her to know Cindy, "Meeting Cindy as a late career PhD and an early career professional, I am impressed by how she stayed at the edge of the geoscience frontier with so many years in business roles. She has an amicable flair while effectively navigating through myriad of problems, classical and unexpected, when it comes to leadership. Being a fellow author on her book, and joining her on several of her short courses and panels, AAPG-sponsored and beyond, her unique skill of pinpointing problems, collecting resources, and delegating tasks to the people with the right skills has inspired me so much. She treats every person with equal enthusiasm and respect regardless of their stage in their career, and never holds back in giving advice. She is the leader that I want to be, and every leader should aspire to be like."

I first met Cindy in 2012. As a new employee at any company just after finishing school, you don't often get to interact with the top brass. This assumption should be especially true at a supermajor. Among my peer group at BP, by far the one who everyone looked up to was Cindy. No last name, just *Cindy*. Because everyone knew there was only one Cindy, and that was Cindy A. Yeilding, Senior Vice President. SVP Yeilding's effective leadership is responsible for the discovery of billions of barrels of oil equivalent worldwide. When I first met Cindy, the Paleogene Trend aka "Deepwater Wilcox" was taking off as one of the final frontiers in the US deepwater Gulf of Mexico. Cindy was in charge of the Paleogene, and it was no mystery why. 20K technology was in high demand to produce from the Paleogene, and Cindy had been interviewed by many, including Oil and Gas Journal, on the progress in the tech development. Advances in technology and engineering were needed to be able to produce oil from such great depths in the Paleogene Trend, an area of nearly 34,000 square miles with fields stretching from the Perdido Fold Belt (original well BAHA-1) to Jack and St Malo southeast of New Orleans at the edge of the Sigsbee Escarpment. As a Paleogene interpreter, I only presented to Cindy a few times, but she was always keenly aware of the team's work. Since retiring from an incredible career with BP, Cindy has joined additional boards in the industry and non-profit sector. She has continued to give back to the energy industry through the Offshore Technology Conference (which she chaired) and other conferences, another AAPG Distinguished Lecture and also spearheading as editor *Deepwater Sedimentary Systems*.

It is amazing how well-connected Cindy is in the energy industry. Everyone knows her. One time, I called to discuss an issue related to the book, and she replied, "Can I call you right back? Armstrong invited us to dinner at SMU where he's receiving a lifetime achievement award. We need to leave soon." Oh, to be on the short dial list of the world's most successful modern wildcatter. Cindy has all the qualities of an exceptionally rare and world-class leader. She has achieved so much in research, resource discovery, inspiring a company and an industry. She is an AAPG Legend of Exploration as one of the top explorationists of all time.

I interviewed SVP Cindy A. Yeilding in May 2020 to learn about exploration leadership and what the future holds for the global energy industry. Read the interview below.

Jon Rotzien (JR): SVP Yeilding, I'm so thankful you had the time to visit today and share your story. Your background in geology and on-the-job business training enabled you to contribute significantly to the global energy industry. Your teams throughout the years with BP invested meaningfully in Super Basins such as the Gulf of Mexico since the 1990s.

Could you share your background, and what led you to your most recent role in BP?

Cindy Yeilding (CY): Jon, thank you so much for the opportunity to chat and catch up! Congratulations on the success of Basin Dynamics, the Houston Explorers Club and all of your other exciting ventures. My background...let's go WAY back. My undergraduate and graduate degrees are in geology, focused on stratigraphy and sedimentary responses to tectonic activity. I began my career with bp in the mid-1980s, including three years of wellsite operations, which really helped ground me in the operational and safety aspects of our industry. I've worked across the value chain and have done almost everything a geologist can do in upstream but most of my career had been in exploration and technology in both technical and leadership roles. I've also had the privilege of working and teaching courses all over the world.

JR: Could you describe your strengths that enabled you to perform those roles at such a high level?

CY: I really thrive on problem solving and creating business opportunities. One of my strengths is busting down dogmas or entrenched thinking. My most successful approach is to constantly test ideas with others and refine where appropriate. I'm not talking about *group think*. This is about using the bigger brain to test and strengthen ideas and also to build understanding and ownership. I'm not sure where I first heard this but supposedly someone has to be exposed to a new idea seven times before the can fully appreciate it.

I used to find different ways to share new ideas with colleagues so that it wasn't just the same approach over and over.

Of course, some ideas should not progress, or the timing may not be right, and you have to learn to read those signs and stop before you diminish them. This teamworking, listening and collaborative approach is what set me up for my most recent job as SVP of Strategic Initiatives (read: big special projects) for BP, where my role was to work across groups of diverse experts to solve problems, answer questions and listen and learn from key stakeholders.

JR: Great points, thank you. Energy stocks took up about~12% of the S&P 500 about a decade ago, now it's about 2%, yet oil and gas represents about 8% of the US GDP. How does the oil and gas industry navigate these difficult market conditions?

CY: Oil and gas are commodities and thus have a volatile or cyclic price. As industry employees know, this has never been a "stable" business but the challenges associated with those fluctuations on the downside often drive technology improvements, simplification and collaboration. The industry has always been able to navigate prices, but never really predict them.

JR: Exactly, it seems the successful companies never forget where they are in that industry price cycle.

Congratulations on your recent conference on Carbon Capture, Use and Storage (CCUS) with AAPG. There have been numerous articles on how the classic oil and gas industry is filling some roles in CCUS, including Hollub's wholesale proposed transition of Oxy. What inspired you to take on the role as the chair of the working team for the National Petroleum Council (NPC) study on CCUS?

CY: Like many in our community, I have friends and family members who question the future of the oil and gas industry and also criticize the history of industrial emissions related to fossil fuel use. In my case, it's my children Tyler and Zack. So, when the opportunity to play a role in helping create a future for CCUS in the U.S. came up, I enthusiastically volunteered to help John Mingé, former Chairman of BP America and my boss at the time, who had been asked to be the executive chair the NPC study. Little did I know that would quickly evolve to leading the 300⁺ person global team of experts to deliver an in-depth analysis of the challenge and a roadmap for the U.S. to move to "At-Scale" deployment of CCUS technology. This was an amazing experience for me and I am so grateful to the experts from a range of energy and industrial businesses, academicians, policy experts, NGOs, the financial community and governments who collaborated on this project. Want to learn more? You can download the 600+ page report here as well as the two-page roadmap and executive summary: https://dualchallenge.npc.org/downloads.php.

JR: Yes, we want to learn more. Thank you for sharing. What is driving the change in industry investment in CCUS?

CY: There have been multiple efforts to begin larger-scale CCUS implementation over the past few decades but momentum has then eroded – most likely based on costs. So, what is different now?

CCUS technology is proven and society's understanding of climate science and the issues facing us is maturing. This is leading to greater acceptance that CCUS offers a solution to the challenge of managing CO_2 emissions today. It's not the only solution but is a critical element of the portfolio of technologies that can be applied to address climate change. CCUS offers so much potential for the world and there are proven technology chains that can be applied now. We need policy help and multi-stakeholder support to catalyze CCUS to help make it into a robust trillion-dollar business. Which gets us to another important point: CCUS will create new jobs and as the industry matures it will also it will also help replace jobs that could be lost in other sectors.

JR: What an exciting path for CCUS – that journey is just beginning it seems. Let's talk about corporate energy industry road maps.

A successful company is built with a vision, correct implementation of a strategy, adequate deal flow, deep subject matter knowledge – a lot of hard work to make smart investment decisions and probably a bit of luck – among other things. Can you describe what it takes to grow *within a company* like you did at BP?

CY: Great question. I've never been a "grass is greener" person and I worked for an amazing company with fantastic leadership and global opportunities, so I focused on progression within the company ra_ than through external job changes. Often, my managers had mc confidence in my abilities than I did, and they often nudged me into roles I didn't think I was ready to take on. Looking back, I really appreciate the support of my colleagues who saw potential in me even when I didn't recognize it. I really enjoyed the technical part of the job, and I didn't want them at first to take my microscope or workstation away! I even hid a microscope in my office for a few years and kept all of my workstation accounts so I could interpret data after hours! I think keeping that technical edge sharp and curious helped me succeed.

It goes without saying but I'll state it anyway: be really, really good at your job! Always deliver on time and aim to have your work exceed expectations. It's important to always be approachable, pragmatic and authentic: not only are these good life skills but your work will benefit from the wisdom of others if you take the time to ask for their insights and listen to their ideas, questions and advice. Finally, always, always, always acknowledge others! I strongly believe in *corporate karma* (this is my term – not sure if others will appreciate it). If you support others in their careers and lives, the universe will look after you as well! Also, it helps to be in the right place at the right time.

JR: If I remember correctly, one of your first big team achievements was the discovery of Thunder Horse (Crazy Horse at the time), thereby providing BP a competitive edge in mapping and interpreting the Miocene GOM with success. Is that correct?

CY: Yes. Thunder Horse and subsequent discoveries in the middle and lower Miocene trend of the Gulf of Mexico are amazing stories in overcoming dogma and persevering with first principles of geoscience. Once the ideas were proven, step changes in drilling, completions and geophysical imaging subsalt were required, which helped us develop the fields and helped advance offshore technologies for other basins and plays as well.

JR: Now, over decades, you've been able to lead and oversee the development of some of the largest data sets available to industry (3D seismic, well data, production data, outcrop analogs, etc. in North America, Latin America, Europe, Asia Pacific) with your other roles

...Head of Basin Analysis and New Ventures, among ...adership roles. You've had an opportunity to see ...resources with great perspective. Can you tell ...what it takes to build "deep knowledge" in a basin through years of drilling, successes (as well as probably some failures)?

CY: Have you got all day? OK... I don't think we do, so here are a few of my favorites:

- Expect surprises and always carry multiple models. It's important to understand that there are non-unique solutions to most geoscience challenges. There's an art to explaining multiple interpretations without confusing the heck out of everyone but learn how to do this as it will serve you well and is part of your job. It's surprising to me I've often had to remind explorers to do this!

- Use all the tools in your tool kit: there is no black box for exploration (or if there is, please let me know!). There are often many tools available, including reservoir quality analysis and modeling, pore pressure analysis and geochemical data and my favorite – biostratigraphy – that can often be overlooked or ignored. Don't let this happen! You'll have conflicting data, but part of solving the Earth's puzzles is to help each piece of data fit and explain anomalies, even where it might appear to be conflicting or contradictory.

- Another element of geologic successes is learning from others: other scientists including local academicians and government experts; insights and data from other basins; technologies and wisdom from other industries. Expertise and experience paired with fresh eyes and first principles of geoscience can be a powerful combination.

JR: Thank you for the sage advice. Your leadership across the various roles in the industry – *as well as outside the industry* – is impressive. Congratulations on your new appointment to the board of Denbury. You chair the Board of the Offshore Technology Conference, you're on the Board of the Center for Houston's Future and have served on the board and executive committee of the

Greater Houston Partnership. Can you share some of your key leadership and philanthropic principles?

CY: It's been such an honor and a privilege to be invited to play a role in the governance and strategic oversight of businesses and not-for-profit institutions. My exploration and technology background has certainly underpinned my candidacy for these roles and I bring lots of fresh ideas and creativity to each one. I actually have to rein myself in sometimes and be sure that I am serving in the role in which they have invited me to serve.

For example, my time with OTC is donated on behalf of the American Association of Petroleum Geologists. Not many people realize that OTC is a not-for-profit, with any net revenues distributed back to AAPG and 11 other supporting societies. I love that I can be a part of such a diverse global technical event that reaches so many people. We had over 108,000 attendees in Houston at OTC in 2014 to focus on safety, technology development, energy transition, lessons learned and, of course, exploration! It's a very fun and fulfilling way to "give back" to AAPG – an organization that has been a part of my life for over 40 years.

JR: You've attended some great colleges and universities. I understand that you're a Mustang first, and then you completed a MS at UNC Chapel Hill. What was it like being a student in geology then? What would be your message to students at these universities interested in making a career in the energy industry?

CY: As my son Zack would say, I went to school back in the Stone Age when rocks were all we had to study! Seriously, we used to say, "She who sees the most rocks wins," and my schools offered excellent field experience: weekend trips; field camps; research opportunities. Be sure to take advantage of any hands-on investigations: fieldwork of course, but also the range data analysis opportunities from the micro to mega-scale.

JR: I wish we could get out into the field again soon!

CY: To get a great education, you should dig deeper than the coursework and take advantage of the amazing opportunities a university offers. Get to know your professors and other students.

Seek out those with real-world experience: folks with energy, government, NGO and previous academic experience can help you understand the real-world applications of geoscience and the types of opportunities available in different industries. There is amazing experience in the academic system and it's not all taught in the lecture halls (*but don't skip your classes!*). Don't ring fence yourself away from the community.

JR: You're famous for your message on *the Explorer's Mindset*. That was an incredibly inspiring presentation you gave at the first meeting of the Houston Explorers Club in February 2019. How did you come to realize what makes the role of exploration so different from other roles in a company, like a BP or ExxonMobil or Shell?

CY: As an explorer, your job is to see opportunities that others can't see, and this can often be contentious at first. You're annoying, you're a dreamer and there are a million reasons people think you should halt. Colleagues will point out that other great minds, often with more experience, have often seen the same data but not come to the same conclusion. You note that they are solving different problems and may miss opportunities or not have access to successful analogs that offer new insights... thus annoying your colleagues even more... or so it seems! If they're telling you to get back in your box, then you're probably doing your job.

You have to be patient and be the right mix of scientist and visionary – not that those two are exclusive in any way but at first people can be resistant to any new idea. One of my favorite performance evaluations stated that, as a development geologist in the late 1980s, I should stop talking about those "airy fairy" deep prospects (now known as the middle and lower Miocene trend of the GOM) and focus on the task at hand (remapping a 15 mmboe offshore field for the 4th time). I later transferred to Exploration, where other like-minded souls were working, and was able to play a role in maturing those notional leads into a new play and a series of drilling prospects.

Technology development is often symbiotic with exploration and goes hand-in-hand with the creation of new opportunities. Often, this is not about what technology can deliver today but realistically, what will technology be able to do in the future and how do you create these enhancements or breakthroughs? Will it make economic sense: if not, then move on. It's also important to explore any policy enhancements that could make this new opportunity feasible.

On another related note, as with any "new" business concept, there is also much dogmatic thinking in CCUS. Just like being an explorer! In my keynote at the AAPG CCUS conference, I made the analogy of how CCUS thinking works today and compared it with how exploration progressed in the deepwater GOM. People are saying, "You can't do that; you can't do this. It's never going to make money." And those exploration plays people originally said "no" to are some of the main producing trends in the world today.

JR: Do you draw inspiration on this perspective from other aspects of life, perhaps sports?

CY: People shut down ideas, not because you can't do them but because of technological limitations and excessive costs. I'm more of a shopper than a sports expert but I really like the Wayne Gretzky-ism of, "Go to where the puck is." What his statement really means is, "Make the puck go there and be ready when it arrives." Deepwater is that way. That great prize created the catalyst to develop technology to discover and produce in the hundreds of thousands of barrels per day from deepwater fields. Trust me, there were a lot of deepwater non-believers out there!

JR: You've been around a lot of oil and gas explorers for decades…you've seen some succeed, and some fail – both in spectacular fashion. However, lessons can be learned from both of these experiences. What is your message for oil and gas explorers today?

CY: Always learn, learn, learn! Be humble in your successes and own your failures by learning from them and moving forward: lessons learned could lead to a new way of thinking and new opportunities. Oil and gas will be a part of our global en come but as explorers, we need to embrace engage in opportunities to create busir solutions to help reduce CO_2 emissions, reduce airborne particulate matter. I encour apply the Exploration Mindset to all aspects busting dogmas just as important (perhaps

CCUS as it is in oil and gas. To me, carbon storage through enhanced oil recovery or saline storage offers an ideal way to utilize the discovery thinking and the creation of new business opportunities.

Thanks again Jon! It's been a pleasure catching up with you and I appreciate your interest in my career and experiences. Hopefully, we'll see you and your colleagues at the Offshore Technology Conference in August if not before!

JR: See you at OTC! Thank you so much SVP Yeilding.

Above: The verdant Ballybunion peninsula and calm Shannon Estuary. Nearly 200 m of stratigraphy of the Carboniferous Ross Sandstone dominated by hybrid event beds is exposed at low tide. This interval is a common analog for fan fringe environments in the deepwater Wilcox Trend, US Gulf of Mexico as described in Marchand et al. (2015) in the *AAPG Bulletin* and other publications.

Richard A. Sears (February 2022)

"The message of peak oil is the wrong message. It's a bad message to carry around. There's a whole bunch of people that imagined the world would be saved from climate change if we'd run out and have to stop producing oil. And that peak would save the world. The message I would like to deliver to this group, and the TED group is a very environmentally active community, the message to deliver to them was, "Don't think oil will go away just because." There's a lot of it out there. Every time we look deeper in the Earth, we find more. If you want to displace oil, you will have to find something new. And that's not going to happen on autopilot. Oil is not going away just because you want it to. 12 years later, I've been proven right by events. Not because I was insightful. I just looked at data and have been living the data for 45 years. This seemed to be the logical answer." – Richard A. Sears

Richard and Patti Sears enjoy a Stanford football game at the Rose Bowl in Pasadena, California, USA.

Richard A. Sears is Adjunct Professor in the Department of Energy Resources Engineering at Stanford University. He began his career as a geophysicist with Shell Oil Company in 1976. During his 33 years with Shell Oil Co. and Royal Dutch Shell, he held technical and managerial positions including exploration geophysicist, technical instructor, economist, strategic advisor and planner, and general management. He spent seven years as Vice President, Global Subsurface Deepwater Technical Services. After retiring from Shell, he was Chief Scientist for the National Oil Spill Commission and is a co-author of the Commission's Chief Counsel's Report which details the technical and managerial failures leading to the Deepwater Horizon blowout and spill, and has served on several committees through the National Academy of Engineering, advising industry and the US Government on safety in offshore energy operations. He received his BS in physics and MS in geophysics from Stanford University, is a licensed Professional Geoscientist, and is a National Associate of the National Academies of Sciences, Engineering and Medicine.

Richard A. Sears is one of the most knowledgeable geoscientists in the global energy industry. Rich has led a distinguished career with many of his roles in leadership. Most recently, he served as lead author in the study titled "Advancing Understanding of Offshore Oil and Gas Systemic Risk in the U.S. Gulf of Mexico: Current State and Safety Reforms Since the Macondo Well Deepwater Horizon Blowout (2023)" which can be downloaded from the National Academies. This was following other distinguished posts including Chief Science and Technology Adviser to the National Commission on the BP Deepwater Horizon Oil Spill under President Obama, and Chair for the Committee on Application of Real-Time Monitoring of Offshore Oil and Gas Operations. Prior to his appointment at Stanford University and his service with the US government, he held various leadership positions with Royal Dutch Shell and Shell Oil Company. He spent 33 years with Shell where he gained significant onshore and offshore experience in oil and gas exploration and production. His latest post as an executive with Royal Dutch Shell, included the responsibility of designing and leading the global deepwater technical services business unit. He also served as Visiting Scientist with MIT to coordinate Shell's external research activities with internal technology strategies.

I first met Rich in 2009 at the Stanford Homecoming Reception for the School of Earth Sciences. I had just completed an internship at the Bellaire Tech Center in Houston, as part of their turbidite research group. Rich was visiting as a member of the Board for the School. When I met him, he had heard about my internship, "Oh yeah, how was working with Shell in Houston?" he asked. I was amazed that an executive at his level kept in touch with the news at the intern level. Years later, now it makes such perfect sense that Rich is truly gifted with understanding people and their contributions to a common goal. Others I've met tell me a similar story about meeting and working with Rich. All of them felt very fortunate to work on his team. Leaders seek to know about members of their team, no matter what level they're at in the company. Since then, we have worked together on a number of deepwater-related projects, most recently as co-editors of *Deepwater Sedimentary Systems*.

I was delighted to get to interview Rich to learn about the energy industry and leadership in deepwater exploration and production. Rich has given me and many others countless bits of important advice. I tend to keep notes when Rich is explaining anything energy related. Expressing the necessity of being on time for deadlines for our deepwater book, both internally and with the publisher, he told me that, "In our industry, if a lease sale is on March 6, and it's on March 6, you're either ready or you're not. There's no asking for an extension. And if *you don't get the lease, you don't get the grease.*" Rich is able to meaningfully connect with employees and colleagues around the world, one of his gifts that makes him an exceptionally rare and talented leader. Enjoy the interview below, *and be sure to take notes.*

Jon Rotzien (JR): Rich, I'm so thankful you had the time to visit today. How did you get started in geophysics?

Richard Sears (RS): That was an interesting story. I was happy in the high energy physics lab at Stanford working with a number of grad students helping to build a gravitational radiation detector. It was a lot of fun. I would think, "Wow this is what real physicists do." I knew I wanted to major in physics, I thought it was really neat. The problem, however, was there were no jobs for physicists. It was the early to mid-70s. Many of the academic positions were filled, and there were no jobs for bachelors. Only the PhDs were getting jobs. But even they were looking around for work. I had a lot of friends who were physics grad students, and I noticed these really smart guys – who by the way were a whole lot smarter than me – were finding it a hard time to get jobs. They would maybe get a non-tenure track assistant professor role, or a post doc, and then when three years was up, they'd be on the market again looking for their next job. "Oh well," I thought, "I like physics, I'll stick with it."

Then in the middle of my junior year, Allen Cox in Geophysics had a habit of putting notes in the mailboxes of the physics undergrads. One note read, "Have you thought of doing a co-term masters in geophysics?"

JR: A co-term is an extra year of school to complete a masters program, only available to students currently enrolled in the undergraduate program. Allen didn't try to point you in the direction of something more meaningful in life, like being a lawyer or studying deepwater depositional systems?

RS: He was brilliant in his short note. The front side was what geophysics was all about, and the back page, Allen was very smart, he had included short paragraphs on people who had done the co-term and where they working – and what they were making. I thought, "The PhDs in physics aren't getting money like that!"

So, I figured geophysics – *why not?* It's almost like physics. So, I talked to Allen and registered for GP51 Introductory Geophysics taught by Allen. He was on the 3rd floor of Mitchell.

JR: Still the main building for geophysics at Stanford.

RS: After I first talked with Allen I went down to Branner Library, walked back to where they kept the journals for geophysical research. At random, I pulled an issue of JGR, opened up to a random page and started reading. Lo and behold, I could understand everything. The science was really accessible. Now if you went into the physics library and pulled out Physical Review, there's a good chance you would not understand everything. However, I found geophysics to be very accessible. You can understand it. It was not a science with deeply embedded language and codes and everything.

I took 51 and thought this was really fun, completed my co-term masters, and Shell offered me a job. 33 years later I left Shell. 45 years later, here I am back at Stanford.

JR: You give a fascinating TED talk on the subject of oil. What is your message about hydrocarbons?

RS: My message there, as I tried to counter what I thought was a whole array of wrong messages floating around about oil and gas....so this was 2010. In 2010, peak oil was a popular topic of discussion. We were running out of oil. The world was going to do the peak oil thing. Peak production, lack of resource, the whole story. In fact in 2010, there was a whole crowd claiming the world had peaked for good on Thanksgiving Day in 2007. There is a website called *Peak Oil*. And that was the date they gave. And we would never get back to that level of production. They cited lack of supply, limited resource and the rest.

Here's the thing, I was never a peak oil adherent. I didn't think it was accurate. Because I looked at numbers. Everyone liked the Hubbert curves. But when you look at what he said, the fact was in the mid-2000s, roughly the 2005-2010 period, the US Lower 48 was producing a million barrels a day more than Hubbert said we should be producing. And by 2015 it was more than 2 million barrels a day greater. Where did all that new oil come from? It came from plays not imagined in 1990s.

It came from stuff like deepwater. 3D seismic was a huge contributor. And shale.

I had come to the conclusion in the mid-80s as Manager of Economics for Shell Oil Exploration, that on the scale of human civilization, the amount of natural gas in the world was effectively infinite. There would always be gas available – at a price – and the price would get higher. But it would be available at a certain price. But I never said that about oil.

JR: Why not oil?

RS: Oil is harder. There probably isn't as much around, but I've since come to the conclusion we're not running out of oil anytime soon either. Every time people predict the demise of oil, someone finds something new. Overthrusts in the Rockies, 3D seismic technology improves, a new Gulf Coast play comes along no one has ever thought of. Then you have the deepwater.

Along with that, it's not just these 1980s phenomena, but this pattern will continue forever. That's exploration. The Head of Exploration for Shell, in 1960s, said, "I'll drink every drop of oil you find in the North Sea." 30-40 billion barrels later, he's full up.

Hubbert was right for what was known then, it makes perfect sense. He reasonably described production from plays known in the 1950s but had no idea what new exploration and new plays would come about later.

All of this to say, the message of peak oil is the wrong message. It's a bad message to carry around. There's a whole bunch of people that imagined the world would be saved from climate change if we'd run out and have to stop producing oil. And that peak would save the world.

The message I would like to deliver to this group, and the TED group is a very environmentally active community, the message to deliver to them was, "Don't think oil will go away just because." There's a lot of it out there. Every time we look deeper in the Earth, we find more. If you want to displace oil, you will have to find something new. And that's not going to happen on autopilot. Oil is not going away just because you want it to. 12 years later, I've been proven right by events. Not because I was insightful. I just looked at data and have been living the data for 45 years. This seemed to be logical answer.

JR: But many people can argue about data.

RS: A lot of people in TED didn't agree with that answer I gave. One guy would hound me in particular. He said he wanted to strangle me. The group sort of invested in this notion, "We can save the world just because we'll have to run out of oil," continues to disagree with this history of oil and gas exploration.

JR: Why are you so interested in deepwater exploration and production?

RS: Well, like a lot of things in my career, it happened due to my role. I became interested in deepwater because I got a job in deepwater. I didn't know I was interested in economics until they made me manager of economics for the company. I thought to myself, "Do I tell my boss's boss that I never took an econ class since high school – and there's a reason why?" Or do I keep it to myself. Plus, it was just a neat title – *Manager of Exploration Economics*.

JR: Cool title.

RS: So, I did that, I did Midcon Exploration. I was Head of Exploration Shell UK. I was also happily running Shell's Michigan business at one point. If you consider Deepwater as Big Oil, Michigan was Small Oil, but it was making a ton of money. We basically owned the oil business in Michigan. We operated hundreds of wells, the sulphur removal systems, and the gas and pipeline network. It was basically a small integrated oil company.

Then I was asked to run deepwater projects in the Gulf of Mexico. Michigan was fun, the econ role was fun, Oklahoma was fun, Williston was fun, seismic acquisition projects were fun. Then with the success we had in the Gulf of Mexico deepwater, we were asked to look at global opportunities in deepwater. How do we prosecute it? Out of that we created Shell Deepwater Services to do deepwater technical work for Shell around the world, and I was named to lead the subsurface organization for the exploration and development projects. I did that for 7 years. So, this interest for deepwater grew out of managers telling me, "Here's your next assignment."

JR: Naturally.

RS: For deepwater, I found out this is pretty exciting. It was exciting for the scale and global nature of it. And it's one of those things I've stayed abreast of, at least as I've done other things. It's most intriguing when you look at deepwater and its development over several decades. It's actually a good analogy of how oil and gas works. In the beginning, the industry imagines there's no resource there. Then someone has a thought. Then you get crummy data, not that it's bad, just that the first data set often looks pretty bad. Then you look back at the growth of deepwater and ask, "How did we *ever do anything* with that lousy data?"

JR: And how?

RS: It highlights the adage, "I never would've seen it if I hadn't believed it." It usually started off with some smart geologist saying, "This could be..." and you fill in the blank. And out of that statement, you think you could see more. And out of that, you drill a well. I was lucky to work for Shell who wanted to spend 10s of millions of dollars on wells to test these crazy concepts. Really deepwater is the oil and gas business in a microcosm.

A funny aside on early lousy data. In the 1980's I was working on strategy for Shell's Exploration VP. There was a show-and-tell for the E&P Executive VP on a developing play and one of the seismic lines they showed was from a decade earlier. It was a critical line because of its location but the quality was terrible. It ran through the middle of a major oil field, there was a lot of surface noise, and it was the first generation of modern data in a new play. Nobody said anything about the vintage of the data, and I don't think anybody in the room knew that I was the seismic party chief responsible for acquiring it. At the end the Exec. VP said let's go forward, but I have one question. Why did you spend the money to acquire this lousy data? I sat there quietly and didn't say anything. He was a production engineer and wouldn't have understood.

JR: Can you tell us about what the dogma was like back in the 70s and 80s pertaining to deepwater E&P?

RS: Deepwater in particular...Shell was pretty busy in deepwater. Shell had been the dominant company in the GOM shelf for many years. And then what a great company it was. Then the industry moved into the flex trend. We missed it, we were not a part of it. And we were not a part of it because we were chasing a geological model that did not apply in the flex trend. When you're so close to something, such as Shell was on the shelf and into the flex trend, you think you know it and how to do it. As you go deeper and deeper the geological models change, but also necessarily the production models have to change. The industry was getting farther from the short cycle, fixed platform developments on the shelf. And in deeper water, the companies wanted to build bigger and bigger fixed platforms. That was some of the dogma within Shell. "There will never be an economic development in the GOM further than 60 mi from shore." People said that. We had limited ourselves into what and why something was working.

JR: Incredible dogma to overcome.

RS: So ok, we missed that. Luckily though, then really deepwater came about, with companies drilling in a couple thousand feet of water.

The first several wells in the really deep water in the GOM were dry holes. People were finding a lot of sand, a lot of shows, but nothing looked like a viable hydrocarbon system, with real traps of scale enough to support a development. So, the conventional dogmas persisted that there were no viable petroleum systems, and that there was a lack of reservoir-seal-trap scenarios. This message seemed to be playing out with the early drilling. And it wasn't just Shell dogma, but also industry wide. In the first days of deepwater, most of the industry just ignored it.

Shell, on the other hand, and that's the funny thing about explorers. They don't let dogma stop them. They sort of had this mantra about them, "There must be something worth taking a look, at so let's go look at it." So, Shell purchased a small amount of spec data, then we were able to acquire much more a little bit later on our own seismic boat. We were seeing interesting things that merited further investigation.

JR: What are those "hey lookies" you've described?

RS: That was coined by Tom Hart, the Exploration VP at Shell for a long time. And he was an explorer, one of the old school types of explorers. Tom was a good geologist and an interesting character. He wasn't much interested in getting down and dirty in the geophysics of things, like seismic response, AVO, rock properties, seismic rock physics. When the geophysicists would start showing bright spots and explain amplitudes, Tom would refer to them all as "hey lookies". Tom had a lot of respect for people who would push the *hey lookies*.

These were looking very interesting, large amplitude anomalies and we had a lot of experience on the shelf with amplitudes as direct hydrocarbon indicators. Tom understood these were early days and could entertain the geophysicists and geologists talking crazy ideas et of water. We don't understand fully what these eant, but boy does it look attractive.

After drilling Mars and Auger, Shell had the good fortune of owning – you can see the picture over my shoulder on the wall – our very own seismic acquisition boat, the Shell America, which gave us a huge advantage in acquiring large data sets over the entire GOM.

JR: That's a good-looking boat.

RS: So, we had a few good wells. Deepwater things appear to be working. Auger looked a lot like the shelf, though it just happened to be in nearly 3,000 feet of water. Mars was a big bright amplitude anomaly in closure, probably with a stratigraphic component. With Shell America acquiring proprietary seismic dataset around the GOM and these wells, we were able to chase trends and attain area wide coverage in the Gulf. As things would play out, this all happened at the same time as the first area wide offshore sales under the Reagan administration.

Instead of having to nominate blocks, the entire Eastern GOM was up for sale and then Western and you could bid on wherever you wanted. We were able to buy up huge swaths of the deepwater. That opened up the whole deepwater GOM for us.

JR: Amazing.

RS: Why wouldn't you be interested in deepwater if you're in oil and gas? You may be making money off of other areas, San Joaquin Valley, shale plays in the Lower 48, but if you're paying attention, you'll have to find deepwater at least marginally interesting.

JR: How about those new discoveries – Graff and Venus – by Shell, Total, NAMCOR?

RS: Shell made a promising discovery, and there seems to be a lot of interest. This is how it goes. In the early days of deepwater we understood the GOM pretty well. By we, I mean Shell. We understood the GOM and understood what made deepwater work. We took those concepts around world, and it led us to places like Nigeria. Angola – that was one we missed. But it also took us to Brazil. The key components we were looking for were simple: a big river system that

empties into an offshore basin with mobile substrat
that's salt. For Nigeria, that's shale. Those elemen
complex basin history, including the GOM and ho
complexity gives a whole array of trap geometries a
of the model we were chasing early on. Big river, deepwater setting, mobile substrate. All that sand onto mobile substrate, and it's going to deform and get complex geometries favorable for traps. Who knows what we're going to see? But we knew we needed those elements to be successful.

And it was sort of working. You can chase this model in lots of places. It's a nice idea, but we weren't always right.

JR: It became dogma?

RS: In your interview with Javier, he had a quote that in some of his exploration drilling cruises, the scientists thought the sand would be soft, and mud would be hard. And they drilled into it and it was not. Similarly, in these deepwater ventures and plays, a well would be drilled into a high feature, and it turns out….it's…Oh my gosh! The sands were hard, shales soft. So, we got it wrong. Then we'd go back to data, take the basin apart, and put it back together again. Ultimately that's how you make new discoveries, in whole new settings and new play types. This happened many times.

JR: What about one specific time?

RS: Going back in time, there was a large structure to be drilled called BAHA, in what is now the Perdido development. BAHA was thought to be a carbonate bank. It looks like some of the big North Sea fields. This idea that you're out in a sediment starved deepwater setting would make sense that it could have been a big carbonate development. So, everyone has in mind this will be a big carbonate structure. We imagine with the seismic analogs we have, that we were going to find North Sea-like carbonates.

The first well didn't make it. There was a pressure problem and we ran out of casing. We went back later, and what did we find? We found Wilcox sand. Way downdip from where it was supposed to be. This changes the whole perspective on the GOM. What you thought you understood was wrong, but you drilled in the right place to

...rstand it. That opens up a whole new play trend in very deep water. We were looking at sand that was thought to never have made it that far.

JR: Now the Wilcox is a major producer.

RS: This same type of thing played out in the shelf. In the early 80s there was this one discovery. Some wells had been drilled, but no hydrocarbons had been found. This was a company named Oryx chasing specific sand intervals, and they found a sand way downdip from the where everyone thought the shelf edge was at the time. They started looking around and tried to understand what that meant. They made one major discovery – several 100 mmboe. Again, this was everyone chasing a play, and most people weren't recognizing how unique and surprising it was when it really said, "Hey, there's a sand here that doesn't belong here."

Most companies said, "Ok it's water wet, let's move on." But a few curious people said, "Hey this sand – what does it mean?" In several years, it meant new plays, new opportunities, new significant discoveries. That how oil and gas works. From the Wilcox in the Western GOM, or deepwater Malaysia or Brazil or Nigeria. That's what makes this business work and what makes it fun. Ultimately, it creates huge value. It is explorers who were really doing the business of exploration.

JR: You started school at Stanford, and now you've come full circle. What do you do at Stanford?

RS: I'm an Adjunct Professor in the Energy Resource Engineering Department, and I develop and teach classes. I teach classes that I think are in some cases necessary, and I'm the best to teach them. There is a gap in what Stanford has to offer students. There is an undergrad core requirement course in engineering economics. This teaches students how money flows through projects and how you measure profitability. It's been a requirement in ERE forever. But no one was teaching it. No one in department was skilled at it. So, they said, "Go take it in the Engineering school at Stanford, in Civil Engineering." Of course, civil engineering projects teach you how to build things, and if it's better to buy or own an apartment building. It teaches you how money flows, but there aren't examples of energy.

I was asked to teach this with a focus on energy, and I'm teaching it in the spring quarter. I was teaching production engineering a few years ago. The Stanford focus in petroleum engineering has long been in subsurface flow. This course teaches you what happens when it gets into the well and onto the surface. In upstream oil and gas, you have three principle types of engineers – reservoir engineers, production engineers and facilities engineers. The stuff in the middle – production engineering – hadn't been taught in a long time.

Other classes I've developed have been important because nobody was talking about this stuff – and it's important. I've taught every year an energy technology, infrastructure and economics course. The idea is to look at the nature of how an energy company works. Admittedly I focus on oil and gas companies and how they're structured. How they look. What's important to them. What advantage do they have in the global energy business. While I focus on oil and gas, which is what I know, I claim this course is good for anyone at Stanford. Period.

JR: Why?

RS: Here's the reason:

There are three big chunks of students at Stanford: a small group is going to get a degree in geology, geophysics, engineering, and go to work for an oil company. They need to understand how the oil business works. This is your chance to understand how your skills interact, how the technology interacts with infrastructure and makes for a profitable business. That's one group. The second group, which is somewhat larger, they're the people that are interested in energy but not oil and gas. They want to lead the future of energy. What does the energy transition look like? How do you deliver energy at scale to people in the world 30 years from now? Oil energy is not going away because you want it to.

The frustrating thing said by IEA last year is, "If we want to meet global climate targets, we can't start new oil projects."

JR: But there are new oil projects starting.

RS: You want to starve people of energy? There's nothing to backfill what you need to take offline. If you want to be leaders in the energy transition, you'd better understand oil and gas because that's what you're competing against. And it's very profitable, very robust, and very resilient. And you're going to have to try to find something better, not just because it's different. Oil and gas has all this installed infrastructure, which is a huge advantage. There are small refineries on the East Coast, really small. 100,000 barrels a day compared to 500,000-700,000 barrels a day capacity along the Gulf Coast. The Colonial pipeline system gets Gulf Coast refined products to the East Coast. These 4-foot diameter pipelines move 100 million gallons a day of petroleum products from the Gulf Coast to the port of New York. What does it cost to move? A nickel a gallon. It you want to power the East Coast, you have to find something at comparable economics at scale to displace oil and gas.

JR: How does this resonate with the class?

RS: If you want to lead the energy revolution, people won't flock to you because you're cheaper. They'll go to you because you're better. Nobody bought a PC in the 90s because they were cheap. No one bought an HP calculator for $400 in the 70s because they were cheaper than a slide rule. They were better. No one bought a car because it's cheaper than a horse. Or an airline ticket because it was cheaper than the train. It's not price that creates big wins in technology revolutions. Many thought leaders don't understand this. If you want to win, you're going to have to win on utility. Price matters, but ultimately utility determines what matters. Price determines the pace of development. People will flock to what works better. Why don't we all still have land lines? Because the cell phone is better than the land line – it's not attached to land.

Those are the first two groups.

JR: And the third?

RS: The third group is the largest group at Stanford. Not going to an oil company. Not going into the energy industry. They'll go off to do something. They'll probably be a thought leader. Whether in media or politics, at some level, they'll be expected to know why the world works. The world works because of energy. You need to know it. I see this in thought leaders, yet they don't know energy at all. They're happy to make pronouncements, yet they haven't the slightest idea of what they're talking about. These three groups make up most of Stanford.

JR: How many students do you get to teach?

RS: So, this course is important to all. How many do I get? About 30 students per year. In this class, I'm sharing real stuff about the world, and most students come out knowing something. Can you think about energy and energy systems? Can you talk about them intelligently?

So those couple of things are where I fill in gaps, which are important things for the curriculum.

I teach another class at Stanford on Deepwater Horizon. This is when tech meets reality. What Deepwater Horizon was, what happened and why. When they mix, they have trouble, and at Deepwater Horizon they had trouble.

JR: I'd like to get a seat in all these classes.

RS: When I got to Stanford to teach the energy infrastructure class for the first time, I shared with the class, "Guess what, it was 40 years ago today that I first sat in a class as a Stanford student. 40 years later, here I am teaching one."

Here I am now it's 50 years later. It was September of 1972 when I started classes at Stanford. Guess that means I have to stay until next fall – don't want to miss the 50th anniversary.

JR: That's a big one. I think you also chose Stanford for the great distance running opportunities. You've been a runner for a long time – competing in marathons all around the world. What is one of your favorite marathon stories?

RS: It was a half marathon in Lagos. I knew it existed, but I'd never run it. I was in Nigeria in 2003 for a meeting of the Nigerian Association of Petroleum Explorationists. It's like the AAPG and SEG of Nigeria. I was in Abuja and thought, "You know, I thought this half marathon in Lagos was around the same time." I contacted an assistant I knew in Lagos. I asked, "Hey could you register me for the half marathon sponsored by the local telecom company." They were right around corner from Shell. I was in Abuja Tuesday through Friday, and the marathon was on Saturday. I knew I could stay over on Saturday and run the half. It was a very popular event and attracted 30,000 locals. Most of them walk it. But many don't walk the entire course. There are a lot of short cuts, and people would go in different directions. For instance, if at mile 1 you made a turn, you were suddenly at mile 11, which makes a half marathon pretty easy. Or at mile 6, you could cut out loop to beach and back.

JR: Lots of opportunities to set a personal best.

RS: I did the whole thing. There were few international competitors there. But it was mostly 30,000 Nigerians. And I managed to get there ahead of the announced start time. And I thought that would be plenty of time. You see, in Nigeria things rarely start on time. But apparently no one wanted to wait for an 8 am start. I managed to make my way to the start, I was dropped off about a km from start. I made my way through the Saturday morning markets, this tall American guy walking through Lagos marketplaces in his running kit. I think I stood out. And I got there 15 min early, but no one was there. I look up about a half mile, and see the back of the group.

JR: The race started early?

RS: It was sort of a tour of Lagos that you wouldn't do under any other circumstances. I had great support from Shell Nigeria, in that I could get picked up at the finish and transported back to the hotel. That was the standout half. It was a typical day in Lagos – hot, humid – miserable conditions to run a race. So, I took it slow to have fun and finish. That would be the standout race. For sure.

JR: Houston probably prepared you well for those conditions.

RS: But at Stanford, we're living in the East Bay and there are over 20 miles of rails to trails and paths. But moving here was not really for that. We were tired of Houston summers. Didn't want any more Boston winters. Getting back to temperate California seemed like good idea. On top of that, Lou Durlofsky asked, "Would you like to teach classes at Stanford?" It was a combination of a pretty place, nice environment, and Stanford offered the chance to develop and teach classes. We always thought, "Hey, if it doesn't work, we can move." We've been here since 2011.

JR: When you look back at the growth of deepwater teams at Shell, what was that growth like? How were teams built – around assets or basins – or both? How were you able to recruit and retain the expertise required for these multi-billion-dollar projects?

RS: I've created a picture for what it looked like at Shell over 30 years. Early in days of deepwater, Shell's organization was traditional, exploration would find something and then toss it over the fence to production. Exploration was chasing prospects, then make a discovery, and toss it to production and let them deal with it. It was a functionally based organization. Exploration didn't care whether you could make money from the discovery. They certainly were not doing things that were going to be a bust. They imagined that every significant find would make money. But literally they would throw the discovery over the fence and let development teams take over. And they would go on exploring.

Now onto GOM exploration and production.

As deepwater developed into a thing, there was really much more to be done. Exploration split into shelf and deepwater. There was a recognition that you needed a team who worked the whole set of technology and geology issues necessary to do deepwater right. To properly understand the play types, skillsets, and multiple ways of prosecuting the plays. Shell started making more discoveries, and there was a recognition that exploration and production would have to work more closely together. There needed to be a focus on how we make money on these things. You have to think about the entire value chain and a prospect through production – going through that whole process. This thinking led to an area-based asset structure. It put exploration and development teams closer together, so that exploration and development were talking to each other about what was necessary to make something work. Once development was happy, they handed the asset off to the production department to manage production. That worked fine for a while.

JR: What happened next?

RS: Then an asset structure developed. In 30 feet of water, it didn't matter. You could do standalone developments for any discovery. But you couldn't afford to do that in deepwater. You could not afford to do separate developments in 4000 feet of water for every discovery. These developed into area assets, and they needed to be more tightly focused. Then skill sets were an issue. What is required to successfully characterize deepwater discoveries and plan for development? The Mars basin differs from in and around the Auger basin. There were many things to consider.

Anyway, Shell discovered a whole array of different things in deepwater. Some were big enough to support their own development, but others weren't. But we had several of them that if they were tied together, could be produced. In this case you'd never develop an individual field in the group, but you could do the whole.

JR: Makes sense to bring together similar smaller fields for a unified development.

RS: So, the Nakika development cobbled together these initial six discoveries. By the way, one of them, the Herschel discovery has just been brought onstream. This Nakika development was led by BP and Shell. Shell led the development, and BP was responsible for production.

So, Shell grew from a very broad functional organization to assets. What happened in the late 90s is we began looking at how deepwater might spread globally. Even still, there was a lot of dogma. People said, "That's fine, that works in the GOM, but there's no reason for it to work around world. We don't know if the GOM thing can be extended globally."

What we learned in the GOM was that you need to have the right people in the right place. And you need to integrate across the bigger chunk of the value chain to make projects work. In the 90s, Shell began asking, "Is there something to be done globally with deepwater? Is there a global play here? If so, should we be doing things differently?"

JR: How did that unfold?

RS: Shell was country focused at the time, so we ha
Shell Oil in the US, Shell Nigeria, Shell Malaysia, and those individual companies were focused on building and retaining skill sets for whatever it took to do the job in those countries. But there weren't enough people with the skills and experience around the Shell sphere to properly prosecute all the deepwater plays separately. At this time, it was unreasonable to move a specialist to Nigeria, then to Malaysia, then to Brazil. We don't have that many to go around. And we can't afford to move all these expats for a two-well program to a different country that in the end, may not work.

So, we developed Shell Deepwater Services. Whoever needed their skills could have them in this Deepwater Tech Center. We had a primary office in Houston, and satellites in other locations. We could develop technology that would work around the world. In a deepwater play in whatever country, and the asset teams would only have to pay for them when they need them.

What we learned from complex deepwater plays and prospects, is that we were able to spread the technology service model across more ventures. We started working shallow water and brownfield developments as well. This morphed into a broader tech service organization responsible for leading tech projects for several years. Again, the idea was to have the right skills at the right time to work on a project. It was also to be able to move people onto something else when they were not needed. They wouldn't be trapped in country not doing anything.

This program had a lot of success.

JR: That's excellent.

RS: In the next evolution, let's divide Eastern and Western Hemispheres so we don't have to operate across 24 hours. So, Shell created tech enters elsewhere. We had offices in Houston and The Netherlands. When I left, they added a third in Bangalore.

JR: Why Bangalore?

.S: The time zones allowed better communication and integration between people and assets. Shell maintained a company-country structure for asset management. I left that world in 2006 for MIT, and it's continued to evolve since then.

In Shell I learned that we make the organization, the organization doesn't make us. But this was a frustrating principle for many people because every few years we were reorganizing again. Every company does this. But I'd never thought about it until I drew up on paper what business we were doing at the time, what assets, and what the opportunities looked like at the time and how the organization matched it.

"Oh my gosh," I thought, we weren't reorganizing for the sake of reorganizing. We actually had smart people at the top that were aware of opportunities we had. The organization was evolving over time to better suit the opportunities.

JR: So, it was nonrandom?

RS: It's good to talk about this stuff in a big company because people grow tired of reorgs. Someone is changing shape and structure. It's very valuable to say to the organization, "I understand what we're doing here, and look at how this has played out over time." This reorg is to meet organizational demands of the geology and geophysics and of the play itself. This is a valuable learning about how the exploration business is done, and how the oil business is done.

JR: On April 20, 2010, offshore drilling changed forever. You were asked to join the Deepwater Horizon Commission staff.

RS: I never thought I'd have in 33 years at Shell, the opportunity to give back to my nation. I was asked to join the commission staff, asked if I knew something about oil and gas, deepwater wells, the fields, the risks. And the primary job of the commission was to answer, "What happened there?"

I don't know if I ever told you this story.

JR: No.

RS: I had retired from Shell. We had gone back to live in Massachusetts. I was hanging out at MIT as a mad scientist. They said, "We're happy to have you here at MIT." But then we sold our house there, and bought a house in California because a department chair at Stanford asked if I was interested in teaching. We were in the process of moving back to Houston to start heading west. We spent some time in Florida along the way. On the morning of April 21, we were on Interstate 10 going over a bridge in Mobile, Alabama. Patti was driving and I had my laptop open. I was looking at emails and headlines and other things. I was seeing the daily reports from the oil and gas industry, and here is this rig on fire in the GOM. I gasped. I said, "Patti, someone has blown up a rig in the GOM." All I could see was this iconic image of a semi-submersible rig on fire with the Coast Guard ships pouring water on it. I don't know what happened, but this looked really bad.

I said to Patti, "I don't know how anyone is ever going to figure out what happened here." The rig was totally destroyed. And little did I know a few months later I'd get phone call from a 202 area code. Didn't know who it was, didn't care. I don't have to answer if I don't know the number. But 202 kept calling. It was the same number all the time. We'd gone over to a friend's house for dinner. Before we stepped in the door, I got a phone call from that same stupid 202 number. I tell Patti, "You go in, I'm going to answer this thing and tell them to stop bugging me."

JR: Who was it?

RS: It was the Associate Counsel from the Oil Spill Commission. They wanted to know if I'd consider joining the staff of the commission to help out. From that, conversations ensued. I joined the staff. And we actually, to a great extent, figured out what happened at Deepwater Horizon.

All of the reports on the spill took a different approach. The Oil Spill Commission worked on systemic risk and how the thing happened. We were tasked to construct a reasonable picture of the root causes.

A number of other groups studied it, to get the engineering details. The National Academy of Engineering and the Chemical Safety Board also looked at the engineering details and technical operational details we didn't look at. BP, Transocean and others also published reports.

Late in 2020 when we were writing our report, the blowout preventer wasn't available, though it had been recovered. It was basically evidence in a criminal investigation, so it was under armed guard in New Orleans. There was nothing I was going to learn about it from outside those walls. And we didn't have the skills to take it apart to find out what went wrong. Others would eventually do that. But I kept thinking this is not a BOP issue. If you're trying to understand the root cause, yeah, the BOP failed, it didn't seal the well. The best we could tell at the time was that someone tried to activate it.

JR: I remember some did not call it the B – O – P, they called it *the BOP* (as in pop).

RS: BOPs are tested in static conditions. They are not tested in wells flowing at 50,000 barrels a day of oil, water and sand, and a whole lot of gas. Those conditions are way outside of the operational envelope for a BOP. The blowout had already happened. The stuff leading up to this incident started happening long before. I argued from the beginning that accidents don't just happen in the moment. Yes, the blowout, explosion and fire occurred around 9:45 pm on 4/20. The important events that led to this event took place hours, weeks and months earlier. This is something that played out over a long period of time. Anyway, that was a long digression.

JR: The Commission described all of this in great detail.

RS: What was pretty amazing was after my career at Shell, I was asked and able to contribute to something as important as understanding Deepwater Horizon. This has an impact on offshore safety and continues to impact how industry operates today and in the future. Not just oil and gas but all industries in the future, to become as safe as possible and in more sustainable ways in the future. It's amazing I've been able to contribute in that fashion. After being an oil guy.

JR: Do people call you that – *hey 'Oil Guy'*?

RS: Jerry Harris, a Geophysics Professor at Stanford, will often say that to me, "You know you really sound like an oil man." I don't know what to say, so I usually respond, "Thank you."

JR: For the Commission, you wrote a brief history of deepwater E&P in the Gulf of Mexico. What inspired you to write this?

RS: It was really interesting, the makeup of the commission. It was an interesting group to work with. I was part of the investigative group with the commission to understand what happened with Deepwater Horizon. There were about 12 of us working on this problem. It was me and 11 attorneys. Now the good news was that most of the lawyers had undergrad degrees in science and engineering. All mostly came from high power undergrad programs like Stanford, Harvard, Yale. All were really smart. They understood science and technology but knew nothing about oil and gas. And nothing about the evolution of oil and gas. And I was worried that they would have these ideas in their minds about what oil and gas was due to the stories that get told in the media. For example – why is anybody going to deepwater in the first place? Isn't there enough oil to go around such that deepwater is unnecessary? The media thinks there's no reason anyone should go there. It's impossible to do anything there. And the only reason to go there is that we've been kicked out of Saudi Arabia. There are these unreal notions about how the oil industry works. I wanted to give the staff and commissioners a bit of grounding in how this business works. It is technology driven. And we don't explore in the deepwater because they can't explore elsewhere. The industry goes to deepwater because a geologist has an idea that should work based on our understanding of the Earth's processes, and the company chases it and tries to understand it. I was trying to convey this to that group so that all we all had a basic understanding of how the oil and gas business works. Otherwise, they'd have this idea that the industry was seemingly doing something crazy in 5,000–10,000 feet of water in the Gulf of Mexico.

JR: Maybe it's a commonly understood fact, maybe not. But the only reason the world knows so much about deepwater sedimentary processes – turbidity currents, submarine landslides, bottom currents, etc. – is because of the exploration and production business. What is unknown about continental margins and deepwater ocean basins today?

RS: That's a goofy question. Well, we don't know what's unknown. You don't know what you don't now. Just consider deepwater and how it's evolved. You see some things that at least look interesting enough, and for some companies, they have the initiative to say, "Let's chase these things in other basins around the world that look like what worked in the GOM." On mobile substrates. With amplitude that look like the GOM, or the reflectors have at least the same seismic expression of sand and shale as the GOM. All of the deepwater activity continues to evolve, and it looks a whole lot different from where I started to when I left.

Back in the 80s, a lot of people didn't want to believe anything of value was in the Mars basin. Hey, it's a different world.

Where are we today? What's just happened? Let's start with Guyana. Lots of companies for decades overlooked Guyana. Now, ExxonMobil expects to produce over 1 million barrels per day there in a few years. Shell and TotalEnergies just announced big discoveries in Namibia. What we see in deepwater is probably, well we call it the deepwater common unifying characteristics. In reality there are many different plays in deepwater. Many people probably think about deepwater as individual plays, and that's not just for deepwater.

JR: What are examples of some plays?

RS: There are several plays in deepwater, not just one. Salt diapirs, shale diapirs, submarine fan strat traps, channel deposits over structure, GOM shelf-like things. Other plays include mid-slope turbidite reservoirs. One of the reasons some companies weren't interest in Angola is that it didn't look like the GOM. There was a lack of salt and structural and stratigraphic combination traps. It didn't look right. It didn't fit some peoples' idea of what an opportunity should look like. Others said, "I see something I like." What's happened in deepwater over decades split into a variety of individual plays that share their own sets of geologic characteristics and have their own geophysical imaging tools and opportunities for imaging. And they're all being pursued individually by companies. Which is just what happened.

What don't we know? We don't know what we don't know. Let's go back to the GOM. We still don't have any idea what's out on the abyssal plain. Shell put spec bids on a whole lot of acreage on the abyssal plain. We didn't do this randomly. We were curious about what it was. But they haven't gotten out there yet. It was the 90s. The industry still hasn't gone below the shale in Nigeria – this would be sort of like going subsalt in the GOM. Someday, someone will do this. These are the unknowns today. These may be huge new opportunities, and maybe not.

JR: One day, future explorers will find out.

RS: You know sometimes these things work out, sometimes not. Where did we get the first penetrations of deepwater rocks in the GOM? We got those on the shelf by people drilling into deeper rocks. These were drilled beneath the existing shelf discoveries. They didn't find anything, but they found rocks that didn't fit a shelf depositional system. But many said, the deepwater GOM doesn't look promising based on these early tests. They said, "I've tested these things, and they didn't work out. We shouldn't go deeper in the GOM." This is how it goes. And as a result, it's interesting to see how things change and how assessments change.

When we were talking in the first part of the interview….sometimes what changes – it can be any number of things. What changed our understanding and assessment in the sands along the Gulf Coast? It was drilled down dip, and sand was found much farther than originally thought based on the geologic models of the time. Then the goal was to find them elsewhere. Where they have oil.

In West Texas, there are all these stacks of reservoir-seal combos throughout the stratigraphic section, it's always had potential. What changed there was the advent of horizontal drilling and fracking and completions. We always knew about these intervals, but nobody had a good way of fully exploiting them. What happens next in deepwater settings? Who knows? A surprise discovery well, the development of new technology – any number of things. It won't be $150 oil.

JR: Many always wish for higher prices. Why isn't this the case?

...s not make for a successful exploration play. It does ...'s on a map. It does not take clay out of the matrix of ...0 oil makes a marginally lousy play into marginally .... chasing price. That's not the secret. By the way, this is something that people miss, even people in the industry. They pretend like high prices change everything. A really good field at $150 per barrel is still good at $40 per barrel. It'll just pay off faster at $150. Maybe. Because all costs go up, too.

JR: How will the offshore E&P industry lead when it comes to the next 10, 20, 30 years of offshore activity – not just for oil and gas E&P?

RS: The answer is, "I don't know." And I'm not dodging the question. Oil companies who tried to reinvent themselves in their careers as broad energy companies have not been successful at that. The whole idea came about in 1970s and 80s. Oil companies at this time had to become energy companies. They did whatever they could do. All bought coal, solar, nuclear, and a few did geothermal. And pretty much all of those ventures that these companies launched all went away in the 1990s. Because the ventures didn't survive during the extended period of low oil price. They couldn't compete. They had no cash, no investment, and they went away. And even some oil companies decided to try to become retail giants. Mobil bought Montgomery Ward.

JR: Who are they?

RS: Have you heard of JCPenney?

JR: I get the point!

RS: Right around the turn of century, oil companies thought they had to become energy companies again. Peak oil was being predicted. Once again oil companies tried to become energy companies. If you go to the very early 2000s, the largest solar photovoltaic company was run by, guess who – BP. It was a lousy business, so they got out of it. By 2005, the largest producer of silicon photovoltaics was Shell. It was a lousy business. So, they got out of it. I don't mean it was a bad business. It just didn't compete with the oil business. Shell was the largest manufacturer in the world, and it wasn't making money. The returns are much lower than what we do in exploration and refining and anything else. We didn't understand silicon. It wasn't a good business for us. So, it was sold to a US solar company. It ended up doing very well, because the solar company understood it very well.

At the same time, Shell was making significant investments in other new energies. We were drilling deep wells in hot dry rock in Central America. To try to come up with new geothermal methods. It worked, but what we discovered is that it works like we thought it would work. But oil and gas vs. hot water? Which do you think makes more money? We got out of enhanced geothermal because it just wouldn't compete.

JR: A pattern. What was the next venture?

RS: Shell made investments in biofuels. It was at the higher end of alcohol production. Turned out the market was not too interested. Most of those investments didn't work out either. It either came down to the technology, the business, but something in the end didn't work. 20 years ago, BP stood for "Beyond Petroleum". 10 years later, guess what it stood for?

JR: Don't know this one.

RS: "Back to Petroleum". Maybe the punch line of all of this is maybe oil companies will lead into the new energy future. Maybe they won't because it's not required. It's not a given. There's no reason to expect they will. If oil companies aren't there as leaders, it's because they couldn't run the business. They kind of go away, and new companies will appear on the scene. Just like coal replaced logging, and oil replaced coal.

JR: The evolution continues.

RS: Oil companies are thinking they can evolve into broader energy businesses. And they're all trying again. With wind, solar, and other ideas. Maybe it will work, maybe it won't.

By the way, one place that had staying power was wind. My contention is why it worked is because it complements the gas business. Better to have dispatchable power behind it when the wind stops blowing. If you see companies buying turbines? Probably buying natural gas from you, too.

Why did Shell organize gas and power? The businesses complemented each other, and that makes sense. And in the extent that business evolves, it's not easy for a company to reinvent itself totally and be very different. It happens, but it's hard. The company doesn't have the skills, the tech, the market knowledge, or the leadership. It's not easy to just reinvent yourself as a new kind of company.

JR: What are the advantages?

RS: What the oil companies have going for them is cash flow from traditional energy sources – oil and gas. They have cash to invest, which should give them something of an advantage. And a lot of installed infrastructure, and some of that could be repurposed to build new energy systems.

In biofuels, people expect to be able to drop biofuels into the existing supply chain. Another footprint is in the refinery. The refineries make bio-gasoline, bio-diesel. And they expect to drop it right into the system. Why they're doing that is that it makes use of all the installed infrastructure, and gives a competitive advantage. They expect to push it right out into the market. The problem with ethanol....ethanol and water mix nicely. But you start putting ethanol in petroleum pipelines, this is a whole problem with water and crud that collected over years and ends up in your fuel. That's why ethanol travels in its own infrastructure. Where it gets mixed into gasoline is right as it goes into the truck to go to the gas station.

If you want to replace oil and gas, you need to rebuild the national infrastructure, which will take decades. It is one of the challenges of evolving energy systems. Oil companies are trying to find a path through this, and participate in new energy, make use of infrastructure, try to do something new and novel. Things change, and in the end, we find out what works and what doesn't.

Oil companies see themselves more and more closely coupled with electricity. They are moving more and more into retail energy markets. Shell tried to do this once before in early 2000s and it didn't work out. Now they're trying again. Maybe it will work out better this time. Maybe not.

JR: Did you have a favorite class at Stanford while you were a student? What is your favorite class you teach now?

RS: My favorite class was during my last year, autumn quarter – fluid mechanics. What I liked about it, what I found fun about it was in that class the focus was on understanding complex physical systems. We were using math to compute things about natural systems. We'd get goofy problems like a space capsule is coming back into Earth's atmosphere, make some simple assumptions like here's shape of capsule, and if it's going to land at X mph, how big does the parachute have to be?

The problems we'd do, you had to understand first principles, some theory, some complex math, and put it all together for a reasonable answer to a complicated question. I liked most of my classes apart from the breadth requirements. That one I particularly liked, since you could learn and could understand complex problems at a different level.

JR: Favorite class you get to teach?

RS: The favorite class I teach now is energy infrastructure tech and economics. It deals with how an energy company works and why. It enables you to think about technology as part of a complex system, and includes business and other things. It focuses on oil and gas, and why it works. Want to do something else? Better understand this. We end up talking about so many different things. What are risks that dominate? Where does irreducible risk come in? How does that make the business run, and how does technology enable it? What enables a tech revolution? And what doesn't? It's not price by the way. Price doesn't reign in tech revolutions.

This cellphone is a lot more expensive than my land line at home. But I use it a lot more. The computer more expensive than the slide rule. Same for air travel, boats, trains – it's about utility. And so it goes. Price matters because you have to pay for something. If it's a better product, it will win in the end. If it's really expensive, it will just take longer.

JR: What was the best part of your job at Shell?

RS: It was Shell. It's just a unique place. And a very strong meritocracy. You did well because you were good at what you did. You were put into jobs because you're good at it. Not because of a good degree, or what you'd done. Lots of people at Shell had PhDs, but the thing was, many people did not have slightest clue of who did.

There were five or six of us in a discussion room. A general manager, middle manager, and the GM asked, "Do all you guys have PhDs?" Two of us didn't. No one had the slightest idea. Didn't know what subject it was in – geology, petroleum engineering, geophysics. No one knows. No one cared. It's all about what you can bring to our very complex problems. The great thing was I got hired as a geophysicist, taught courses in geophysics at Shell's training center (it was a big stretch, but vaguely I knew what I was talking about). At one time, I was the Chief Geologist, at one time Manager of Economics. It didn't matter I hadn't taken econ in college. It mattered I could understand problems, and I love that environment where people were able to find what they're good at and contribute. Could have a whole variety of assignments if they were interested.

Some were very technical at Shell – the specialists. That's what they did. At Shell, there was room for all of these people. Shell was where they all had opportunities to contribute and do what they were good at.

JR: Did you find out what you were best at?

RS: I learned what I was best at. I was not the best deep detailed technical contributor. But I was good at synthesizing the work of lots of other people and lots of other disciplines and pulling it together in a way bigger than any individual discipline. I relied deeply on all technical specialists. I had no illusion I'd be better at that than they were. I took the pieces together and made it work as a whole, for instance running the E&P business. Or building academic relationships – really any job function I had at the time.

JR: Like the Michigan business.

RS: Michigan was like a small integrated oil company. We had 600 wells, owned two gas plants, owned a sulphur plant, and a lot of pipeline. We couldn't get eaten up by thousands of competitors. We could run it that way very profitably and do things that were unique. Exploration, processing, transportation, all separate functions. We could do deals across a whole lot of things. When I sold a deal in Central Michigan, the buyer had the obligation to transport produced gas on our pipeline network to our plants. After the sale, we ended up making as much money, and had captured them into bringing gas into our gas plants. We had the tariffs, plus we were stripping the liquids out. Those are the kinds of deals we were able to make looking across the whole value chain. A strictly E&P business wouldn't make those deals. They might see the sale as a net loss. But for an integrated company, we saw it as a net gain. And it required no additional capital, no additional maintenance. Now my guys wouldn't have to drive hours into Central Michigan to workover wells. It was a win-win all around.

By the way, the least favorite class I teach is production engineering. It's fun in its own way. Not nearly as fun as understanding why that's important.

JR: And the least favorite part of your job over the past 4+ decades?

RS: Understanding new, different bosses. I never had bad boss, just had different bosses. You get into a new position, and wonder, "But what is driving this person? How do I work with them?" I need to still work for them but would like to do the job in the way I think it should be done. It's a bit of the people side of being in a big company. It's the people side of managing upward. When things change, you have to be able to deal with that. Occasionally the bureaucracy would get you down, but that happens.

Rarely did bureaucracy get in the way of doing good work. The organizations I've worked with since leaving Shell, some of these companies are run by bureaucrats, and you can't do what's best. Because bureaucrats tell them how to do the work. This didn't happen at Shell, where business decisions were being done by some sort of goofy rule of an administrator of some sort. When I needed to hire somebody, an HR issue of where they lived or where they come from could arise. So, you need to think, "How do we make this work?

Who's doing the hiring, who is financing this position?" Organizations I've worked with since, this doesn't happen. A technical person is told where their boundaries are, what they have to live within.

JR: So, you're happy with your role now. Not going to go out and buy an oil company and drill more wells?

RS: As my career has evolved, I'm still happy, and I don't know what I'd do differently if I had to do it over again. Shell people have told me I've had a really different career. Acquisitions, teaching, interpretation, lease sales, drilling, economics, exploration management in Oklahoma, North Sea, West Texas, Michigan, deepwater, to global deepwater, and finally to quasi business-academia at the end of my career. And now teaching and working with the National Academy of Sciences on projects. It's worked out exactly right for whatever reason.

JR: That's so awesome.

RS: I like to think I got lucky, in a less modest moment, the better you are the luckier you get. Maybe I've had something to do with how this turned out. But I don't tell myself that too often.

JR: What would you like the world to know about Rich Sears?

RS: I'm one little piece of a big system, trying to do work that I like and that I've found to be useful. I found out I could play a role in helping to find new oil and gas resources. Then it was helping the world understand Deepwater Horizon to help prevent something like that from ever happening again in offshore safety and operations.

JR: What is your message for explorers today? For those in the broader energy business?

RS: Understand what you're good at. And focus on that. Don't flail around just because you get into new stuff. Gotta be good at it if you want to succeed. Companies that tried to evolve into different things often failed at those things. Some companies through 80s, 90s and early 2000s didn't really know what they wanted to be when they grew up. Trying all sorts of things, doing nothing particularly well. Then they started going back to what they were good at, at the time. They

focused on traditional oil and gas plays in regions
feel as an energy company you need to be doing so
you need to figure it out and get good at it. Before y
out there to change the world.

Try this. You don't see too many football players trying to break into the NBA. It doesn't work, it requires a whole set of different skills. You need to have the specific skills for what you're trying to do. You also have athletes trying to cross over, where the skill sets are kind of the same. A football player who transforms into a track athlete in the Olympics. That works and makes sense because he can beat anyone running down the street. But it's not the 300-lb lineman that does that. It's the running back or receiver who's able to do track as well as football. But this is very rare. You need to have the necessary skills to do what you're trying to do.

For explorers in the international business of oil and gas E&P, it's still a market. It may be somewhat smaller in the future. Rather than being a specialist in certain environments, be a specialist in subsurface exploration, development, redevelopment, and optimization of subsurface resources. From a geoscience or engineering standpoint, that's probably the direction people are going more and more.

And then there are all these geoscience skills, petrophysics skills, geophysics skills that are important skill sets for the new energy economy. If we are going to get serious about carbon sequestration, the projects that have failed are not because we don't know how to cool CO_2 to supercritical levels, they failed because of the misunderstanding of the subsurface. The carbon uptake didn't work. This new energy economy will require these skillsets to.

JR: Thank you so much Rich.

Above: Deepwater deposits of the Paleogene Annot Sandstone. Highly regarded as the birthplace of the Bouma Sequence, these outcrops provide a stimulating training environment for geoscientists and engineers working deepwater depositional systems in the global energy industry.

Scott W. Tinker and Richard J. Chuchla (October 2019)

"One thing that unites BEG studies is that they are underpinned by the rocks. We have the largest collection of core and cuttings in world in – a couple million boxes. We recently opened a new core facility, with core labs, an SEM floating-slab lab, and several more focused labs. We look at outcrops, cores, and cuttings to get at the fundamentals of scientific inquiry." – Dr. Scott W. Tinker

"Have the courage to challenge dogma. Dogma is perhaps the most opportunity-limiting element in the business. There are over a dozen "facts" that I was told by experts and superiors in the company that were diametrically wrong. These were not trivial "facts". There were "facts" that affected the strategic direction we were taking and on which hung very costly decisions. Exploration of different point of views and opinions is very important, and it recognizes that each of us look at "facts" in a different way. One of the most impactful roles a leader can have is to have the back of a subordinate standing up to dogma." – Richard J. Chuchla

University of Texas and the Bureau of Economic Geology have a deep bench of talented geologists, and by way of Michigan and Chile, Dr. Scott Tinker and Richard J. Chuchla have added significantly to that reputation for Texas geology and inspired the world. Their leadership styles complement each other so well, it was hardly a difficult decision to do a joint interview with them in early 2020.

Scott Tinker works to bring industry, government, academia, and NGOs together to address major societal challenges in energy, the environment, and the economy. Dr. Tinker is director of the 250-person Bureau of Economic Geology, the State Geologist of Texas, and a professor holding the Allday Endowed Chair in the Jackson School at The University of Texas at Austin. Tinker co-produced and is featured in the award-winning energy documentary film *Switch*, which has been screened in over 50 countries to more than 15 million viewers and is used on thousands of K—12 and college campuses. Dr. Tinker formed the nonprofit Switch Energy Alliance and just completed a new film on energy poverty, *Switch On*. He is the voice of *EarthDate*, a 2-minute weekly program produced by the Bureau of Economic Geology that focuses on remarkable stories of Earth, and is featured on nearly 400 public radio stations in all 50 United States. He has served as president of the American Geosciences Institute, the Association of American State Geologists, the American Association of Petroleum Geologists, and the Gulf Coast Association of Geological Societies. Dr. Tinker is an AGI Campbell Medalist, AAPG Halbouty Medalist, GCAGS Boyd Medalist, and a Fellow of the Geological Society of America. In his visits to some 65 countries he has given nearly 800 keynote and invited lectures.

Richard J. Chuchla is the Energy and Earth Resources Graduate Program Director and the Leslie Bowling Professor in Geological Sciences for the Energy and Earth Resources Graduate Program at the Jackson School of Geosciences. A geologist by training, with an undergraduate degree from Cornell and a master's from the Jackson School of Geosciences, Richard started in base and precious metals, moved to coal, and then oil and gas, working in exploration, development and research. The assignments took him from Tucson, Arizona – where he accepted his first industry job two days after earning his Master's – to Europe, Latin America and West Africa. It was then back to the United States, where he spent the better part of his last 10 years launching ExxonMobil's unconventional resources program including two years at the corporate headquarters in Dallas advising the Management Committee and CEO, Rex Tillerson.

I first saw Scott present a screening of *Switch*, his first famous documentary, at Stanford in 2012 and was blown away by his concise and impactful message about energy. Following the screening was an interview with a panel of Stanford professors. Scott enlightened the audience with a impactful conversation on important energy issues. If anyone knows energy in its broadest sense, it's Scott. Years later when I became a full-time Texan we connected in Houston and in Austin at the Bureau of Economic Geology (BEG), where he currently serves as Director and State Geologist. His latest documentary, a follow up to *Switch*, titled *Switch On*, is shown in classrooms around the world, including down the road from the BEG at the McCombs School of Business. Many of us don't know how Scott does it. He *must* have superhuman energy. The travel, the presentations, the research, the documentaries, the Switch foundation – all while attending to his day job as Director and State Geologist – and being the most caring family man. When he concluded a BEG core workshop on reservoir quality in Houston in early 2015, he quipped, "My son is currently a student studying geology – and he would love to work for your company this summer in an internship." That worked out well – his son has gone on to drill a lot of great wells as a full-time oil-and gas-finding geologist. Scott has done it all – from research as a carbonate specialist in sequence stratigraphy, to leading the largest state survey (and in the world), to documenting the world's energy challenges in greater detail than any other effort in history. His efforts have changed the world. He has brought energy to the forefront of conversation, which was necessary and turns out – only he and his teams can do. Dr. Tinker keeps everyone wondering, "What will he show the world next about energy?"

"You look too wise to be an undergrad. I thought this short course was for undergrads mostly," I said to the gentleman dressed as a professor in the second row of the classroom. "Nice to meet you, I'm Richard Chuchla," he said as we shook hands. Very humble greeting, considering Richard is in many ways responsible for the great success that ExxonMobil has had in Latin America, West Africa and most recently with the shale explosion that led the USA to be the number one producer of oil and gas for a few years. That was the first time I met Richard, when I gave a 3-hour deepwater systems crash course to about 40 UT undergrads (and Richard) in September of 2017. Most of the time when I give university presentations, professors don't stay the whole time. Richard stayed the whole time, and apparently took notes. "Most of what you said lines up with what I know," he mentioned, "And I learned a few new things, too," which I took as a huge compliment I'll never forget. His depth and breadth of exploration, appraisal and development program execution is among the best in the world, recently leaving his post as an executive at ExxonMobil to build the Energy Resources Program at the Jackson School of Geosciences at University of Texas at Austin. I'm always amazed at Richard's ability to condense the world of oil and gas drilling, basin analysis and the macroeconomic conditions of the world into simple easy-to-understand interpretations. It's one of his many gifts as a leader, and no doubt helped his teams succeed in big ways. He is also a deep thinker on the "how and why" in a project, and the concept of motivation. He is one of the most beloved professors at University of Texas, and a favorite among the students. "The one who hoods the most students wins," he mentions every year as Director of the Energy Program at UT Austin. He's not bragging, just getting the job done because his students end up with some of the most impactful careers in the energy business following graduation.

Dr. Scott W. Tinker and Richard J. Chuchla have made numerous contributions to the global geoscience community and the energy industry and continue to inspire the Bureau of Economic Geology and Jackson School of Geosciences to new heights.

In February 2020, I interviewed Scott Tinker and Richard Chuchla. Read the interview below.

Jon Rotzien (JR): Mr. Chuchla and Dr. Tinker, I'm so thankful you had the time to visit today and share some of your recent achievements. You have similar backgrounds in that you have published peer-reviewed technical articles and reports ranging from carbonate depositional systems to structural restorations of various types of sedimentary basins, yet you've had different career paths for the last few decades. Now, you're both living in the same city of Austin and get to work with some of the most innovative and hardworking scientists at University of Texas at Austin and the Bureau of Economic Geology.

Could you share your backgrounds and what led you to your current roles?

Scott Tinker (ST): My father was a geologist with Shell for 39 years, so with that influence I went off to university to be anything *but* a geologist. However, I took a geology class freshman year, and was hooked! I worked for a year in Houston for renown geologist, Dr. Bob Sneider. Bob promised he'd fire me after one year so that I'd go back to school and earn a Masters. He was true to his promise, and I headed off to the University of Michigan.

I mostly worked East Texas Basin – the Pearsall Group, James, Pine Island Shale – and that was a lot of fun. At the end of it, I had a several offers in Houston, but I took one in Denver where I had lived as a kid, and loved it. I ending up working for Champlin/Union Pacific and then Marathon for 17 years. During my time at Champlin, I worked Canadian sedimentary basins, carbonate rocks and regional studies. I was lucky to work with great geologists like Neil Hurley, Dave Eby, Kent Kirkby, Jim Ehrets, Charlie Kerans and many others. People matter in your career, Jon. Great people – that's the bottom line. At Marathon I worked Yates Field in west Texas, and we built some of the industry's first 3D geocellular reservoir models. We had tight collaborations with engineers, geologists, petrophysicists and geophysicists. I learned a lot about computer programming and the power of multidisciplinary teams.

Those were terrific years, and very busy years. My wife Allyson was running her own business, we were having kids, and I did a Ph.D. on the side under David Budd at the University of Colorado. I was fortunate to work on the world class exposures in McKittrick Canyon in The Guadalupe Mountains.

JR: Then how did you transition to the BEG?

ST: The writing was on the wall by 1999, with most of the industry research labs closing left and right. It looked like Marathon's lab was going that way, too, unfortunately. Charles Kerans, a long-time friend told me the BEG was looking for a new director. I was 40 years old. No one else was qualified, so they got stuck with me! I came to Austin from Denver in January 2000. There were about 90 people at the BEG then, and they had just been through some tough years. There was a need to build back the culture and morale.

It's been a good run at the BEG. We now employ a great group of about 250 full-time equivalent scientists and staff, and bring in government, state, federal and industry support through consortia, federal and state grants and foundations. We look at energy, environmental, and economic challenges and avoid "good and bad, clean and dirty" labeling. Instead, what are the key scientific questions across the 3E space? We've had some success and I've certainly learned a lot. The best part for me is the chance to work with and meet great people; fellow state geologists, leading academics, industry giants, government and NGO visionaries. I've been lucky to ride the coattails of legends and leaders.

Richard Chuchla (RC): Frankly, my career path has been a random walk and a wonderful one at that. However, there is some context that is meaningful. I was born and raised in the Atacama Desert, in a small mining town in Chile. I was surrounded by spectacular geology. In Atacama, you can see it all since there is no ground cover. Dad was a mining engineer at the El Salvador porphyry copper deposit and that was another connection with geology. My best friend was the son of the Chief Geologist for the district which included the El Salvador and Chuquicamata ore bodies. He'd take us out on the weekends in his four-wheel drive truck. Our town was on the Inca Trail scattered with ruins and pottery, so it was not just geology, but also the unique native cultural history that made this area interesting. There were spectacular exposures of fossil beds in which we found gorgeous little stars which I learned many years later are parts of crinoid stalks. All of that made for an upbringing that developed my love of the outdoors, an understanding of the history and fragility of the area in which I lived and an interest in rocks and geology. And, it deeply infected me with the travel bug and a desire to see more of the world. While I think Mom would have loved to see her eldest son go into medicine, and Dad did _not_ want me to be a mining engineer there was not a lot of question about my major at Cornell.

After my Master's degree here at University of Texas, I worked in mineral exploration for about 6 years looking for base and precious metals. It was hard to believe I was being paid to have so much fun. We closed down our U.S. minerals company so I had a mercifully brief stint in the coal company working in the Appalachian and Illinois basins.

My guardian angel plucked me out of the coal company and I found myself at Exxon Production Research Company. I worked at the lab for 7 years, mostly on research applications and regional studies. I could not imagine being surrounded by a better group of geoscientists. They also turned out to be wonderful mentors and friends. I had so much to learn but incredible colleagues to help get me there. I'll be forever grateful to them and it reinforced my view of the importance of mentors and peer-to-peer learning.

Before that time, I had never really worked in "operations". My first assignment in the Exploration company was Mexico. That was 1995 and we thought Mexico was about to open its upstream! Then came opportunities in the deepwater of Brazil, Angola, Equatorial Guinea, São Tomé and Príncipe and Nigeria and, on African terra firma, in Chad and Niger. While I really enjoyed my time in the Development company, I've spent most of my career in exploration, which aligns best with both my skills and personal passion for prospecting.

Chasing new opportunities in South America is perhaps what I enjoyed most. It always felt a bit like coming home, even though, try as I might, Chile was not on our list of prospective countries. But maybe my biggest professional challenge came in trying to sell ExxonMobil on the idea that unconventional resources (hydrocarbons in tight rocks) should be a part of our portfolio. That was a good part of what I did in Dallas, although I played a very small role in the XTO acquisition. Ironically, I finished my ExxonMobil career where I started in the Exploration company: heading up our Mexico project following the opening of the upstream there.

Now, through very serendipitous circumstances, I'm here at UT prospecting for and developing young student minds, directing this program at a time when the energy industry is undergoing profound change. Many of my students are interested in renewables so I am broadening my understanding of energy. I'm learning again. That has been a recurring theme in my professional life and is responsible for whatever success I have had.

An important point pertinent to my professional wanderings: all of this requires a very tolerant and supportive life partner. I could not have done this without my wife, Elizabeth Green, who not only shouldered the raising of our kids, dealt with some really unnerving uncertainties as we shut down Exxon Minerals Company, but who also provided the kind of encouragement that anybody who is out there trying to take on big challenges needs!

JR: Thank you very much Scott and Richard. Both of you have and continue to engage in energy leadership roles. How were you able to develop your leadership through time? What are some important principles for good management and leadership – from your experience leading the BEG to leading an industry supermajor?

RC: I'd say my leadership skills were developed through practice and making mistakes. I was not a natural leader; in fact, I had very little interest in leading during the first ten years of my career. I was truly content as a technical hand studying the subsurface. However, when I first had a leadership role thrust on me, I found it fulfilling and challenging, in a completely different way.

On being a good leader:

First, I think that keeping an open mind and listening to new ideas is vital.

Second: have the courage to challenge dogma. Dogma is perhaps the most opportunity-limiting element in the business. There are over a dozen "facts" that I was told by experts and superiors in the company that were diametrically wrong. These were not trivial "facts". There were "facts" that affected the strategic direction we were taking and on which hung very costly decisions. Exploration of different point of views and opinions is very important, and it recognizes that each of us look at "facts" in a different way. One of the most impactful roles a leader can have is to have the back of a subordinate standing up to dogma.

JR: Dogma can be dangerous in the business, and the promotion of different perspectives in the interpretation of the subsurface is valuable. Did you observe any examples of these types of leadership?

RC: Lots of them but lots of examples of good leadership as well. It's so easy to default to dogma and we all do it all the time. I had taped a number of my favorite quotations on the wall of my office. One of them, from John Kenneth Galbraith is: "*The conventional view serves to protect us from a painful way of thinking.*" For any student of exploration, it's obvious that discoveries are made because somebody recognizes opportunity that perhaps thousands of geologists, looking at the same basic information, could not see.

Mother was very curious and her time as a child in a Russian concentration camp imbued her with a certain fearlessness and the courage to speak her mind, irrespective of what others were saying. I like to think I inherited a measure of those qualities. At ExxonMobil, I found that while senior management often challenged divergent ideas, they recognized the courage it took to buck the tide.

Another challenge for any leader, and his or her team, is learning from failure. As explorers, we fail much more than we succeed and I have experienced both the exhilaration of leading a team to a discovery and the pain and humiliation in a dry hole. But, that dry hole may contain the keys to the next discovery. Another of my favorite quotations is from Enrico Fermi (in his quotation you could substitute the word "hypothesis" with "well"): "There are two possible outcomes (*of an experiment*): if the result confirms the hypothesis, then you've made a discovery. If the result is contrary to the hypothesis, then you've made a discovery." A dry hole is a discovery, painful as it is, but it is only a discovery if you learn from it.

JR: Those are great quotes, and very applicable to the business. How did you promote this powerful way of thinking?

RC: First, you model the behavior. Another thing I did was to start a newsletter called *Creative Contemplations*. It began as a cathartic experience, growing from my frustration about the way new ideas were being promoted or challenged and what I thought was insufficient creativity in the Exploration organization. While there was some philosophical meandering, I tried to keep it grounded in the business. This newsletter ended up exploring several themes, including the fascinating psychology of perception; how "we see things not as they are but as we are". I sent it to a few people, but through the sharing power of the internet, it ended up on the desks of hundreds of employees and, while never intended for this, some issues got outside the company. A student at Rice University responded that the challenge of sharing new ideas in academia was as challenging as in the corporate world.

By the time I left, I had 120 pages of Creative Contemplations. As leaders, you're not always contributing to a discovery. But you can contribute to employees' professional fulfillment: how they tackle a problem, their creativity and innovation and how much fun they have. You will never know what the impact of this dimension of leadership is but I think it is huge...inspire people to be brave, develop new ideas and make big discoveries.

JR: Wholesome thoughts...and that'd be great to bring back *Creative Contemplations* for the industry.

RC: I'd like that and I have many more stories I'd like to add! Some of the inspiration for writing Creative Contemplations came from John Lienhard. I arranged John's first visit to ExxonMobil which was awesome...a small auditorium filled with geoscientists and senior executives in rapt attention as this mild-mannered and mellifluous speaker talked about innovation. I believe John is still at UH as an emeritus engineer and I continue to listen to replays of *Engines of our Ingenuity*. There must be hundreds of episodes now.

JR: The UH community is very fortunate. Thank you Richard, it sounds like we all need to check out *Engines of our Ingenuity* – website is https://www.uh.edu/engines/.

ST: I've made plenty of mistakes. You need to recognize your mistakes, the earlier the better, and don't be shy about addressing them. Don't be too proud to adapt. Nonetheless, there are a thousand ways to skin a cat, and you have to start somewhere. Move forward and adapt. Work really hard, try to lead by example, and be willing to do as much or more of what you ask of anyone else.

We have a very diverse group of nations represented at the BEG: 25 nations from 6 continents – it's a bit like a United Nations meeting when we all get together. Different cultural, religious, educational and socioeconomic backgrounds. This diversity helps us to achieve big goals. Diversity sounds great, but true diversity is not easy. You have to be open to different perspectives and upbringings. Many people wouldn't even like each other working together back in their home countries.

My goal is to create an environment that supports them, but not tell them what to do. This takes letting go. Keep a sense that these are talented people. It's a bit different from a corporate approach, which can be a bit more top down. In the academic realm, it's bottom, top, middle, so that each person in each group has the capacity not only to thrive – but shine and lead. We try to make sure they have the right resources, from labs, to field equipment, to infrastructure, make sure they're compensated well, and can truly thrive at what they're trying to accomplish.

The BEG is not for everyone, but for those it fits, it's fantastic. We sit between academia, industry and government. It is a fun, unique construct. My role is always to be looking into the future, in terms of burgeoning technology, science and also in terms of financial support.

You have to look way out in front to anticipate the challenges facing society. For example, in the past 15 years, we established one of the leading subsurface nanosensor research groups in the world (Advanced Energy Consortium); a leading earthquake seismology group (TexNet and the Center for Integrated Seismicity Research); and a world class carbon utilization and storage team (Gulf Coast Carbon Center). Another BEG strength is in water and energy. Our only recent national academy member in the Jackson School is Bridget Scanlon, a hydrologist at the BEG.

JR: Congratulations, those are huge accomplishments.

ST: We were also very early into unconventional resources: tight gas, coalbed methane, and then shale. We have a couple of key industry consortia on mudrock systems, resources and reserves, studying from the nanopore to full-basin scale. Bob Loucks, Steve Ruppel, Rob Reed and others were the first to discover porosity in organic material, in the Barnett. We have a team that has done leading basin-wide studies of four major shale gas basins including the Barnett, Fayetteville, Haynesville and Marcellus and three shale oil basins including the Eagle Ford, Bakken and West Texas.

One thing that unites BEG studies is that they are underpinned by the rocks. We have the largest collection of core and cuttings in world in – a couple million boxes. We recently opened a new core facility, with core labs, an SEM floating-slab lab, and several more focused labs. We look at outcrops, cores, and cuttings to get at the fundamentals of scientific inquiry.

JR: How about that new rock garden?

ST: Our new Stoneburner Texas rock garden is laid out like the geology of Texas. The 5–8-ton boulders in place are matched to the outcrops one would find... be sure when you visit you take the audio tour as you walk through it. To complement this, we published a major book a few years ago on Texas geology, with Tom Ewing as the lead author. It was a massive undertaking. An accompanying handbook shows the best places to view Texas geology. It takes a team to complete these jobs, you need to commit, raise the money and then just do it.

I knew Jack Jackson and was pleased to be part of forming the Jackson School. Larry Faulkner was president of UT when the School formed, and Peter Flawn, Bill Fisher, Jim Langham and I as the "kid" were lovingly referred to by Jack as his "Jackson 5." Since we formed the school, I have served with 8 department chairs, 5 deans, and 3 university presidents. Quite a ride.

JR: That is such a flourishing research program – with engagements around the world. Dr. Tinker, I remember when you gave a presentation at Stanford, during a screening and interview on your documentary film *Switch*. It must have been about 2012 or so. Now, you've been live blogging your recent global travels to different energy markets. Can you tell us more about that inspiration, and what you've learned?

ST: I have an Instagram account... @doctinker. My adult son, Derek, an engineer and IT whiz who heads up tech development for the Switch Energy Alliance, created it and brought me into the 21st century.

JR: Good intergenerational support network!

ST: Harry Lynch has been my partner in all things Switch. Harry is an outstanding documentary film maker and a very smart guy. He and I made the original film *Switch*, in which energy is the star. It has been seen by over 15 million viewers. But we left off a third of the world that doesn't have access to energy, and decided we needed to make a new documentary, focused on energy poverty. To do this, and many other projects, we started a 501(c)3 called the Switch Energy Alliance.

The new film, *Switch On*, is a feature-length film in which we visit Colombia, Nepal, Ethiopia, Vietnam and Kenya to look at energy poverty. We focus on off grid, under the grid (slums) and clean cooking. A third of the world still cooks indoors with biomass, which represents a huge health issue. When you cook inside with wood, it's like smoking a couple packs of cigarettes. Women and children suffer the most from diseases like pneumonia, cancer, cataracts – and there are other smoke related diseases, too. It kills more people each year than Malaria and AIDS combined. It's a very human piece, and is now screening by request on educational and corporate campuses, festivals and a limited theatrical run.

We discovered recently that many high school teachers nationally are using Switch videos—primers, 101s, the energy lab, site visits—in their classes. One very popular high school class is AP Environmental Sciences (APES). 200,000 kids took it last year in the United States. We formed an advisory group of APES teachers to help develop curriculum to serve with our videos and provide heavy supplementary content for the APES class. The program is pilot testing this spring, and will release more broadly in the fall. Our goal is to provide an opportunity for students to think critically about important energy issues. "Clean and dirty" is too simple a construct.

Similar conversations are happening on higher education campuses. Not just in STEM, but in business, policy, law, liberal arts and more. There is a tremendous need for non-partisan, objective energy education.

JR: A very informative documentary for universities around the world.

ST: Another thing SEA is doing is a 4-minute, highest production quality museum film. It shows why energy matters in our lives, featuring Hollywood quality movie magic. We have lined up the Houston Museum of Natural Science and the Denver Museum of Nature and Science to screen it, and will offer it more broadly to other museums. Each of those museums hosts more than 2 million visitors a year. It's a great opportunity to expose a broad audience to the power of energy in their lives. I have a short cameo as the school bus driver...

JR: *A bus driver!* Can't wait to see *Switch On*, the Museum Film and all of these other great projects.

Richard, I'd like to come back to you for this one on global energy markets. The global energy market is never always changing. You have been leading the Energy and Earth Resources Masters Program at the Jackson School for years now. How do you collaborate with industry and academia to prepare your students and researchers for roles in the private and public sectors?

RC: You are right...the global energy market today is truly exciting and exceedingly relevant. When I was finishing graduate school, the energy business was synonymous with the fossil fuels business. It is much more than that today.

I came to this job as another step in my random career walk. About 6 months into retirement, I got a call from Dr. Bill Fisher, who asked me and Dr. Mark Zoback at Stanford to participate in a review of the graduate program.

Bill Fisher conceived the idea in 1980 of what ultimately grew into the EER Program. Interestingly, it was tied to funding that provided my fellowship while I was a graduate student at UT, so maybe I'm randomly walking in circles! Mark and I spent a day reviewing materials prepared by the Jackson School and interviewing students and faculty. At the end of it, I compiled our recommendations and observations and sent them to Bill mentioning that I might be interested in being involved in their implementation.

So here I am. My motivations are two-fold: to provide the opportunity to give back and share my personal experience and a very parochial, selfish interest – to continue to learn. Energy as related to the oil and gas business will be a significant part of the energy equation for quite some time. But, around me, is an enormous interest in renewable energy, of which I knew very little. In fact, right now, of our students interested in energy, slightly more than half are interested in renewables. Renewables are a very rapidly growing story for all the right reasons and they are not going away. Climate change is a near and present danger which we must try to mitigate but to which we will have to continue to adapt.

Our program is multidisciplinary, taught by 37 professors from Jackson, Cockrell, McCombs, LBJ School of Public Affairs, and the Law School. We have diverse students with diverse interests. Central to the EER proposition is that energy and resource solutions are inherently multidisciplinary. They 1) must feature sound science and technology; 2) must be financially viable to attract investors; and 3) it must be acceptable to society at large. All of our students are schooled in these three themes: tech, finance and policy. It was Bill Fisher's prescient thinking that led to the creation of this program 40 years ago and I think it is how graduate schools ought to prepare our future "energy practitioners".

JR: Sounds like a wonderful and innovative program, and again, *the rule of three*, like the 3Es mentioned by Scott earlier. How do you teach and encourage collaboration?

RC: This program teaches multidisciplinary thinking which, by nature must be collaborative.

In my case, the role I play includes creating context for the program. This means develop an outlook of the energy business and the society in which it operates. This provides a basis to understand, and convey to students, the fascinating kinds of jobs they might ultimately pursue. Relevant companies and sectors include oil and gas, renewables, utilities, energy efficiency, investment banking, regulation. However, we also look at water and other earth resources. Energy has a nexus with everything.

To bring this random walk full circle....The town in which I spent my childhood is named El Salvador, after the rich porphyry copper deposit being mined nearby. That same area of the Atacama Desert, is where 65% of the world's lithium reserves are. These are produced from shallow subsurface brines below salt flats. The brines containing lithium are pumped to the surface where 18 months of evaporation in huge ponds results in precipitation of lithium carbonate. As the driest spot on the earth, evaporation is efficient but the very resource being evaporated is exceedingly scarce. *And*, that water is also needed to process copper ores from the most richly endowed copper mining district in the world in the same area. So, is this consistent with sustainable energy solutions?

JR: Sounds like many more solutions for your graduates to provide for decades to come.

Scott Tinker, continued...

"Energy, economy and environment, are inextricable. This 3E waltz is critical. Energy underpins healthy economies, and healthy economies invest in the environment."
– Dr. Scott W. Tinker

JR: You have traveled to some pretty far out places – both in terms of travel distances and cultures. Rex Tillerson mentioned in an interview with David Rubenstein that our industry sends our employees, "...to places you wouldn't want to send your worst enemy...yet we do it gladly, and with a great deal of pride and purpose." What are some of the most interesting places you've been – from either a cultural standpoint, or the business potential?

ST: I've been lucky that way, about 65 countries. Each country offers something unique; economic extremes, climate extremes, governmental extremes, landscape extremes. Svalbard is about as far north as you can go at N79 latitude and is cold and dry. Versus the heat and humidity of equatorial countries such as Colombia, Ethiopia and Indonesia.

There are wealthy places with stunning beauty preserved, like New Zealand and Iceland, and you read about those places and anticipate them. But more surprising are the human impressions you get from the poorest nations. Given the levels of poverty that often exist, they are remarkably well balanced and "in tune" with their environments.

Travel has made me more aware of, and hopefully more tolerant of, human difference. Especially those of us with a lot of stuff, who really don't know how fortunate we are. Programs like the Peace Corps offer that type of opportunity – I'm very supportive of that sort of service, for example in gap years or right after graduation.

Travel also exposes interesting ironies in areas that are of high interest in my area of study. For example, the worst environmental impacts in the world in terms of local pollution—soil, air, water—are in poor nations. They simply can't afford to clean it up. By contrast, wealthy nations, although large consumers, have regulatory processes and the wealth to invest in the environment. Energy, economy and environment, are inextricable. This 3E waltz is critical. Energy underpins healthy economies, and healthy economies invest in the environment.

The historical approach to poverty has been to provide aid. But we are seeing that it is more effective to invest in base-level services that allow micro-markets to form that are fit for purpose to the culture of the region. These are more lasting. Teach to fish, rather than give fish.

But first you have to get everyone up to certain economic level, and this is more complex perhaps than people appreciate. A-B-C: energy-economy-environment. Can't just go A to C. For example, eliminate fossil fuels and clean up the environment. In fact, the reverse would happen. Eliminate fossil fuels, damage the economy, harm the environment. Counter-intuitive perhaps, but very real.

That's the amazing part of travel – you can see these things, hear the sounds, smell, touch, taste for yourself. The memory doesn't fade. And that is the difficult part of travel as well. To watch kids die from pneumonia caused from breathing smoke that comes from open-fire cooking indoors, or a tooth infection, or dysentery. It's wrong, because most of it is so solvable.

Another big issue tied to poverty is population. Education is tightly related to fertility rates. In modern, educated economies, fertility rates are low. In poor countries, with poor education, parents have 5 to 10 children. Many die before becoming adults. Lifting a country out of poverty starts a virtuous cycle. It's very solvable, but not easy, particularly with the simplified, and misleading, energy politics today. Good and bad; clean and dirty.

The greatest factor preventing the end of energy poverty is corruption: regional, national, public, private – even education – corrupt investment practices. It happens at all levels. Coming out of poverty increases education levels and leads to more structured societal practices. It reduces corruption. A virtuous cycle. I tell students that getting engaged in real energy conversations, not oversimplified ones, gets you involved in meaty, nuanced issues.

For example, the world is urbanizing – 150 million people in the world move to cities each year. This requires a lot of energy in a small area. Dense energy, like nuclear, natural gas, coal, or some combination of the above. These sources provide dense "always on" electricity. Affordable, reliable, available. That's why they are used. Rather than removing the fuels, as some propose, and damaging economic growth and environmental investment, better to address the emissions and clean those up.

JR: As we learn in the industry, companies cannot predict the future (we are fairly bad about predicting oil prices as Tillerson has said before). Instead, many executives plan their company to be able to deliver value in a variety of different scenarios. We are prepared to think about the future of the energy industry unfolding into various scenarios. Can you dive into some of these scenarios for the future of our energy industry?

ST: All forms of energy are resources – oil, gas, coal, sun, wind. Resources, are not the same everywhere. Some places have great wind, others great sun. Some neither. A portfolio of resources is important, so you don't put all energy eggs in one basket. Because resources vary, we can't impose one set of standards from a particular geographic area onto another. California doesn't have what Maine has.

A sustainable energy transition is one in which the world is lifted out of energy poverty, modern economies remain healthy with secure energy, and the environmental impacts of all forms of energy on all forms of the environment—land, air, atmosphere and local air—are reduced.

There is a good/bad, clean/dirty mantra today that is not only inaccurate, but prohibits real progress. I think the impacts of coal, oil, and even natural gas are real, fairly well understood, and certainly pointed out extensively by modern media and in schools. What is not as well discussed is the environmental damage from low density forms of energy like solar, wind and batteries. There is a massive impact from mining to extract all of the metals and materials to build all of the panels, turbines and battery backup systems required to transition to renewables. These are simple machines that require extensive materials.

For example, the U.S. installs about 2200 MW nameplate of rooftop solar energy year. That represents millions of solar panels each year! But the actual generation from all of these panels, using a reasonable capacity factor, is less generation than one nuclear reactor. And the nuclear reactor does not require redundant backup at night when the sun isn't shining.

Another example is electric vehicles, which are called *green*. A Tesla S has over 7000 lithium-ion batteries, each about 3" by 1". To electrify 600 million vehicles, about half of the world's vehicle fleet, would require over 3 trillion lithium-ion batteries. And in 10 years they wear out. It's a number no one likes to think about, but we have to. It would take 95,000 years to count to 3 trillion 1 second at a time. Stacked end-to-end and side-by-side, 3 trillion batteries would cover a U.S football field, end zones included, in a stack nearly 30 kilometers tall! That's above the ozone layer.

Where will all of these materials come from? How will they be manufactured, and where will they be disposed when they wear out? Is that green? Further, China makes more than half of the EVs in the world. And they charge those EVs mostly with coal electricity emitting CO_2 into the single global atmosphere. Is that green? The environmental impact of renewable energy is massive, because the stuff to make panels, turbines and batteries is not renewable.
Renewables have an important role to play, but it will take energy honesty and critical thinking to consider the energy future. It's not a transition from carbon to no carbon. That's a political framing, not a sound technical or economic evaluation. Such critical think largely missing in political discourse today.

JR: These are big points that aren't discussed source – quite stunning. Dr. Tinker, at our Septer,

Explorers Club leadership luncheon, an energy executive mentioned that you are "the best at portraying the need for exploring for and producing energy" around the world to "end energy poverty." This is very high praise from an executive at a supermajor. You also won the prestigious Michel T. Halbouty leadership award from AAPG.

ST: Sounds like a brilliant person! Awards are nice, but at the end of the day they sit on a shelf and collect dust. I work with a lot of extremely talented people on these very significant issues. The achievement that would mean something to me would be when students at universities and in high schools are having rigorous, civil, critical thinking conversations about energy issues. When they do, we will solve these issues.

I don't know what is going to happen. If the next generation can work together, in the radical middle, look at the data, compromise and be willing to be wrong, they will iterate towards viable solutions. And I'll feel like I've played a small part in accomplishing something.

The other big thing I'm passionate about is addressing energy access, which means providing energy for the whole world while also managing atmospheric emissions and other environmental impacts of energy at scale. Between 20 degrees north and south latitude, it's very hot and mostly poor. Warming will affect this region mostly negatively. However, energy will offset the negative impacts of climate change, just like it does in Houston. It would be tough to live in Houston in August without AC. Same with Stockholm, Sweden in February without heat.

With improvement in education and economic growth, a nation can afford environmental health – and we begin a virtuous cycle. Those are the measures of impact that I consider. No award for that stuff. When I see someone light up with understanding–that's a good feeling.

I met two students from Ohio who mentioned they had seen *Switch* and said they do an energy case competition across campus. That's the kind of award that matters to me. Engaging and thinking critically with civil dialogue.

JR: Amen! Wish we could get more screenings of *Switch* and *Switch On* on more college campuses around the world.

You've been around a lot of oil and gas explorers for decades…you've seen some succeed, and some fail. However, lessons can be learned from both of these experiences. What is your message for oil and gas explorers today?

ST: Exploration is evolving. My son is a geologist at Hilcorp and he's found a lot of oil in vertical and horizontal wells. To me, the biggest change is being able to access and analyze data; big-time data analytics on multiple kinds of data sets. That will provide a look into the earth that is different from what we have done in the past. Both in conventional and unconventional, and existing and frontier basins that are still out there.

Today we see a much more quantified approach to exploration. There are a lot of oil and gas molecules in the world, and we don't know everything yet. An open-minded approach to exploration is critical, so that we can continue to invent, to dream, to see things where someone else might not have seen it in the past, based on a new vision, new data, new ideas.

The message I try to give to all energy professionals is that what you do in bringing energy to the world is vital, and is lifting nations out of poverty. This is especially apparent in the exploration and production of natural gas, which has lower CO_2 emissions. The petroleum industry is a vital industry. Sometimes in the US and western Europe the industry can feel a little beat up – but I think that is mostly owing to a severe lack of complete understanding and critical thinking. The energy industry must continue to improve and minimize environmental impacts, not leaving a trail of debris but leaving it better than you found it. That is true exploration.
But that all said, energy professionals should be proud of what you do. You lift the world out of poverty. It matters.

JR: Thank you so much Dr. Tinker.

Richard Chuchla, continued…

"One ingredient of success that I have brought to productive ventures has been energy. If you can convey the excitement and joy of the task at hand, you infect others and motivate them." – Richard J. Chuchla

JR: You have traveled to some pretty far out places – both in terms of travel distances and cultures. What are some of the most interesting places you've been – from either a cultural standpoint, or the business potential?

RC: I was born and raised in Chile and did not become a U. S. citizen until 1988. Unlike most Americans who are citizens as an entitlement of birth and grow up in a remarkably prosperous and sheltered part of the world, my earliest views of the world were quite different. My parents were both survivors of WWII, Dad from some of the most brutal battles of the war and Mom from a Soviet concentration camp where most of her family perished. At age 11, Mom traveled from Poland to Siberia and, several year later, from Siberia by foot and train through Russia, Kazakhstan, Persia (now Iran), Syria and Palestine where she ended up in an orphanage. They both saw the world under extreme hardship but they both talked unceasingly of the wonders of the world at large. For these reasons, I was infected by the travel bug early in life.

So, segue to travel with ExxonMobil…Yes, ExxonMobil sent us to all sorts of places. I've lost count of the number of countries I have visited. One might worry about some of them but we were so well taken care of that I never felt in danger. I loved it. If you did a principal components analysis of the fulfillment I got from my job, something close to 50% was in one way, shape or form tied to the travel necessary to conduct the business of a multinational corporation. While getting out of the office was necessary, it was also intellectually liberating and freed me of the day-to-day office nonsense so that I could think. The joy of travel was indeed tied to learning about new cultures and meeting people who view the world and the business differently. When I went to Luanda, Angola for a JV technical or management committee meeting, I was not just in a different city. I was working with people who invariably viewed the issues on the agenda from a different perspective. While sometimes frustrating, this enriched discussions and led to better solutions.

I'll always have a warm spot in my heart for Latin America; for its geology, people, food and cultures. Maybe one of the most fascinating projects I worked on there was the Tambopata block in the Peruvian Amazon. Tambopata was in the Andean foothills south of and along strike of the giant Camisea complex. We ended up drilling a well on the Candamo structure and while we found a lot of gas, we also found a reservoir that would probably not deliver volumes at commercial rates. The most interesting part of this (ad)venture was the environment in which we were doing business: among the most ecologically diverse places on earth. Just to be there was a privilege. The area has "uncontacted people" so very basic issues like having a cold or the flu that could infect people with no natural immunities to these illnesses were critical considerations. Business had to be conducted in a very careful and responsible way.

When you hear people talk about the oil and gas business, you get the impression that the environment is a secondary consideration. That could not be further from the truth. We always regarded environmental stewardship as part of our social contract...our license to operate. You realize the consequences and how high the stakes are for doing business in places like the Peruvian Amazon.

JR: Fascinating how complex the work can be in these frontier regions for exploration and appraisal – what an experience to share with our generation.

RC: I can't leave South America without talking about the lead our team took in entering the Vaca Muerta play. In late 2007, we had highlighted the Neuquén Basin and the Vaca Muerta, in particular, as a top tier shale opportunity. We were well ahead of the competition although we did not pick up acreage until 2010. Watch this space....there will be continuing challenges for international shale plays, but they are not going away.

Working on our Angola and Nigeria assets as the West Africa Deepwater Geosciences Manager was another international experience that was memorable. That included working with Total to unravel the intricacies of channel systems guided by high resolution

3D seismic data with a vertical resolution of 6.5 meters and ultimately drilling the first 13 development wells on Girassol. As the Angola-Congo Area Manager, another uplifting experience was drilling 12 consecutive discoveries on Block 15. The magic was in the beautifully calibrated 3D seismic data and working with outstanding teams of passionate, motivated geoscientists. We worked hard, were successful and we had fun doing it.

JR: Wow, that is a great string of discoveries – congratulations.

RC: I've taken numerous business trips to China. My first was in 2008 just before the Olympics. At that time, we were talking to PetroChina and Sinopec about jointly pursuing shale opportunities. China was in the midst of delivering double digit GDP growth and it was pretty easy to see how this rapidly growing economy would be playing a central role in the world's energy future. By virtue of its economic growth, China is going to continue to drive the energy world and directly or indirectly create the incentive to find and deliver more oil and gas. It is an amazing country with highly driven, ingenious and industrious citizens fully intent on achieving the living standards of our country.

JR: Thank you Richard – good things to watch from the Vaca Muerta, offshore West Africa and China.

Companies cannot predict the future. Instead, many executives plan their company to be able to deliver value in a variety of different scenarios. Can you dive into some of these scenarios for the future of our energy industry?

RC: Actually Jon, the Energy and Earth Resources graduate program is about exactly this topic. But the imperative is a lot greater…it's about preparing students to shape the energy future. So, in this regard, my role as Director, is to look at the many scenarios for the energy future, share them with students not as proselytizer but in a way that allows them to make up their own minds about the energy future in which they want to play a role. Remember the adage, "We see things not as they are but as we are." All the while, I am a student myself, continuously readjusting my opinions based on new data and insights. My ideas and perspectives have changed. I believe renewable energy resources are critical to the sustainable development of Earth and I believe climate is the central theme of this part of the energy age.

As much as I think renewable resources are critical to our future, I don't think it's reasonable to assume that in the next several decades we're going to have an energy ecosystem divorced from fossil fuels. These fuels have been central to our prosperity and while I hope to see coal fade from the mix, fossil fuels will provide the majority of our energy in 2050. But the trend to renewables is entirely consistent with the energy trend we have seen in the U.S. over the past 200 years: each succeeding fuel has had higher hydrogen to carbon ratios and emits less CO_2 per unit of energy than its predecessor. So, the next step is to get rid of that one last nasty carbon molecule in methane...much easier said than done. More tractable, but still a major challenge is to strive for zero net carbon, and capture and sequester the CO_2 from combustion.

So where do oil and gas companies play into this story? My personal opinion is that they are struggling to understand how renewables will fit into their business models. This is not a trivial exercise but it is how successful oil and gas companies will remake themselves into true energy companies. They have to continue to deliver earnings to shareholders, and they have to produce energy safely and reliably and at the necessary scale...that will not change irrespective of the move to renewables. Their shareholders and our energy dependent global population depend on it.

JR: Great points. How will this happen?

RC: It is clear to me that investors are indeed looking to the future with the expectation that renewables will play a major energy role. I think that total global capital investment in energy is close to a trillion dollars annually. Capital investment in renewables is around $400 million per year. The pot of money for energy investment is not infinite so oil and gas companies are, in a very real sense, competing for their share.

As renewables have grown, it has become fashionable among their detractors, to point to related issues. This is fair but not if it's done in an impartial way. For example, I have attended presentations where a point was made of the growing demand for Rare Earth Elements

(REEs) for use in renewables power components against a dystopian background of one of the main REE mines in China (actually an iron ore mine that produces REEs as a byproduct). That mine is an environmental mess but presenters fail to note that the main use of REEs is in catalysis in the oil and gas business. And, if we are going to worry the environmental degradation caused by mining, which we absolutely should do, we also need to worry about the 120,000 orphan oil and gas wells in the U.S., un-reclaimed coal mines, coal ash tailings…the list goes on.

My final comment is about the inexorable and exponential progression of technology. Whether it is allowing us to explore in increasingly deeper water or increasingly tighter rocks or capture CO_2 in a commercially viable way or increase the efficiency of solar cells and batteries, it will be responsible for improvements in our lives that, today, we can't even imagine. So, when you think of a better energy world, know that it will happen sooner than you think and in ways that will surprise to the upside.

JR: Many complex factors will play a role, as you have mentioned – thank you Richard.

Your leadership across the various roles in the industry is impressive. Can you share some of your key leadership or management principles? While we know you can't give away your best secrets, we'd appreciate some tips for people starting their own businesses.

RC: Honestly, I'm not sure my leadership has been either that impressive or that critical. I have had the good fortune to work with talented people and high performing teams that, with just a bit of direction and nourishment, were quite capable of doing the work without me. There hasn't been any success I've been involved in over the course of my career that was due to my efforts in isolation. So, if you want to look good, surround yourself with good people.

One ingredient of success that I have brought to productive ventures has been energy. If you can convey the excitement and joy of the task at hand, you infect others and motivate them.

JR: It sounds like a little enthusiasm can go a long way.

RC: A second ingredient a good leader brings is listen...carefully and sincerely. As a leader in the business, you are torn by the expectation that you be c simultaneous knowledge of the enormous uncerta   ... ui the business. Every Energy and Earth Resources student at UT Austin has to read Michael Lewis' book titled *The Undoing Project*. It's about two Israeli psychologists, Daniel Kahneman and Amos Tversky, who showed that in the context of uncertainty and risk, we are prone to make non-optimal decisions due to biases rooted in the way we think. The book itself expounds on the quotation from Voltaire, "Doubt is not a pleasant condition, but certainty is absurd." One way to bridge our own cognitive biases as we contemplate the uncertain world of energy is to listen to and understand the views of others. I was reminded of this continuously by categorical statements made by experts in my own company which were shown to be diametrically wrong (like shale gas will never compete with imported LNG or you can't commercially produce oil from shale, or the Santos pre-salt reservoir will be a tight, volcaniclastic sandstone and the source will be overmature for oil...I have a dozen of these). Unfortunately, I'm sure I too have contributed to this erroneous dogma.

JR: Some great quotes to keep in mind, and a powerful way of thinking. In 2019 at our first Houston Explorers Club luncheon, we had an executive speak from BP, and they too encouraged awareness of dogma in the industry. It sounds like an important theme – and sage advice.

A few more questions for you Richard...next one....you've been around a lot of oil and gas explorers for decades. You've seen some succeed, and some fail. What is your message for oil and gas explorers today?

RC: The first one is, another profound grasp of the obvious: start with the big picture. You have to develop context for whatever you're doing, and that's critical in trying to unravel the mysteries of the subsurface.

JR: This sounds similar to how Siemon W. Muller coached his geologists during mapping projects in California.

..: Yes. In the energy business, it starts with the "outlook": is there a market, and how am I going to connect to that market? How will that market change? Where are the basins with the most prospective geology? What are the fiscal regimes of the countries in which these basins occur? We talk about developing understanding from plates to pores. Without the context of plates, you will never fully understand the pores. And then given the diverse datasets we use, integration is critical. This is an exercise of intellect and computational data analysis.

I attended the most recent UrTEC conference, and I was taken aback by how poorly integrated a lot of the thinking is in the shale business. The shale renaissance in energy production has been disproportionately driven by large engineering staffs, who think that we can manufacture good results with completion design and logistics. You can't squeeze blood from a turnip, and you can't squeeze oil from crappy rocks and make money doing it. Shale resources are no different from any other resources (energy, minerals, etc.) on Earth. All are log normally distributed. There are relatively few basins that command most of the value, a larger population with moderate quality resources that are commercially viable and then a very large population that erodes value. You must be selective about the basin, the play and the part of the play you pursue. Much of that workflow comes from the minds, and careful analysis of geoscientists which is then integrated with engineering considerations. In spite of the high levels of production, the performance of the shale business, as a sector, has not been encouraging: negative free cash flow for a decade. That's a metric to think about. However, the upside for shale, done right, is enormous. It is not going away and it will grow as international opportunities find their legs.

JR: That's a surprising financial metric. I see how the future might be much more positive.

RC: There are many more attributes of effective explorers but I'll offer this last one. Conceiving an idea in exploration is an exercise in science but it requires a deep emotional commitment. That emotional commitment is critical in sustaining an explorer through the ups and downs of prospect generation and maturation. However, a trait of explorers is the ability to evaluate their results dispassionately.

You need to be continuously testing discoveries against their commercial viability.

JR: Thank you so much Professor Chuchla. I really appreciate your time today.

Kurt Rudolph (September 2020)

"When I became Chief Geologist, I also helped lead an annual review of exploration technical learnings. It included a number of cold statistics that had a range of topics: from, "Here's how we did on success, how it was rated and volumes, all in different basins, play types and regions of interest." But we also tied the clinical statistics discussion to a number of case studies that illustrated the program-wide learnings and results. It was presented yearly to both management and technical staff, including different offices around the world. People were always curious, and can certainly learn from the experiences of other parts of the world." – Kurt W. Rudolph

Kurt W. Rudolph received a B.S. in Geology from Rensselaer Polytechnic Institute and an M.A. in Geology from the University of Texas. He began his career as an Exploration Geologist with Unocal in 1978, until he joined Exxon Production Research in 1981. He held a variety of positions at Exxon/ExxonMobil, including Research Geologist, Chief Interpreter in Kuala Lumpur, Technical Advisor for the Africa and Middle East Region, and Hydrocarbon Systems Resource Manager. From 2002 until his retirement in 2015, he was Chief Geoscientist with ExxonMobil Exploration Company in Houston. Since then, Kurt has been an Adjunct Professor at the University of Houston and Rice University.

His interests include seismic attributes/DHI analysis, risking and assessment, sequence stratigraphy, basin analysis, and tectonics and sedimentation. Current research includes the Cretaceous Western Interior, Paleozoic orogenic systems of North America and northern Europe, and integrating subsurface uncertainty into assessment and economic analysis.

He won Wallace Pratt Awards for the best AAPG Bulletin paper in 1994 and 2017, was an AAPG-SEG Distinguished Lecturer for 2001-2002, was the AAPG Michael Halbouty Lecturer for 2007, won best paper award for the Mountain Geologist (RMAG) in 2015, and will be an AAPG Distinguished Lecturer for 2023-2024.

Kurt is an encyclopedia of geologic knowledge. Kurt has the ability, as described in the previous conversation with Richard Chuchla, to see the basin from "plates to pores." Some of his most recent keynote presentations characterize the evolution of plate margins. He brings context into any scientific endeavor because he's worked nearly every basin where there's oil and gas. Whenever I go to a new place, I always ask Kurt, "What was it like to work there?" He often gives a sincere and vivid description as if he was in that country or city last week. To us in the applied geosciences, we admire Kurt's landmark contributions to understanding petroleum geoscience. But Kurt doesn't think about these great achievements often. Talk to him any day, and he is busy on any one of a number of what he calls "side projects." To him they may seem like side projects, but is the Paleozoic history of North America a side project? Many would say it sounds more like an entire research lab's body of work over several decades. Kurt has the rare ability to be able to fit all geologic data into his head at one time, and then articulately explain the nature of the basin's evolution. What would make most people's head hurt, Kurt is in his element weighing multiple data sets of varying accuracy and uncertainty. Few people in the world could take on projects of such scale for many reasons: i) the project is too open ended and could many multiple, compounding implications; ii) the project is too extensive from a data and data type standpoint, and; iii) few people have taken the time (a lifetime, or better part of a career) to immerse themselves in the geology of an area so large, so as to understand it, understand which questions to ask, and how to solve the problem.

Kurt is not just a brilliant geologist. He takes time to invest in people. He has coached AAPG Imperial Barrel Award teams, has taught courses at Rice University and University of Houston and many other universities around the world. And he's seen a lot of success with these roles too because he is so approachable. He's able to disentangle the difficult geoscience lexicon and translate it into meaningful conversation with students and peers. With his unique ability to understand the complex evolution of continental margins and basins all around the world, it's no surprise that he was able to lead as Chief Geologist of ExxonMobil for an unprecedented (in modern history) 13 years.

Anyone who knows Mr. Rudolph understands he has made decades of contributions to the global energy industry, and continues to lead in the exploration geosciences. In this interview from September 2020, you'll learn about leadership in the energy industry, working with university geoscience programs, the prospect review workflow and global exploration trends.

Jon Rotzien (JR): Kurt, thank you for your time to visit today and share some of your insight on the energy industry.

Could you share your background and what led you to your current roles with Rice University and University of Houston?

Kurt Rudolph (KR): I started in the industry in 1978 at Unocal, in a small office in Jackson, Mississippi. I'll actually talk more about that than you'd expect. I came out of school at a really good time. It was the time in the industry that every company you interviewed with gave you an offer. I wanted a mid-sized company, so Unocal worked well. I got the offer, and they said, "You can go anywhere you want, any office." Those included Anchorage, Los Angeles, didn't have an office in Denver, their Rockies office was in Casper. I asked, "Where's your most active office?" There was a long pause, and they said, "Actually it's Jackson." I thought, ok I'll go there.

JR: What was it about Jackson?

KR: Jackson was unique in the sense that you probably wouldn't find an office like it today in a medium to large company. There were only 6-7 geoscientists in the office. They gave me a four-county area, and you're responsible for everything. Developing prospects, field development, seismic interpretation, overseeing seismic acquisition and processing, log analysis, sitting wells, working with landmen, etc. I probably did a crappy job on many of the more specialized things, but you get comfortable with a lot of fundamentals and how things integrate. It is hard to get that experience now, and so quickly, at a major.

JR: But you didn't stay there long?

KR: 3 years later, I'd learned a lot and was plateauing. I hired on with Exxon research in their sequence stratigraphy group with a lot of names you're familiar with – Vail, Mitchum, Posamentier, etc. I got exposed to really smart people, and it ramped up my learning a lot.

JR: Where did you go next?

KR: At the end of '89, we went to Malaysia. I was there almost 6 years and had an advisory job in Kuala Lumpur. Malaysia was super active drilling both exploration and development wells. It had excellent 3D seismic data, for the time. I had transitioned from a deep research group in Houston to an operationally active environment, where you have instant punishment and reward. I was responsible for QC of prospects and the development program, especially on the seismic interpretation and analysis.

When we came back to Houston, Exxon made me advisor for the Africa/ Middle East Region. This was in 1995, right before all the big deepwater discoveries started being made. Especially for us in Nigeria and Angola. I got to, again, see all this great stuff, help guide it a bit. But also learn a lot at same time.

JR: What about the Exxon and Mobil merger? What was your role?

KR: This isn't too interesting. I was on the merger transition team co-located with Mobil staff. At least in geoscience, I think I was the only technical person I was aware of. Everyone else I worked with was in management, so it was pretty new to me. I helped design how geoscience in the new company would work, in terms of technical assignments, career development and quality assurance. Not long after the transition period, they named me Chief Geologist and had that position for 13.5 years until I retired at 60 and a half.

JR: How did you manage to keep up with the technological advances during your career?

KR: I was lucky in that I got to see a ton of stuff around world, data, technology, global exploration, development and production programs. In my last position, I also experienced the generational changes, and to see my replacements coming in, and perhaps help them a bit. That was very satisfying.

One thing I tried to do all the time was to stay technically connected. It's easy to make ridiculous recommendations if you don't stay current with the technology including software like Petrel and Petromod. I always had a side "hobby project" to maintain some level of practitioner skills. In that way, I was able to stay grounded and not lose touch with how much it takes to interpret seismic, correlate wells, make maps, etc. I also taught the sequence stratigraphy field schools in West Texas, Utah and Wyoming.

JR: Then how did you make the transition to University of Houston?

KR: Shortly after retirement, a senior manager at ExxonMobil who was the chair of an industry advisory committee said, "Hey you know, this would be interesting for you to serve UH [as an Adjunct Professor] – go talk to the chairman there." That's how I got attached to UH. I work with grad students – over time, I've been on 9 committees, with several of those students graduating. The research spans a lot of areas, but the projects usually have a stratigraphic component, and that's mostly what I've been doing at UH.

JR: And what about Rice?

KR: Another friend of mine, Kevin Biddle, was putting together a course to teach at Rice. It was a Tom Sawyer type of thing, he asked if I could "maybe handle a few of the lectures and exercises." I told him, "The way you explained it, it could be different in a few ways." In the end, I ended up teaching half the course! It's about decision analysis in the energy industry, and it's all about assessing, risking, and providing economic analysis of opportunities in upstream. In other words, how technical information gets translated into business decisions.

JR: How is the course formatted?

KR: We have two big projects the students complete, where they take an opportunity all the way from identification of the risk and volumetric elements to a drilling decision and development.

One project uses conventional prospects in deepwater West Africa, using public domain information only. We look at several prospects, risk and compare them as drilling opportunities. Then we focus on one, provide more information, and they mature their risking and a probabilistic assessment. This gets translated into risked economics including NPV, IRR. After drilling, they calculate the reserves with the well information in hand. The economic analyses explore probability weighting for different outcomes, value of information analysis, etc.

The other project is very similar in intent and goals, but is based on an onshore unconventional example (the Barnett). The lesson is, even when the geology and commercial context is very different, the same principles and methods apply.

Working with students keeps you connected to younger people, which helps keep me grounded at my advanced age.

JR: In 2013, energy stocks took up a significant (double-digit) part of the S&P 500, yet now that percentage is low single digits. Recently, ExxonMobil was removed from the S&P 500 ending a decades-long run. Some talking heads would say not to invest in oil and gas companies at all. What do you think about the future of the oil and gas industry?

KR: I've seen a lot of cycles, since I started in 1978. The most serious one was in '86. Oil price was single digits for an extended period of time. There have been a lot of discussions in the past (and now) asking if this is the end, as we know it. Alternatively, it's a common refrain that the period we are in now is just another cycle, and things will return to normal.

I don't think it's the end, but I think it may be different than previous downturns – for two reasons.

First, there are the structural changes in society and in industry. Coal is a cautionary tale when you look at what's happened to mining industry. On the supply picture, we'll possibly have chronic oversupply for the near to medium term. It'll probably get worked out due to the lack of investment that goes along with the reduced adding of reserves.

It's also different now because we have this buffer of unconventionals that can be turned up and down more easily, whereas deepwater takes many years. The unconventional trends are in North America, obviously, but also emerging in places like Argentina and China. And the availability of unconventionals is new. That wasn't as big a factor in previous equations of upstream cycles.

JR: What about global economic trends?

KR: There has been a correlation between energy use and economic development – this is likely to continue in some form. However, there has been a change in the nature of the global economies; we are now more service- and information-based. And now alternatives are very competitive. And the policies and societal challenges associated with climate change will likely remain and grow.

So, I don't think this is the end of the industry, by any stretch of the imagination. But it is also going to be a different world. I don't know if it this is a black swan event, but the future will probably look different for those reasons.

JR: Congratulations on your AAPG award-winning paper with Frank Goulding. Can you tell us more about your inspiration and outcomes of that project?

KR: This is a long narrative, so apologies. In 1996, the corporation requested we evaluate how good exploration was in delivering what was predicted in terms of success and volumes. We looked at predicted vs. actual values, but also technology applications associated with our exploration program. And the answer in short was, "Ok, we did a pretty good job," and the corporation was satisfied. As always, there were some anomalies.

At the closure of project, some of us saw that this shouldn't be an isolated event, but rather a systematic tracking that should be ongoing and on a forward basis.

JR: How did the workflow get implemented?

KR: It was viewed as it could be used both as a technical stewardship and learning tool at different scales – at the local, play type and portfolio level in terms of what was performing in terms of results.

It could also be used to guide technology development, and used to look for specific anomalies. As always, you tend to focus on the disappointments and what went wrong, but it's also important when you miss things and it's a high side outcome. You want to do more of that in case it's not just a one off.

JR: How did this workflow change the way you viewed exploration?

KR: It brought a bit more discipline to the exploration workflow. Over this long period (1996–2015) the tracking and reporting was stewarded by a few different groups. I chose to stay involved because it was really interesting. But it finally became firmly institutionalized when we made it part of the base business process. It became a key part of stewarding the prospect inventory, from earliest characterization through drilling.

When I became Chief Geologist, I also helped lead an annual review of exploration technical learnings. It included a number of cold statistics that had a range of topics: from, "Here's how we did on success, how it was rated and volumes, all in different basins, play types and regions of interest."

But we also tied the clinical statistics discussion to a number of case studies that illustrated the program-wide learnings and results. It was presented yearly to both management and technical staff, including different offices around the world. People were always curious, and can certainly learn from the experiences of other parts of the world.

JR: How did it change the discussions during prospect review?

KR: The workflow was also pretty useful in making discussions more enriching when you're evaluating prospects. You start to touch on those outcomes in the past that might be analogous. Is this scenario reasonable? Is it much better or worse than other things in the p when you have similarities (or how is it different)? As a result, te can have a much deeper discussion on key risks, uncertaintie success cases.

When I retired, I said to Frank, who's now Chief Geologist, "We ought to think about publishing this." While we weren't able to publish specific cases obviously, at least we got the generalized, program-wide learnings published.

Above: Photopanel of a section of the Miocene-Pliocene Capistrano Formation, San Clemente State Beach, California, one of the premier outcrop belts used for training deepwater exploration and production geoscientists.

> *"Being overly responsive to events is not always a good thing. You need a long-term view, to take out anecdotal outcomes. We're [exploration is] in a statistical game, and you need a balance between the immediate results and overall drilling program."* – Kurt W. Rudolph

JR: Successful exploration seems to be accomplished with a vision, correct implementation of a strategy, adequate deal flow, deep subject matter knowledge – a lot of hard work to make smart investment decisions and probably a bit of luck – among other things. Can you describe what it takes for a large company to run a successful exploration program?

KR: This may be a little bland, maybe too corporate. What I think are the keys are three kind of elements: i) being disciplined; ii) being consistent; and iii) having a long term view and not over responding near term noise, if you will.

laborate on those?

hing, one thing we were good at for a long er the work was done in KL, Lagos, Houston e, at least not too different. It helps to have a little local creativity and approaches, and in the end, those nuances might be adopted as part of the global best practices. But if you need to rank and prioritize drilling and acreage opportunities, you need to have consistency. As a base case, you need to have a consistent workflow and criteria to characterize, sort, and prioritize the portfolio. Some might view this as impeding creativity. I've thought a lot about that, and will touch on it later.

Being overly responsive to events is not always a good thing. You need a long-term view, to take out anecdotal outcomes. We're [exploration is] in a statistical game, and you need a balance between the immediate results and overall drilling program.

JR: How do you approach discipline?

KR: By discipline, I mean trying to be objective, not, you know, swayed by bandwagon effects or emotions or all that stuff. Just trying to get back to facts without squashing creativity.

JR: In your experience, what are the ingredients for a high-performing exploration team?

KR: I think there's really two big things for me. First is diversity. Different kinds of people, skills, experience, work styles, all that stuff. I'm not talking specifically about just gender, age, nationality, etc. But that goes hand-in-hand because people from different backgrounds are going to think and work differently. That's good, and can be highly complementary. You definitely need creative types on the team. They might be a little loose with the data, but that can have a certain advantage. And you also need careful analytical scientists to keep those creative folks grounded.

JR: What if you had all of one type or the other?

KR: If you have all of the first type, the company will probably go broke (and I have some stories on that). But if you had all of the latter types, coldly analytical, you're probably never going to do anything. So, you need both.

Another thing is that as technology has advanced, you have to have depth. By that I mean expert specialists who *really* know their discipline. But also, broad integrators who can fit it all together. If you had all broad-thinker people, you might not get the level of detail to achieve great results, and you definitely need experts to evaluate contrarian facts that don't seem to fit. Also, people with lots of experience need to be on the team, but experience comes with bias. The people who are less experienced are also unencumbered, and come to the table without too many paradigms. It's also helpful to have people with deep experience in the basin or play, but then you also need people who have global experience in other basins all over the world. They can say, "Hey, I've seen this play from this other basin, and it may work here," or something to that effect.

JR: What about communication on objectives?

KR: You also need very good clarity on shared objectives. And that concept works top to bottom. You need some alignment up through senior management, but it also needs to work side to side, and within different components on the team. Team members need to understand, for example, what does success look like? What does failure look like? What is the value proposition for what I'm doing? Everyone on the team needs to see how they fit into that context.

JR: Your recent research on foreland basins in the US has great applicability to the Shale Revolution? What have you found?

KR: First of all, realistically, for a lot of unconventional plays, virtually all have been found not through high science, but by empirical information identified by really smart people. But to extend these concepts in lightly explored places, we can take the learnings from, say, North America to places like China and Argentina, obviously.

It's not universal, but there is a common correspondence of big increases in basin subsidence and source rock deposition. This doesn't only apply to compressional basins, but also extensional basins as well.

My interpretation of this is that rapid increases in accommodation, whether it's the Marcellus with onset of Acadian (Appalachian) orogeny, or the Kimmeridge Clay during the Late Jurassic extension, is that the rapid subsidence creates an instant starvation event before sediment transport and depositional processes (for coarse sediment) can catch up and fill in the basin. It's an effective way to prevent dilution by coarse clastics.

JR: What about the asymmetry of most basins?

KR: More importantly, subsidence events are not uniform. Often basin margins are going up, while basin centers are going down. That relief creates enhanced basin physiography for upwelling and nutrient enrichment.

The basin differentiation creates an enclosed basin, which increases anoxia. In the end, those three things give you the lack of dilution by clastics, increase in organic productivity, and preservation. Overall, it's good for making organic-rich marine source rocks.

JR: Do all foreland basin systems show this?

KR: A lot of foreland basins follow this theme, unless it's like the Andean system, which is overfilled. Not a good situation for source rock development. When you look across North America (like the Utica, Marcellus, Niobrara, Pebble Shale, Wolfcamp), many source rock examples occur at rapid increases in subsidence associated with orogenesis. And many, as a result, are also unconventional plays.

Another important thing, shale reservoirs (and I hate that term), it's not just the kerogen that matters, but are they "frack-able"? In other words, are their mechanical properties sufficiently brittle. This is most often due to the presence of biogenic silica (radiolarians) or carbonate (coccoliths), like the Eagle Ford, Marcellus, Vaca Muerta and the Niobrara. (While it's a common scenario, it's not a universal truth.)

JR: What do you tell students and people early in their careers when they ask about how to succeed in the energy industry?

KR: Now is probably as bad as it's going to get. My advice is to stay flexible, cast the net really wide, hope to get employed and then if you do get a lower-level job, use that position to advance. More energy jobs are in unconventionals now because that's where a lot of the demand is. For most geoscientists working unconventionals, they're operationally based. Which isn't always the most exciting experience for everybody. But you can be exceptional and push boundaries in any role. So, if you're landing wells, and that's probably gets kind of repetitive, do everything you're responsible for and then find side projects. That'll make your job a helluva lot more interesting. That's one of the few things I've told students.

JR: How is this generation better or worse prepared for the energy industry?

KR: One thing about this generation, they have a very good network. But some folks try to overly engineer their careers. They say, "I want to do a, then b, then c." Because they think it'll enhance their career. Sometimes what you thought was going to be the best job ever, wasn't that great, and sometime what you think was going to be the worst was actually a fantastic role. Make your wishes known, but it may not be what you think of it when you finally arrive.

My comment on unconventionals may need some clarification. What I think makes your job most gratifying....you must do everything that's asked, but try to find something extra. In the worst case, you probably learn something that won't have any impact, but in the best case can broaden your opportunities and expand your career as well.

JR: You've been around a lot of oil and gas explorers for decades...you've seen some succeed, and some fail. What is your message for oil and gas explorers today?

KR: One thing I'd emphasize, and I see this in academia, too. Stay linked to the fundamentals. Don't get overly enamored by high-end tools. They have their place, and they're really important. But you have to have tie it back to basic science.

Another thing is to not become overly wedded to your own ideas. Listen to others, their ideas might be valid. In the last 20 years of my career, I tried to include that in my work model and to use a hypothesis-based approach. You can honor diverse opinions, and characterize uncertainty better. It's really important not to just to pick your favorite scenario, but to keep several alive. That makes you a better observer. You're not just looking to validate what you thought was right, but you're seeking alternatives.

As people, we're always looking for the bright new shiny object. Azimuthal seismic data, or sequence stratigraphy....You can't think to yourself, "Ok, I've got this cured. I've got my toolkit and this is going to solve world hunger."

JR: Is there one thing you've learned in the last ten years about how we do our science that you'd like to leave me with?

KR: This is gonna be weird. But the older I get, the less I know. By that I mean you've had a long career, you start to realize how many times you've been wrong in things you had tightly held beliefs in. You have to have humility.

It's kind of a rare thing dealing with really incomplete information, and being forced to make a prediction. In our business, after you make the prediction, it gets tested by drilling, which is when the real learning starts.

JR: Are there any other professions that come close?

KR: The closest analogy I've found is in meteorology. You're audited everyday by predictions. Most other earth sciences, you don't have this "in your face" feedback loop, as we are embedded in all this natural complexity. We apply art, judgment and experience, it's not all hard science, all the time. That's a blessing and a curse. On the bright side, unlike math and physics, a geologist isn't washed up by the time they're 30 or 40.

What I've also learned in the last 10 years, is that bias is in all experienced professionals. And this bias is implicit, and we are generally not aware of it.

Kahneman (who won the Nobel Prize in economics) and Tversky (who alas, died before it was awarded), showed that we're not the rational beings we think we are. The biases color our judgements. Kahneman wrote a popular book about ten years ago that made their work accessible. In it, he describes these two modes of thinking – fast thinking and slow thinking. And another concept, Prospect Theory, in how we respond emotionally to gains and losses.

When humans evolved on the plains of Africa, they had fast choices to make. Quick decisions. That's what fast thinking is about. Run when you see a lion, or escape the crocodile. It's efficient, fast, easy, and really takes no mental effort on your part. When you think of it in terms, heuristically, people tend to do things on gut feel. In our case in exploration, people tend to use easily available analogs and implicit rules.

When faced with choices, we'll often default to this really easy way of thinking. Which can be a huge pitfall for complicated situations.

Confirmation bias is one of the most important types of bias. You get information in, and you already have a model in mind. You tend to embrace information that fits the model, discard info that doesn't fit the model. Unconsciously, you're selecting things that support your point of view because we as a species experience this terrible dissonance about being wrong. This avoids that pain if you will.

Another example is called narrative bias. If you can tell a memorable story around something, it gets embraced and remembered much better than statements of cold hard facts. This is the salesman part of the job. I used it myself. But just because it's a good story doesn't make it right. You need to be able to peer beyond the gloss of the storyteller.

In my decision analysis class at Rice, we talk about these biases. We do a simple experiment of anchoring bias. This is where your initial estimate of something colors your final estimate, and it's hard to move away from that.

JR: How do you teach this in the class?

KR: In the class, we come up with two less well-known countries, so the students have only a vague notion of the population. At first, we ask the students to just shout out what they think the population is, say, for a country like Uzbekistan. And then for another country that's equally poorly known, we'll ask the students to write down the population on a card and turn it in. In terms of the mean, the second country comes in much closer to the actual, but has a larger standard deviation. And it's for a simple fact that when the first student says, "12 million!" for the first exercise, there is a much tighter range, and, in the end, a much worse answer. Everyone anchors around the initial estimate.

It's one of the things I used to do in assessing, risking and ranking of a prospect. I like the wisdom of the crowds approach to start. In this way, the loudest voice or highest salary grade doesn't get all the attention, you ask people to write down estimates on pieces of paper. You get more information than what you'd get in anchoring environments, where the answer is modified by what people say. After you get everybody's unvarnished estimate, then you talk it out and try to understand why everybody thought the way they did. At the end, you don't just take the average of the estimates but try to get the best of independent thinking and consensus.

We all have these biases, we all do it. You need this self-awareness and slowing down. The first president of the exploration company had this saying he used a couple times. And it took me years to understand. "Often you have to go slow to go far." You can't be always ready to answer and make a decision on the fly using gut feel because often that is terribly flawed. When somebody asks a complex question, I think one of best answers is, "I don't know yet, let me get back to you." Often it is better to step back and think a bit, this takes out cognitive biases in our system. And time to seek others' wisdom. But saying that takes courage.

JR: Thank you very much Mr. Rudolph.

Above: Outcrop exposures of the seismic-scale Miocene Awakino mass-transport deposit, Taranaki Basin, North Island, New Zealand.

Leadership in Applied Research

It is rare that a leader in geoscience does not have superb technical skills for solving scientific problems. Some leaders take their findings to develop a new market; some prefer to pursue scientific truth purely as a noble cause. This next section is devoted to those who are on the cusp of finding new prosperous avenues of geoscience research. These researchers travel to some of the most remote places on Earth to conduct their studies, and use the most advanced computation methods available to solve complex problems with implications for the energy industry, climate change and how we as humans interact with Earth. These leaders show that it is in strong relationships that great success is achieved. Not just in personal relationships, but also in relationships among university, corporate and government teams. These leaders in applied research excel in understanding how to create value for multiple parties in collaborative research environments, such as joint industry projects (JIP), which are common for scientists whose research is highly valued by companies and government agencies. This section features four accomplished geoscience researchers.

Dr. Sebastian Cardona is one of the most influential, well-respected and successful leaders in deepwater sedimentary systems. He has held numerous academic and industry positions that have taken him to some of the most remote places on Earth. He describes the aspects of what it takes to thrive as a well-rounded, applied geoscientist.

Dr. Anshuman Pradhan is a talented geoscientist and pioneer in the field of modeling, engineering and statistics including AI/ML workflows. His thoughtful approach toward applied research will help anyone in the field of scientific inquiry design and implement impactful studies.

Professor Sumit Verma and Dr. Shuvajit Bhattacharya demonstrate how industry, academic and government research partnerships yield amazing results. They have worked in various technical leadership roles in Asia-Pacific, Europe, Africa and North America and are inspiring the next generation of researchers dedicated to evaluating Earth's resources using high-tech imaging methods.

Sebastian Cardona (July 2021)

"I live by a simple motto: being a human-kind—that is being humane and kind! The best leaders I have interacted with have been humble and encouraging. They lead by example and empower others. I've been fortunate to have worked with great leaders in the scientific and professional community and I am just paying it forward."
– Dr. Sebastian Cardona

Sebastian Cardona is a sedimentologist and marine geologist with interests in geohazards, marine geology, and exploration geology. He worked for Equinor US in Houston as an exploration geologist 2019-2020 while completing his Ph.D. Sebastian is originally from Medellin, Colombia and holds a M.Sc. in geology from The University of Texas at Austin (2015) and a Ph.D. in geology from Colorado School of Mines (2020) working with Lesli Wood and Brandon Dugan. He has conducted and published research addressing the sedimentology of submarine landslides (also known as MTCs and MTDs) using outcrop, core, wireline, and seismic data. He also participated in the IODP Expedition 372: Creeping Gas Hydrates Slides as shipboard sedimentologist investigating the interaction between submarine landslides and gas hydrate. Sebastian will join the Sediment Mechanics Lab led by Julia Reece at Texas A&M University as a 2021 Geoscience Future Faculty Postdoctoral

Research Associate Fellow this September to investigate the genesis of weak marine slopes.

I sat down with Dr. Sebastian Cardona in June 2021 to learn about the broad processes associated with submarine landslides, also known as mass-transport deposits (MTD) and mass-transport complexes (MTC). Sebastian commands in-depth knowledge of gravity driven processes, petroleum exploration, and how to characterize deepwater depositional systems using a variety of data types. I first met Sebastian when he gave a comprehensive presentation on submarine landslides at the GeoGulf Convention in Houston in 2019. His talk was part of the GCSSEPM-sponsored Deepwater Symposium, in which we had many countries, oil companies and universities represented in the full day of talks. His presentation and interpretations were so impressive that I've invited him on a number of occasions to present at other conferences and colloquiums as well. In my opinion, there is no one better at being able to map out the anatomy of an outcrop than Dr. Cardona. It's one of his many gifts – to be able to peer past the distractions, weathering profile, unevenness of the outcrop cut – to see the structural and sedimentological traits that allow him to accurately characterize the rock. But these aren't just any outcrops that anyone could interpret. These are highly folded, complex wads of pervasively 3D-mixed sandstone, mudstone and conglomerate consisting of dismembered and sheared beds. Take for instance Sebastian's interpretation of the Rapanui Mass-Transport Deposit in the 2020 issue of Sedimentology. Geologists have been visiting and studying this outcrop for decades, and yet Sebastian, for his PhD dissertation no less, studied the outcrop and provided the most thorough qualitative and quantitative assessment of any MTD in the world. Not only does this resonate with basic science and how and why MTD form and move, but also has major implications for the energy industry – specifically how MTD affect a total petroleum system and may act as seals or carrier units. That study in particular ignited studies of MTD around the world. It put these deposits on the global stage again since the original treatise was published in 2010.

Sebastian is not just a world-class scientist, but he presents convincingly, and with a lot of great analogies to make sure his team understands the goals and importance of the work. This is why he is always my first choice when it comes to explaining deepwater processes. He connects with the audience. He has done everything from marathons to triathlons and has worked in research labs on land and by sea. A master of many languages, Sebastian is experienced at leading in many settings.

Read the interview below from July 2021.

Jon Rotzien (JR): Sebastian, I'm so thankful you had the time to visit today and share your story. Could you share your background, and what led you to your current role?

Sebastian Cardona (SC): Always happy to chat with you and thank you for the interview invitation. I am originally from Medellin, Colombia and I moved to San Antonio, Texas almost a decade ago where I completed my BS in Geology at the University of Texas at San Antonio. While pursuing my bachelors, I was fortunate to intern for an independent exploration company at San Antonio, Welder E&P, where I learned a great deal about conventional exploration from my mentor Raymond Welder—I even learned the almost extinct 'craft' of picking faults with paper logs! From there I went to the University of Texas at Austin to pursue an MS in Geology with Lesli Wood and Lorena Moscardelli. I was fascinated by 3D seismic data and I got to work with an amazing dataset from offshore Gulf of Mexico. I remembered I finished my MS right in the middle of the 2014-2016 oil crash, so job opportunities were scarce. On the positive side, working with Lesli was so fun and there was a PhD opportunity for me to continue my research on submarine landslides, so I followed her when she took the Weimer Distinguished professorship at Colorado School of Mines. I recently completed my PhD in Geology (May 2020) from Colorado School of Mines working with Lesli Wood and Brandon Dugan where I investigated the sedimentology of submarine landslides—these are also known as mass transport complexes (MTCs) or deposits (MTDs) among the industry. During the last year of my PhD, I moved to Houston in October 2019 to take on a job as exploration geologist at Equinor. Unfortunately, I was one of those that got let go during the most recent crash in 2020. It seems that my graduation dates are a bit in tune with oil crashes!

On the brighter side, I was awarded the 2021 Geoscience Future Faculty Postdoctoral Fellowship at Texas A&M University where I will work with Julia Reece at her Sediment Mechanics Lab. I am really looking forward to starting this opportunity and doing experimental and numerical work in submarine landslides. The goal is to advance geohazard assessment of areas at risk—in a way we want to improve our understanding of the preconditioning and triggering factors in submarine margins, so we can potentially identify where submarine landslides may happen before they do happen. Understanding marine hazards is becoming ever more important as seafloor infrastructure keeps growing driven by global connectivity and the energy transition—check out the exciting wind farm joint-project between Equinor and BP, offshore East coast that will provide New York State with wind power.

JR: Congratulations on those recent developments, and go Aggies! I've seen you present a number of times and have learned so much every time, including at the GCSSEPM Deepwater Symposium as part of GeoGulf in Houston in 2019 and earlier this year at the South Dakota School of Mines Depositional Systems Colloquium. What inspired you to undertake detailed studies of MTD around the world, and in some of the most renowned outcrops in Taranaki?

SC: That's a funny story! I am indebted to Lesli Wood and Lorena Moscardelli for nurturing my deep interest in submarine mass-transport deposits. It's been more than a decade now studying these deposits and they don't cease to surprise me. The idea about studying the deposits in Taranaki was born from a conversation with Lesli. We recognized that much of the previous work on these deposits was based only on seismic data—pioneered by Lorena—so we wanted to bridge this gap by providing detailed outcrop studies that could help those working with remote-sensed data (e.g., seismic and wireline). The outcrops in Taranaki are just world class—as I am sure you know—and I encourage all geoscientists, especially those working with deepwater deposits, to visit them in the future and take your class in Taranaki!

JR: Your paper on the Rapanui MTD (Taranaki Basin) in *Sedimentology* describes the anatomy of that system in unprecedented detail – a must read for anyone working submarine landslides. On another topic – GeoGulf is in Austin this year. Are you and colleagues leading a session on deep water?

SC: Unfortunately, I won't be presenting any of my work this year, but I am planning to attend. There are several new themes this year such as Geohazards and Sustainable Energy that I am looking forward to.

JR: Some great themes. Energy stocks took up about~12% of the S&P 500 about a decade ago, now it's about 2%, yet oil and gas represents about 8% of the US GDP. How does the oil and gas industry navigate these market conditions?

SC: That's a hard question but in my perspective, I feel the industry has been very "reactive" overall. I wish the industry was more proactive in developing and nurturing new ideas that disrupt status-quo rather than keeping the 'reactionary' approach. The oil and gas industry does not have any excuse not to be positioned in a leading role in the energy transition—it has the economic and know-how muscle—yet it feels that there is still much reluctance. As a result, much of the young talent is not being retained or even attracted in the first place.

JR: Can you tell us about your favorite project or well so far in your career?

SC: So far my favorite professional project was proposing a prospect in the deepwater Perdido area, offshore Gulf of Mexico. I really enjoyed working with several specialists in different disciplines, and it exposed me to the great amount of detail that goes into exploration. Hopefully I get to see the press release about a discovery if it gets to be drilled. On the scientific side, my favorite project was to sail as a sedimentologist in the Expedition 372 of the International Oceanic Discovery Program. We sailed from Fremantle, Australia to Lyttelton, New Zealand and collected core from a submarine landslide on the seafloor suspected to be reactivated due to gas hydrate dissociation. While on the *Joides Resolution* (JR) research vessel, I got to work with amazing geoscientists from every continent.

JR: How is your swimming, biking and running?

SC: Mmmmm the pandemic hasn't helped me much to stay on top of my training, but I am getting back at them this summer.

JR: Would you consider racing on the Basin Dynamics Multisport Team?

SC: Absolutely!

JR: Excellent.

You're a great leader in deepwater depositional systems. You have a profound grasp of sedimentary geology principles, a rare ability to connect with a large audience, and a deep curiosity for our science – including its origins, history and its applications. Can you share some of your key leadership principles?

SC: Thanks for those words, Jon. I try to replicate what I have learned from other great leaders in our scientific and professional community. I live by a simple motto: being a human-kind—that is being humane and kind! The best leaders I have interacted with have been humble and encouraging. They lead by example and empower others. I've been fortunate to have worked with great leaders in the scientific and professional community and I am just paying it forward.

JR: You were a student not too long ago. What would be your message to students at universities interested in making a career in the energy industry?

SC: This is a really tough question. From first-hand experience, I would advise students to focus on gaining skills rather than choosing a particular topic of research, especially if those skills are transferable and valuable in other disciplines. Although the awareness of geosciences has increased more and more, it does not seem that career options are growing. Perhaps it's a function of the pandemic and I hope things pick up soon.

JR: What is your message for oil and gas explorers today? Or for those in the broader energy business?

SC: You were saving the hardest question for last! I've been tinkering about this exact question as I navigate my own transition into the broader energy business. I clearly don't have a silver bullet answer, but I am happy to share my experience. For me, it has always been important to foster my scientific curiosity and to keep learning new things. A way to do this is to keep volunteering and participating in the several scientific communities and their activities. The energy landscape is certainly changing in front of our eyes, so it's important to keep learning and adopting new ways of doing things.

JR: Thank you so much Dr. Cardona.

Above: Dr. Cardona examining the Miocene Lower Mount Messenger Formation, Taranaki, North Island, New Zealand. The Tongaporutu Beach locale is best visited during low tide, where tourists and geologists alike can examine the uniformly fine- to very fine-grained turbidites interpreted to represent a channel-lobe transition zone (CLTZ) documented in a PhD thesis. This is a popular stop for many tourists as the coastal erosion regularly produces isolated sea stacks from the sandstone. Two of the *Three Sisters* monument are shown in the background; one sea stack recently collapsed. In the distance, the Whitecliffs and Mt Taranaki are barely visible through the low clouds.

Anshuman Pradhan (October 2021)

"Successfully addressing the groundwater and energy challenges of the future will be critically dependent on improved understanding of the geological processes operating in groundwater and hydrocarbon basins. Given (1) the large uncertainty associated with the subsurface, and (2) advancements being made with respect to the data acquisition technologies, for instance fiber optics acoustic sensing networks and high-resolution remote sensing satellites, we will likely see a strong shift towards data-driven approaches in informing our geoscientific analyses and studies. Thus, it is critical that geoscience students actively seek to train themselves in applied statistical and data sciences early on in their academic studies. This will allow them to practice geosciences knowledgeably and responsibly in the data scenario of the future." – Dr. Anshuman Pradhan

Anshuman Pradhan exploring alluvial fan deposits in Death Valley, California, USA.

Anshuman Pradhan is a postdoctoral scholar research associate in Computing and Mathematical Sciences at California Institute of Technology. He has a Ph.D. degree in Energy Resources Engineering from Stanford University. He holds a bachelor's and master's degree in Applied Geophysics from Indian Institute of Technology (Indian School of Mines), Dhanbad. His research interests include geophysical inversion, geological modeling of aquifer systems, hydrocarbon basins and deepwater reservoirs, rock physics, Bayesian statistics, machine learning and artificial intelligence.

In September 2021, I interviewed Anshuman Pradhan while he was a postdoctoral researcher in the department of Computing and Mathematical Sciences at Caltech. Anyone who has met Dr. Pradhan or read his work understands his in-depth expertise in geophysical inversion, geological modeling of aquifer systems, hydrocarbon basins and deepwater reservoirs, rock physics, Bayesian statistics, machine learning and artificial intelligence.

What you might not know about Anshuman is that he and his graduate advisor practically invented ML/AI algorithms as they pertain to basin analysis during his PhD. As a result, Anshuman gave our first keynote presentation at a GeoGulf Convention in Houston. In this presentation, he outlined the steps on how to effectively model deepwater channel complexes using AI/ML/DL methods. This was a bold prediction to use these methods to model reservoir distribution in highly complex reservoirs. Most PhD geologists, some of them Chief Geologists in their respective supermajor companies, in this subject area would say, "Well what about _____ (slope, provenance, grain size, flow rheology, diagenetic properties, water saturation – any number of traits)?" Anshuman's models account for many of these variables. And for that, the reservoir characterization and modeling world changed forever.

Anshuman thinks and explains highly complex mathematical algorithms with poise and ease. He translates the mathematical world to the modeling world to be used by geoscientists. In this way, his expertise crosses disciplines better than anyone I've ever observed. Most would say that "a little bit of enthusiasm goes a long way." Anshuman shows that a lot of enthusiasm can go even further. You can't help but get excited about reservoir modeling and prediction when Anshuman explains the method, results and outcomes. Anshuman has accomplished so much so early in his career, we're all wondering, "What geoscience challenge or dogma will he tackle next?" At the time of this interview, his postdoc was keeping him quite busy. In this interview, you will learn about reservoir characterization using advanced statistical methods, among many other skills.

Jon Rotzien (JR): Anshuman, I'm so thankful you had the time to visit today and share more information on some of your recent work, research and achievements.

How are you enjoying your postdoc?

Anshuman Pradhan (AP): Thank you, Jon, for giving me the opportunity. It is always a pleasure to talk to you. Thanks for asking, I am very much liking my postdoctoral experience at Caltech. The campus is very pretty, plus the weather is gorgeous all year round. I am in the department of Computing and Mathematical Sciences at Caltech, working on machine learning assisted predictive hydrological modeling and geo-hazard mitigation.

JR: Before Caltech, it was Stanford. What was the inspiration for your research and your dissertation on *statistical learning and inference of subsurface properties under complex geological uncertainty with seismic data*?

AP: Yes, I finished my Ph.D. at Stanford last December. Given that human demands for energy will see significant increases over the next few decades, the need of the hour is to develop novel geoscientific methods that facilitate reliable and efficient decision-making such as to sustainably explore and develop subsurface energy resources. A major challenge in reliably characterizing hydrocarbon reservoirs is the large uncertainty associated with the complex geological and spatial heterogeneity of the subsurface. I am motivated to develop methods and strategies that allow obtaining improved subsurface images, building better models, and efficient decision-making in challenging geological settings. During my Ph.D., I worked on three different real-world subsurface characterization problems and addressed these challenges by employing inter-disciplinary techniques and principles from geology, geophysics, machine learning and Bayesian statistics.

JR: I remember when you presented the keynote at GeoGulf in October 2019 in Houston titled *Integrating Basin Modeling and Seismic Imaging for Joint Uncertainty Reduction*. It was a great summary of the GCSSEPM *Global Deepwater Reservoirs*

Symposium. What do you think are some of the biggest challenges facing basin modeling and subsurface interpretation today?

AP: Yes, I really enjoyed presenting at GeoGulf back in 2019. In that presentation, I had talked at length about some of the major challenges facing basin modeling today. In my opinion, one of the biggest challenges for basin modeling is the uncertainty associated with our understanding of the geological history of hydrocarbon basins, for instance, in terms of the scientific principles governing the depositional processes or the evolution of stratigraphic properties across time. Direct measurements of the present day subsurface which help reduce this uncertainty are sparse and many conventional modeling workflows rely on manual, ad hoc calibration of model parameters to data. What is needed are methodologies and workflows that allow imposing data constraints in a "statistically rigorous" and automatic fashion into basin modeling endeavors. I think same holds for subsurface interpretation. I believe the geoscientific community can leverage recent research advances in the machine learning and statistical learning sciences to address these challenges. We have recently published a paper in *Geophysics*, where we introduce an automatic Monte-Carlo sampling based workflow to reduce basin modeling and seismic imaging uncertainties with seismic and borehole pressure and temperature data. Using a real-world study from Gulf of Mexico, the work shows how statistical approximations can be employed to improve modeling of the subsurface and make reliable predictions in interdisciplinary problems, where exact solutions are analytically impossible or computationally infeasible to obtain.

JR: GeoGulf is in Austin this year. Are you attending?

AP: Yes, I looked at the technical program for GeoGulf this year, some really very interesting talks in there. Unfortunately, due to some prior commitments, I won't be able to make it this year. I look forward to attending next year.

JR: We'll miss you. This year's keynote has big shoes to fill.

Your research strongly benefits those who work in the conventional exploration and appraisal business around the world. What are the broader impacts of your research? Perhaps you can tell us a little more about your postdoctoral research?

AP: In addition to the exploration and production industry, the methodologies I develop are generally applicable to other subsurface characterization problems, for instance, modeling and decision-making for sustainable groundwater extraction, development of geothermal resources or subsurface carbon sequestration. In my postdoctoral research, I am working on developing novel machine learning based approaches to predict and mitigate environmental hazards such as land subsidence associated with groundwater overdrafting in California's Central Valley. The general objective is to compensate for the limited knowledge of Central Valley's hydrogeology by learning from the diverse datasets that are available in the valley, for instance, well hydraulic head and lithological data, remote-sensing measurements of land surface displacements, climate data such as precipitation and evapotranspiration, and vegetation and land use data. To deal with the spatio-temporal nature of these datasets, I am employing spatio-temporal Gaussian process learning to improve understanding of the underlying aquifer system and help design hazard-free groundwater pumping strategies.

JR: What's next for you and your career?

AP: I am passionate about the subsurface and am interested in continuing to conduct novel research that helps improve our understanding of geological processes and sustainably interact with the subsurface. Beyond my postdoctoral appointment, I am interested in pursuing a research career in the academia or industry that allows me to keep making novel contributions in interdisciplinary geoscientific research.

JR: What is seismic Bayesian evidential learning?

AP: Previously, we talked about the numerous challenges encountered for building reliable models of the subsurface. However, the final goal in many cases is not the earth model itself, rather some low-dimensional variable such as the drilling location of the next production well or total volumetric proportion of sands in an aquifer. An interesting research question that may be posed in this scenario is whether we may directly estimate this low-dimensional variable from data without inverting for the full earth model? If yes, can we retain desired complexities of physics and geology while dispensing with the limitations associated with building large-scale subsurface models? Seismic Bayesian evidential learning is a statistical framework that allows fast decision-making with seismic data without needing to perform computationally expensive inverse modeling of the subsurface. It employs machine learning to directly learn from seismic data features relevant to the decision problem.

JR: What are some of your recent discoveries in seismic deep learning? Congratulations on your new preprint in arXiv.

AP: Thanks, Jon. We published the preprint about a month back, I am glad you were able to take a look at it. Recently, we have seen a tremendous interest in application of deep learning models to seismic reservoir characterization. A major challenge that impedes straightforward application of deep learning models to subsurface problems is the lack of labeled training data that is used to train the deep learning model. Note that we observe the subsurface sparsely at the wells, thus the labels, or subsurface properties, are missing at a number of locations.

A popular approach to address this challenge is to create the training dataset synthetically. However, it is imperative that creation of synthetic data conforms to the established geological understanding of the subsurface system, associated uncertainties and geophysical principles. In this study we found that, even if the deep learning model is performing well on a synthetic dataset, it does not necessarily give reliable predictions with real data. This can happen if the synthetic dataset is not consistent with the true subsurface heterogeneity. We proposed several strategies that enable us to ensure consistency of the synthetic training dataset. We successfully used the methodology to constrain a large-scale reservoir model of a producing deepwater reservoir, containing more than a million grid cells, to 3D seismic data using deep learning. This study reinforced the fact that successful application of established machine learning models in subsurface problems requires novel geoscience domain specific approaches.

JR: What is your message to students pursuing basin analysis as an area of study, or as a career?

AP: Successfully addressing the groundwater and energy challenges of the future will be critically dependent on improved understanding of the geological processes operating in groundwater and hydrocarbon basins. Given (1) the large uncertainty associated with the subsurface, and (2) advancements being made with respect to the data acquisition technologies, for instance fiber optics acoustic sensing networks and high-resolution remote sensing satellites, we will likely see a strong shift towards data-driven approaches in informing our geoscientific analyses and studies. Thus, it is critical that geoscience students actively seek to train themselves in applied statistical and data sciences early on in their academic studies. This will allow them to practice geosciences knowledgeably and responsibly in the data scenario of the future.

JR: Thank you so much Dr. Pradhan.

Sumit Verma and Shuvajit Bhattacharya (April 2021)

"Geoscience is the science where most of the time the questions do not have any definite answers. For example, we might not know whether a certain rock layer is a limestone or a sandstone just by looking at a seismic image, so, we have to create an environment where all the researchers on the team can present their point of view. Such an open environment leads to creativity, which is a required skill for geoscientists." – Professor Sumit Verma

Dr. Sumit Verma is an Assistant Professor of Geophysics at UTPB. At UTPB, he also served as the acting Chair for the Department of Geosciences in 2019 and was Program Coordinator (2017-2019). Dr. Verma is co-principal investigator of the Attribute Assisted Processing and Interpretation (AASPI) consortium. Dr. Verma received his M.S. (2007) in Applied Geophysics from the Indian School of Mines - Dhanbad, and his Ph.D. (2015) in Geophysics from the University of Oklahoma. After earning his PhD, he worked for one year as a Postdoctoral Research Fellow at the University of Wyoming. Dr. Verma also worked with Reliance Industries Ltd. E&P for four years (2007-2011) as a development geoscientist. Dr. Verma's research areas are Seismic Interpretation, Quantitative Interpretation and Reservoir Characterization. His scientific records include more than twenty technical papers in well-known geoscience journals and over forty abstracts. Dr. Verma serves as Deputy Associate Editor for the peer-reviewed scientific journal *Interpretation*.

"For research methods and results to be successful, you want it to be reproducible and implementable in other areas. For example, Sumit and I worked on seismic attributes in identifying complex fault styles in a rifted-margin setting affected by structural inheritance in Alaska. Structural inheritance implies the episodic reactivation of basement faults and the generation of new faults in the shallow subsurface. We found that a suite of attributes including curvature and aberrancy/flexure was really helpful to image these features. Now, such features are not rare. There are areas in Norway and SW Australia, which are also affected by similar fault styles. Industry can apply these attributes in those areas for greater business success. This can go both ways." – Dr. Shuvajit Bhattacharya

Dr. Shuvajit Bhattacharya is a researcher at the Bureau of Economic Geology, the University of Texas at Austin. He is an applied geophysicist/petrophysicist. Previously, he was a tenure-track faculty at the University of Alaska (Anchorage). He has been working on energy resources exploration (including geothermal), induced seismicity, and carbon sequestration for many years. His research focus includes seismic interpretation, petrophysical analysis, and machine learning for subsurface geosciences. He has published more than 50 technical articles and conference papers.

I first met Sumit when he was a standout intern at BP. Sumit was by far and away one of the most advanced interns, with a challenging project usually fit for a new PhD. I later found out Sumit had years of experience drilling wells in India, prior to his PhD working for the legendary geophysicist Dr. Kurt Marfurt. Marfurt only selects those with exceptional qualities, and Sumit exceeded even those standards. Years later, I had the opportunity to collaborate with Sumit and Shuvajit on work on the North Slope of Alaska following the giant discoveries of Pikka, Horseshoe and Willow. We worked together on seismic attributes that are useful in delineating mass-transport complexes and slide blocks associated with the Torok and Fish Creek Slump. Sumit and Shuvajit are incredibly curious and masters of their skillsets. Not only are they so technically gifted, they also attract like-minded, energetic, thoughtful, cheerful and focused team members. They are great team builders. For example, they're well-known for their leadership in building and stewarding the Attribute-Assisted Seismic Processing & Interpretation (AASPI) Consortium, one of the premier collaborative seismic interpretation consortiums in the world. Sumit has attracted a lot of top caliber scientists to his program with UT Permian Basin, and has won many awards for his visionary analysis in geophysics, including best talk at GeoGulf 2023 in Houston. Shuvajit contributes to nearly every industry research group at the Bureau of Economic Geology. Shuvajit, a petrophysicist by training, is particularly industrious, often having the most abstracts at regional technical meetings such as GeoGulf. He has also written a new book on artificial intelligence and machine learning in the geosciences. These are two incredibly bright scientists who are leading the way for geophysics and petrophysics.

In March of 2021, I interviewed Sumit Verma and Shuvajit Bhattacharya to learn about current research in AI/ML workflows, petrophysics, seismic attributes and deepwater mass-transport deposits.

Jon Rotzien (JR): Sumit and Shuvajit, I'm so thankful you had the time to visit today and share some of your recent achievements. You've had a variety of exciting roles so far in your career – from drilling exploration wells to conducting research in the US, Canada, Australia, New Zealand, South Africa and India.

Could you share your background, and what led you to your current role?

Shuvajit Bhattacharya (SB): Thanks, Jon, for allowing me to talk about my research and its implications today. My professional background is in geosciences, specifically geophysics and petrophysics. I completed my Master's in Applied Geophysics at the Indian Institute of Technology Bombay and Ph.D. at the West Virginia University. It's been more than ten years since I have been practicing in this field. Fast forward to late 2019, I was a faculty at the University Alaska Anchorage, teaching and researching geophysics and subsurface mapping. I graduated a few students; all of them are working professionals in the industry or at the state or federal agencies now. At that time, I applied for a research position at the Bureau of Economic Geology. They were looking for a researcher who could help them develop and implement new workflows in petrophysical and geophysical analysis, especially for tight reservoirs. I had the kind of academic and industry experience they were precisely looking for. BEG is one of the leading geoscience research organizations in the world. Quite a few stalwarts and people I deeply respect work there. So, I joined BEG last year.

Sumit Verma (SV): Thanks, Jon. My professional background is in applied geophysics and I specialize in 3D seismic interpretation. I completed my Master's in Applied Geophysics at the Indian Institute of Technology (ISM), Dhanbad in 2007. I worked for four years in an Indian Exploration and Production major known as Reliance Industries Limited as a development geophysicist. In 2011, I received an opportunity to work with Professor Kurt Marfurt for my PhD, so I moved to Oklahoma. I gained knowledge about seismic attributes and seismic data processing in my PhD and finished my PhD in 2015. After my PhD, I learned about Rock Physics for CO_2 sequestration during my post-doctoral research at University of Wyoming, where I was for a year. Since 2016, I have been teaching geophysics courses and researching subsurface geological interpretation with seismic attributes at the UT Permian Basin. Here, my students are motivated to find all the potential of the greater Permian Basin, whereas collaborators including Shuvajit have enthusiastically involved me with the work on the North Slope of Alaska. My AASPI consortium at UTPB, which runs in collaboration with University of Oklahoma, keeps me connected to industry related challenges in the area of subsurface seismic attribute assisted interpretation.

JR: Energy stocks took up about~12% of the S&P 500 about a decade ago, now it's about 2%, yet oil and gas represents about 8% of the US GDP as many CEOs have currently mentioned. How do your industry funded research groups navigate the current market?

SB: Jon, that's a great question. I would say that researchers need to be flexible with their research problems, research methods, and funding agencies. As you research, trends and business priorities change, so you have to be aligned with it. In industry, it's more dynamic. Here is an example. I know of an exploration group in a large company that was very much involved in producing oil and gas from fractured and fault-bound reservoirs for many years. Then, very recently, they changed their focus to new exploration and moved on to shelf-edge reservoirs, defined by stratigraphic traps. Automatically, your research methods used to identify and analyze such reservoirs need to change. Being a geophysicist/petrophysicist, I had to develop and implement new algorithms and workflows to solve the new problems. It worked out and received funding from many companies. Here at the Bureau, researchers (including me) work on various projects on carbon sequestration, geothermal energy, induced earthquakes, and hydrogen storage. Again, research flexibility, deliverability, and vision are the keys.

SV: The times are no doubt tough for both industry and academia. I agree with Shuvajit, that we need to adapt to the time. We need both funds as well as data. Currently, we are receiving more data sets from the industry than funding. That enables us to do better research, but we are only able to hire a limited number of research students.

JR: Your research employs a number of geophysical methods and algorithms to highlight the importance of thorough subsurface interpretation – many of these algorithms you create or code yourself. Can you explain why it is so important to apply these methods in exploration and production projects globally?

SB: For research methods and results to be successful, you want it to be reproducible and implementable in other areas. For example, Sumit and I worked on seismic attributes in identifying complex fault styles in a rifted-margin setting affected by structural inheritance in Alaska. Structural inheritance implies the episodic reactivation of basement faults and the generation of new faults in the shallow subsurface. We found that a suite of attributes including curvature and aberrancy/flexure was really helpful to image these features. Now, such features are not rare. There are areas in Norway and SW Australia, which are also affected by similar fault styles. Industry can apply these attributes in those areas for greater business success. This can go both ways.

In the last year, I was working on a deltaic reservoir in Alaska. In many areas around the world, for example the US Gulf of Mexico and Malaysia, the industry has been exploring and developing these types of reservoirs for many years. One of the interesting things about these reservoirs is that you find intervals of laminated shale and sandstone, which results in a suppressed resistivity response and erroneously low estimates of hydrocarbon saturation. Therefore, many of these reservoirs were overlooked in the past. The Nanushuk reservoir in Alaska was no exception. I implemented new workflows used in the other areas to interpret this reservoir. I concluded that it is a low-resistivity reservoir, published the findings, and now this interval is well-known in the industry community. This led many companies to look at this reservoir using new techniques and workflows. Again, some of these algorithms and workflows are globally implementable, and these can drive business success.

JR: Those workflows are so important. Sumit, I remember we were preparing to co-present in a subsurface interpretation workshop for the 36th IGC in Delhi – until it was cancelled due to COVID. I was really looking forward to co-teaching that workshop with you – hopefully soon. Can you tell us about some of your current and upcoming research?

SV: Yes, Jon I hope we will be able to conduct the workshop in India. Last year, it was Holi (an Indian festival) when we were planning to be in India for AGC workshop. It has been one year since then. I am looking forward to having the COVID things over, so that we can get back to planning our workshop. There have been some limitations due to COVID, but on the bright side, I was able to accomplish quite a bit of research over the past year. There are few works that Shuvajit and I are working on together, including machine learning projects on facies classification, continuation of our research on the North Slope with your collaboration as well as geothermal research in Netherlands. In collaboration with Dr. Annapurna Boruah, I am working on macro-seepage analysis and CCUS in the Grayburg–San Andres Formation, Permian Basin. We are also developing the implementation of machine learning tools in AASPI, which is like Convolutional LSTM for facies classification by Miao (post-doctoral researcher). I still think there is much more we can do on the side of geological characterization with the Alaska data set.

JR: The North Slope has so much potential. Many more like Pikka-Horseshoe to be found over the next decades.

Can you tell us about some of your current research projects, Shuvajit? You have so many.

SB: Well, I'm working on quite a few research projects now, all focused on subsurface interpretation. Currently, I'm involved in two large projects: i) characterizing tight sedimentary rocks (shale), for example, the Wolfcamp and Spraberry in the Permian Basin; and ii) 3D velocity modeling in the Delaware Basin in West Texas. The first one is more on the exploration and development of petroleum resources, and the second one is related to induced seismicity. Apart from these two main projects, I am also working on several other projects, like carbon sequestration in Texas and Michigan and geothermal resources mapping. I just completed a small-scale study on the feasibility of hydrogen storage in carbonate reefs in Michigan.

JR: Let's talk deepwater now. How did you ever decide to get involved in the odd world of deepwater mass-transport deposits (MTD) and slide blocks?

SB: That's a long story. I was working heavily on the subsurface geology in Alaska. As you know, it's a frontier area. There are not enough publications in that part of the world, and the geology is very complex. On one occasion, I was working on a large 3D seismic survey to interpret a shelf environment and observed large blocky features distributed over ~400 km^2. It was baffling and intriguing. By chance, we got to look at two nearby 3D surveys and integrated the observations from all the data, now covering a much larger footprint – around 2,000 km^2. Having all the data helped us interpret these peculiar features as large submarine slide blocks. We also interpreted that these slide blocks moved along the slope of the basin as one system. These geologic features are important because they can serve as seals for underlying reservoirs in the deep subsurface and potential geohazards in the modern-day environment. There are many areas where modern-day slide deposits are found including the Gulf of Alaska and offshore California as well as Norway. We then took the research one step further and used machine learning to automatically identify and predict the distribution of slide blocks.

SV: There are two places where you might have seen my name attached to MTD – one in Alaska and the other in the Permian Basin. I would say, Shuvajit got me involved in the MTD project in Alaska. For the Permian Basin data set, I was not sure what were the tiny thrust faults and duplex structures. So, I gave this task to my graduate students. Fortunately, at the same time, some of my students, including Paritosh, attended Dr. Henry Posamentier's presentation at a conference, and we also saw similar examples from Netherlands. Then, Paritosh characterized the MTD with seismic attributes. Like Shuvajit said, MTD can be considered a geohazard in some basins, whereas in other basins they can function as an important part of the total petroleum system. In either case they are really beautiful on seismic attributes.

JR: Your algorithms and newly developed attribute combinations have a way of uncovering exceptional detail in mass-transport deposits, some of the best I've seen. What about your current work in AI/ ML/ DL?

SB: I have been working on machine learning for the last 11-12 years. I use AI/ML mostly for petrophysics and seismic interpretation. I recently came up with a new approach to predicting rock properties reliably and consistently using subsurface data. It's more on multivariate time series-based analysis and ensemble ML modeling. As you know, ML is mostly based on pattern recognition; however, we have patterns and anti-patterns in the data. One of the fundamental problems with using geologic data in ML is that ML assumes all attributes in the model are independent, whereas we know several geologic features are highly correlated or at least conditionally dependent on each other. This affects ML models' trust, and they will fail – sometimes miserably – especially in areas where we find rare events (or anti-patterns). Anyway, the new approach helps to derive more geologic insights and build meaningful models. I am giving several invited talks on this topic organized by the professional societies, including the Australian Geophysical Society, European Association of Geoscientists and Engineers, and here in the US.

SV: I am looking into lithofacies classification via machine learning using both well and seismic data. We have recently implemented convolutional LSTM in our AASPI consortium software. We also saw good results of classification in the area of geochemistry. I think that the broad field of geoscience can benefit from the application of machine learning and AI.

JR: It seems to take vision, strategy, deep subject matter knowledge – and probably a bit of luck – among other things to create a successful research group in the geosciences. Can you describe what it takes to be a successful research group in the broad field of geosciences?

SB: Jon, you have already mentioned a few. I'm a young scientist, and I know that I have a lot to learn. Based on my experience, I can tell there are quite a few factors in play, including research vision, technical strength, deliverability, collaboration, knowledge-sharing, and flexibility. First and foremost, you need to have really deep technical knowledge to formulate the research problem and understand its implications. Then, you find out what funding agencies are out there (industry, state/federal agencies, and private foundations). Each of these organizations has its own research agenda and priorities, and expected types of deliverables. Rarely, you'll find that the same research problem and the same approaches you are using in a proposal to one agency is of interest to another agency. Some agencies are more into basic sciences, some more applied, and others for broader impact. Industry proposals are more dynamic and need focused studies. When you continue to deliver high-quality products to the sponsors consistently, you build a portfolio and credibility. And I think that's the key.

SV: I agree with Shuvajit on this in most parts. I would like to add that geoscience is the science where most of the time the questions do not have any definite answers. For example, we might not know whether a certain rock layer is a limestone or a sandstone just by looking at a seismic image, so, we have to create an environment where all the researchers on the team can present their point of view. Such an open environment leads to creativity, which is a required skill for geoscientists.

JR: You also serve in other areas, such as chairing multiple technical conferences per year, leading the AAPG IBA competition for your universities (you even competed in that one year, right!). You have multiple roles as editors and reviewers for industry geoscience journals such as *Interpretation*. Can you share some of your key leadership principles? While we know you can't give away your best secrets, we'd appreciate some tips.

SB: Thanks for asking that. I serve on the editorial board of the SEG/AAPG journal *Interpretation*. I am involved in many other committees including the SEG carbon solutions task force, the technical committee for ARMA geothermal resources, and the SEG and AAPG annual conference, where I chair, review and judge several technical sessions. I really enjoy these roles, and I continue to get invited, which means I do a decent job in those roles. My participation in these committees allows me to learn from others and also to give back to the community. Just two weeks ago, I was giving an invited talk at the AAPG CCUS-focused international meeting (held for the first time in the history) and then took part in a long round table discussion on the needs for future research in carbon sequestration and how we can attract students into this new field of research.

For tips, I do think there are a few important things including passion, perspective, and being proactive. If you are passionate about leadership, have the right perspective on why you want to do this, and look for opportunities proactively, perhaps you can positively impact the organization.

SV: Like Shuvajit, I am also a deputy editor of *Interpretation* and serve on the SEG carbon task force and the SEG annual conference. I am also heavily involved with the Permian Basin Geophysical Society. Also, I help organize the free geoscience virtual workshops. I think these workshops are the way to connect geoscience students, industry professionals and researchers without any borders when in-person meetings are not possible. For example, we organized one workshop in collaboration of Dr. Boruah from India and had more than 1500 participants. As you mentioned, I also prepare my AAPG students for the IBA competition.

I am not sure I know about any profound secrets pertaining to leadership. I can say that, most of the time leadership activities can be very time consuming, but it brings me joy to be able to participate in any activity which gives me a sense of giving back to the society.

JR: What is your message to students interested in making a career in the energy industry?

SB: That's a great question. I always say that energy is the basis of our civilization, and many people around the world are living in energy poverty. They need affordable, clean, and reliable sources of energy, and they will eventually get that. Having said that, the outlook in the short-term does not look very bright if you want to work in the oil and gas industry, compared to 10 years ago. But, things can change quickly. Also, keep in mind geology will continue to play a big role in the coming years. For new energy resources, including geothermal energy, batteries, solar, and wind energy, you need to know geology and the utility of geologic materials (i.e., mining). Many energy companies (e.g., ExxonMobil, Chevron, Shell, and Oxy, etc.) are creating new divisions and even start-ups and joint ventures for geothermal resources, carbon storage, and hydrogen storage now, all of which need deep technical knowledge in the subsurface. Many of these activities may help to mitigate climate change. I think the future economy will be a mix of different renewable and non-renewable energy resources, including oil and gas. So, there will be a need for those who want to work in the energy industry.

I have heard from many senior geoscientists that they flocked to study geology due to the Arab Oil embargo in the 1970s, which resulted in a massive uptick in oil price globally. They were considered heroes who could work in distant offshore rigs and remote areas in the Arctic and provide energy resources reliably and affordably to the people. I think it will happen once again as we move towards an energy transition to mitigate climate change. Geoscientists are in the best position to acquire and analyze climate data and provide solutions.

SV: This is a tough question to answer. I agree completely with Shuvajit on this one.

JR: You've been around a lot of oil and gas explorers for decades... including companies such as RIL, ONGC, EOG, COP, BP...you've seen some succeed, and some fail. Lessons can be learned from these experiences. What is your message for oil and gas explorers today?

SB: Well, I would just say two things here. First of all, try to find a balance between science and technology. Every now and then, there are some new software releases. Just because they're there, it doesn't mean that we have to use them. Software is just a tool to solve a problem quickly. What's more important is the "science"—for example, understanding the geologic processes that form rocks and geophysical algorithms that can image them. Second, be flexible and open to new ideas and methods. Be more data-driven rather than trying to confirm a preconceived notion (or confirmation bias). Confirmation bias is very real in geology, and it has led to numerous research and business failures. Use data analytics and machine learning to provide more data-driven solutions.

SV: Yes, we have seen all the companies fail sometime, and get success another time. As explorers, we need to learn from not only our mistakes but mistakes of others. Although, sometimes the geological problems are too tough to solve, and in the end, teams still cannot find out why the well was not a success. So, rather than trying our luck the second time, we should focus on why we were not successful. Knowing the reason of success or failure is critical if we want to be successful on the next try.

JR: One final question for you Shuvajit and Sumit. Collaboration has been a central theme in your discussion today and is one of the drivers of success in science and technology. How do you identify good collaborators?

SB: See, we cannot do everything by ourselves. We need good collaborations. When I'm looking for collaborators, I really look for their technical strength (and novelties of their work) that complement the team. There is also a big human factor, including moral integrity, negotiability, humbleness, and the ability to be receptive to peer criticisms. These attributes are also important to me.

SV: Interests in similar areas, willingness of collaboration, complimentary skillsets, and integrity are the key qualities that I look for in a collaborator. I am fortunate to have you both as my collaborators.

JR: Thank you very much Dr. Verma and Dr. Bhattacharya.

Above: Sunny skies illuminate outcrops of the Upper Miocene Urenui Formation, Wai-iti, Taranaki Basin, North Island, New Zealand. Located along the Tasman Sea, Wai-iti Beach is a pleasant and convenient outcrop locale to observe and study these siliciclastic deepwater deposits. This 900-m-thick slope channel-overbank succession is comprised chiefly of turbidites, debrites and hemipelagic mudstone. *Photo courtesy of Y. Gavillot (2020).*

Power of the Team

Seldom are big results or solving big problems achieved by a single person. While we hold leaders and CEOs in high status, they are typically brilliant at bringing together the right mix of people, data, funding and are exceptionally good at identifying valuable questions to solve. The leaders in this section devoted to the *Power of the Team* share their principles on what it takes to win big – with big teams.

Oftentimes, leader is a singular term. When in meetings, there is one leader. This person is usually interpreted to be the smartest person in the room. Whatever they say, people tend to follow. However, there is power in numbers. By seeking the perspective of many, you'll often get closer to the right answer. While every leader in this book is gifted with team skills, this section is specifically devoted to those who share their principles on what it takes to identify team opportunities, build a team and lead and inspire a team to success.

The Drifters Research Group, started at Royal Holloway, University of London, studies deepwater sedimentary systems with a specific focus on drifts formed largely by bottom currents. This research is made possible by the intersection and collaboration of industry, academic and government teams. The Drifters describe what it's like to build and be a part of a large team effort to understand the applied science of deepwater sedimentary systems, their tectonic evolution, and their impacts on global ocean circulation patterns. This research is relevant as ever as giant turbidite-contourite fields have been found on both sides of the Atlantic and western Indian oceans.

Paul Mann shares his leadership principles on how to build and lead the Conjugate Basins, Tectonics and Hydrocarbons (CBTH) Research Group at University of Houston. Arguably the most successful and prolific long-standing industry-funded research group in its class, CBTH studies petroleum-rich continental margins to better understand the predictive attributes of hydrocarbon systems – many of them located in Super Basins.

F. Javier Hernández-Molina, the dynamic, energetic and visionary faculty leader of The Drifters started at Royal Holloway, University of London, describes the formation of The Drifters and what it takes to lead in understanding the Earth's ocean and deepwater frontiers.

The Drifters Research Group (February 2021)

The indefatigable Drifters going airborne in the Sahara Desert (Merzouga Desert, Morocco) in October 2019. From left to right: Wouter de Weger, Zhi Lin Ng, Sandra de Castro, Adam Kirby, Debora Duarte, Sara Rodrigues and Estefania Llave (IGME).

"For me, the most interesting area towards which my research can contribute, is by using contourite morphologies to decode deep paleo-ocean circulation and better understand oceanographic processes which interact with the seafloor. This assists the prediction of lithologies in deep marine settings." – Adam Kirby

"The structural control of deepwater systems tends to be an underappreciated area of research, which is now under development. In my research, I'm aiming to comprehend how regional setting (e.g. tectonic-controlled morphologies and diapirism) influences deposit distribution." – Debora Duarte (not pictured)

Adam Kirby studies paleo-ocean circulation as part of The Drifters Research Group.

"Years ago and still today, energy companies have primarily focused on gravitational processes to determine reservoir presence and quality – for turbidite reservoirs. However, our findings show that bottom currents are a significant agent in deepwater environments, forming entirely new deposits as well as altering those related to density currents. A deep knowledge of bottom currents and how they influence sediment transport and deposition can improve depositional models with key implications for reservoir geometry, distribution, and rock properties." – Oswaldo Mantilla

"The knowledge of deepwater sedimentation and the influence of oceanographic currents in continental margins are a valuable asset in reservoir characterization and especially in research and development for carbon capture and storage (CCS). Also, the high concentration of microplastics we find on the seafloor is still poorly understood. Bottom currents can concentrate microplastics (mainly comprised of fibers from textiles and clothing) within thick sediment accumulations, especially in contourite drifts, which researchers have termed "microplastic hotspots"." – Sandra De Castro (not pictured)

Oswaldo Mantilla works to understand how bottom currents affect the distribution of sediment in the oceans.

The Explorer's Mindset

"Industry professionals tend to want to look at the "big seismic picture", however, seismic studies only provide relatively low-resolution acoustic data, and cores contain very little information about lateral facies changes. Particularly in the case of deep-marine sedimentary systems it can be very hard to envisage these systems. Looking at outcrops can change that, allowing you to get a feel for the sedimentary deposits below the exposed surface observed in seismic data and cores." – Wouter de Weger

"Using the Gulf of Cadiz CDS as an analog to understand the effects of bottom-current processes on past depositional environments on a margin, and its wider implications on paleoceanography and paleoclimate, we could apply this knowledge to reduce the uncertainty in the seismic-stratigraphic interpretation and the evaluation of petroleum system elements on other Atlantic margins potentially affected by similar bottom-current processes." – Zhi Lin Ng

This interview is with Adam Kirby, Debora Duarte, Oswaldo Mantilla, Sandra de Castro, Wouter de Weger and Zhi Lin Ng to learn about contourite and mixed deepwater sedimentary systems.

In 2017, a very special research group assembled at Royal Holloway, University of London under the leadership of F. Javier Hernández-Molina to study along-slope processes, bottom currents and mixed deepwater sedimentary systems. This group would soon be named *The Drifters* for their work in contourite drifts, among other deepwater sedimentary phenomenon. Their research would almost instantaneously reach the top level of deepwater research in the world.

I can't hold back a smile when I think about *The Drifters*. They are the one of the most productive and hardest working crew of graduate geoscientists I've ever met, plus they conduct their research with a great deal of hard work, enthusiasm, integrity and levity. Their work strongly goes against the conventional paradigm of deepwater systems, and they've been able to skillfully observe and interpret deepwater systems – both ancient and modern – with a fresh set of eyes to offer the most unapologetically honest scientific appraisals of deepwater sedimentation on a global scale. And they present their work with a great deal of pride and joy. These are the scientists that are the future of ocean science and discovery. These students (now professionals) deserve a big applause for correcting the trajectory of deepwater research and aiming it at unsolved problems that were very poorly defined before their research was published. I am grateful to have met them and learned from them, and continue to seek their advice when it comes to interpreting mixed deepwater sedimentary systems. At the time of this interview, these colleagues were PhD students, now they are Doctors of Philosophy (PhDs). *NOTE: See their biographies below while they were graduate students. Their work in progress at the time of the interview is now published and accessible by anyone who is interested.*

Adam Kirby is a PhD candidate studying deep marine sedimentology in The Drifters Research Group based at Royal Holloway, University of London (RHUL). He holds a BSc from the University of Plymouth and an MSc in Petroleum Geoscience from RHUL. His thesis centers on the identification and classification of contourite depositional and erosive features in seismic reflection data, the primary case studies for which are in the Cenozoic record of the Argentine and Uruguayan margins in the Southwest Atlantic. He previously studied Cretaceous contourite deposits on the West Iberian Margin which led to his interest in the field. Adam's current and future research interests reside in understanding the complex lateral and temporal evolution of alongslope systems, he does this by interpreting their sedimentary stacking pattern and decoding the local and regional depositional and oceanographic processes interacting with them.

Debora Duarte is a PhD researcher working on tectonic control on deepwater sedimentation and salt tectonics in the Drifters Research Group based at the Royal Holloway, University of London and in the Portuguese Institute for Sea and Atmosphere (IPMA). She holds a BSc and an MSc in Petroleum Geosciences from the University of Lisbon. Her PhD work aims to investigate the role of tectonics and diapirism on the evolution of the Gulf of Cadiz Contourite System, based on a seismic reflection dataset along the SW Iberian Margin. Previously, Debora worked on the characterization of fluid escape structures (pockmarks) and migration pathways on the Estremadura Spur, West Iberian Margin. Debora's research interests are focused on understanding the control of regional tectonic episodes, and reactivated structures on deepwater sedimentation. She also aims to investigate the influence of salt tectonics and related fluids on deepwater sedimentary systems.

Oswaldo Mantilla Muñoz is a fourth-year PhD student at Royal Holloway, University of London. His doctoral research investigates deepwater deposits, focusing on the evolution of bottom-currents and its interaction with gravitational processes. He works in the Northern Carnarvon Basin (Northwest Shelf, Australia) in sequences from Early Cretaceous to Quaternary. His work includes a multidisciplinary approach that encompasses seismic stratigraphy with 2D and 3D multichannel seismic reflection, structural geology and oceanography to reveal the regional controls of sedimentary processes and paleoceanographic pattern variations throughout Mesozoic and Cenozoic in the Northern Carnarvon basin. This study has implications for the sedimentary evolution of the East Indian Ocean as well as in the exploration and development of hydrocarbon accumulations (distribution and geometry of reservoir rock). He previously studied Cretaceous and Cenozoic deepwater deposits of the Colombian Caribbean offshore.

Sandra de Castro just submitted her PhD *"Modern sandy contourites: conceptual and economic implications"* at Royal Holloway, University of London. The aim of her PhD is to characterize modern sandy contourites and differentiate them from other deepwater deposits at core scale. She graduated from the University of Basque Country (Spain) in 2012 with a Bachelor's Degree in Mining engineering and in 2015 with a Bachelor's Degree in Geology. In 2016, she graduated from University of Granada (Spain) with a Master's Degree in Geology applied to energy resources. She started her research career in the Spanish National Research Council (IACT-CSIC) on the stratigraphy of transgressive sandy large-scale bedforms in continental platforms and the influence of seafloor irregularities on their formation (doi.org/10.1016/j.margeo.2017.02.007; doi.org/10.1007/s00367-017-0508-4; doi.org/10.1016/j.csr.2018.04.005). Later, she jumped into a deeper environment. After three years diving to unravel contourite-dominated deepwater processes, Sandra is ready for a change. She is looking forward to putting her scientific skills into practice and to transitioning towards an applied field in the geosciences.

Wouter de Weger is a PhD student at the Royal Holloway, University of London. He is a member of The Drifters Research Group under the supervision of Prof. Dr. F.J. Hernández-Molina. For his PhD, he is studying ancient contourite deposits to improve the understanding of processes, products and characteristics of bottom current induced sedimentation and the implications for the hydrocarbon industry. Wouter, a Dutch national, graduated from Utrecht University (The Netherlands) in 2013 with a Bachelor's degree in Earth Sciences. In 2016 he graduated from the same University with a Master's degree in Earth Sciences, having completed the *Earth, Life and Climate* and *exploration geology* program. After his graduation Wouter gained some industry experience but he remained interested in studying outcrops, particularly those related to contourites as they are very much underexplored.

Zhi Lin Ng is a fourth year PhD student at Royal Holloway, University of London. His doctoral research investigates the role of bottom currents and their interaction with other deep-marine sedimentary processes in shaping continental margins, using the Gulf of Cadiz contourite depositional system (CDS) from the Late Miocene to the present as an example. His work includes a multidisciplinary approach that encompasses sedimentology, stratigraphy, structural geology and oceanography, and has implications for the evolution of the Mediterranean-Atlantic water-mass exchange and Atlantic overturning, as well as the Messinian Salinity Crisis. He holds an MSc in Petroleum Geosciences from Royal Holloway, University of London, and a BSc (Hons) in Geology from Universiti Malaysia Sabah, Malaysia, and completed sedimentology-based research projects under the tutelage of Prof. Javier Hernández-Molina and Prof. Sanudin Tahir during the master's and bachelor's degrees, respectively. He is currently a postgraduate representative for the British Sedimentological Research Group (BSRG). In 2018, he was awarded the Graduate Student Poster Prize for his contribution in the BSRG Annual General Meeting at Heriot-Watt University, Edinburgh. He was also the recipient of the Book Award in 2015 from the senate of Universiti Malaysia Sabah as the bachelor's program best graduate.

Read the interview from February 2021.

Jon Rotzien (JR): Debora, Adam, Sandra, Oswaldo, Lin and Wouter – wow, I'm so thankful you had the time to visit today and share some of your recent research accomplishments and what they mean to the energy industry.

Let's get started. Your team has had many recent publications on contourite and mixed depositional systems in high-profile journals including Geology, Marine and Petroleum Geology and Sedimentology to name a few. Congratulations! Can you tell us about your recent research achievements?

Debora Duarte (DD): Hello Jon! Yes, we have had many successes as a research group. As for me, I am currently finalizing a manuscript about the structural control on the Gulf of Cadiz Contourite Systems. More recently, I co-authored a paper on fault-controlled drifts of the South China Sea (https://doi.org/10.1016/j.margeo.2021.106420) with Dr. Shan Liu (School of Marine Science, Sun Yat-sen University), a close collaborator and friend of The Drifters, and our supervisor Dr. Javier Hernández-Molina.

Wouter de Weger (WW): Hi Jon, always a pleasure to sit down with you. Before answering your questions, I would like to express my gratitude for the interest you have shown in our research activities over the last couple of years and for the stimulating discussions we had.

JR: Wouter, it's been a blast so far.

WW: For my MSc Thesis I joined Dr. W. Capella on a fieldtrip to Morocco to find and study the sedimentary succession capturing the closure of the Rifian Corridor in Morocco. It was during this project that I realized bottom currents related to the overflow of dense Mediterranean water played a significant role in sedimentation in the region during the late Miocene. For my PhD project I focus on the topic of contourites in the same study area for which I consider myself very lucky. The first publication for my PhD was about the intermittent overflow behavior of a late Miocene contourite channel system in the Rifian Corridor of Morocco in *Geology*. This paper, due to the *Geology* format, is very condensed and sets the stage for the more elaborate articles to come. The second paper which has been submitted a while ago describes a slightly younger contourite channel system in the same region. Herein the focus lies on the lateral migration of contourite channels and its associated changes in sedimentary facies. Furthermore, we discuss in detail about the observed tidal signatures within the sandy contourite deposits. The third paper, which is nearly ready for submission, focusses on the channel morphologies, erosional events, and sedimentary infill sequences. The two last contributions describe in detail sandy contourite channel facies and their lateral and vertical facies changes. In these contributions new facies models are proposed for sandy contourite deposits.

Sandra de Castro (SC): During my time at Royal Holloway, University of London as a PhD student, I, along with The Drifters, developed a new deepwater depositional model related to the activity of deep-marine currents. This model is based on the analysis and interpretation of sediment cores (ichnofacies and microfacies analysis), especially on the intermittency of sedimentary processes during the deposition of Bottom Current Reworked sands (doi.org/10.1016/j.margeo.2020.106267). I also implemented a statistical analysis to analyze large quantities of data for the discrimination of different deepwater deposits such as hemipelagites from muddy contourites and turbidites from sandy contourites (grain size and X-Ray Fluorescence) (doi.org/10.1111/sed.12813). I have recently submitted my third-authored research article to Marine and Petroleum Geology. It is focused on the textural and geochemical characterization of bioclastic and siliciclastic contouritic sands in collaboration with Institut Français de Recherche pour l'Exploitation de la Mer (IFREMER).

Zhi Lin Ng (ZN): I have recently submitted two first-authored research articles to various journals pending the peer-review process. They are focused on the long-term sedimentary evolution of Late Miocene CDS of the Gulf of Cadiz, and the relationship with multiple control factors such as the changes in tectonic processes and oceanic gateway exchange.

Oswaldo Mantilla (OM): I am working offshore Western Australia, and my study has revealed the evolution of bottom currents since the Early Cretaceous to Recent and their interaction with gravitational processes. Moreover, extensive and thick contourite deposits in the Northern Carnarvon Basin demonstrate that marginal plateau development is required for and promotes the intensification of bottom currents.

Adam Kirby (AK): Hi Jon, thanks for giving us this opportunity to talk about our research. As a group we are very proud of our publications and look forward to seeing where our research takes us in the future. I have not yet published my PhD work as a first author, but recently co-authored a paper (https://doi.org/10.1016/j.marpetgeo.2020.104768) with my colleague Sara and PhD supervisor Dr. Javier Hernández-Molina, which looked at a Cretaceous mixed turbidite-contourite system in seismic data from the Argentine Margin. I'm currently working on two exciting projects, the conceptual results from which will be presented in two papers. The studies focus on Cenozoic contourite features in seismic data from the Argentine and Uruguayan margins, and take a look at the complex lateral and vertical evolution of asymmetric mounded drifts and plastered drifts.

JR: I'm always amazed at how industrious your group is and look forward to reading those papers that are in review soon. Next question for you. You have many energy companies (including operators and service companies) interested in your research. Can you describe how your research is enabling the energy industry to discover and produce more energy resources? Also, what are some of the other applications of your research that you're most excited about?

OM: Years ago, and still today, energy companies have primarily focused on gravitational processes to determine reservoir presence and quality – for turbidite reservoirs. However, our findings show that bottom currents are a significant agent in deepwater environments, forming entirely new deposits as well as altering those related to density currents. A deep knowledge of bottom currents and how they influence sediment transport and deposition can improve depositional models with key implications for reservoir geometry, distribution, and rock properties.

My research also provides new observations on major zones of erosion and intervals where density currents were more affected by bottom currents. Moreover, clinoforms have been traditionally related to gravitational processes. However, my data show that many of these aggradational and progradational clinoforms are related to contour currents, representing a change in the conventional models for continental margins. These new models also have a significant impact on novel play types in hydrocarbon exploration.

WW: We do, for which we are incredibly grateful. Every year we have a joint industry project meeting combined with a field excursion. The first year we went to Cyprus to see the Eocene-Miocene calcareous contourites. The evenings are used to discuss the progress of our research activities. These discussions are always very fruitful for and contributive to our work. In 2019 we went to Morocco which was particularly nice for me as I got to show my study area. The amount of positive feedback was amazing, and it was great to see the excitement and the interest of the participant looking at the outcrops I study.

For me, being a field geologist, my contribution to the energy industry can sometimes appear a bit less straightforward. Industry professionals tend to want to look at the "big seismic picture", however, seismic studies only provide relatively low-resolution acoustic data, and cores contain very little information about lateral facies changes. Particularly in the case of deep-marine sedimentary systems it can be very hard to envisage these systems. Looking at outcrops can change that, allowing you to get a feel for the sedimentary deposits below the exposed surface observed in seismic data and cores. By studying these outcrops in detail, I managed to construct facies models that contribute to recognizing and understanding contourite channel systems and to determine their hydrocarbon play potential.

Besides the interest to the energy industry, contourite deposits, and in my opinion particularly sandy contourite deposits as their resolution is higher, contain significant information about global ocean circulation and climate change. This topic is addressed in our *Geology* publication (https://doi.org/10.1130/G47944.1).

DD: Sometimes, the structural control of deepwater systems tends to be an underappreciated area of research, which is now under development. In my research, I'm aiming to comprehend how regional setting (e.g. tectonic-controlled morphologies and diapirism) influences deposit distribution. Despite not being directly linked to hydrocarbon exploration in the area, it does have analog value and sheds light on potential resource distribution and migration pathways.

AK: Working at the seismic scale my research contributes towards a greater understanding of deep-marine depositional systems. I classify contourite features from a local to regional scale, and coupled with the research of my colleagues this can enable the development of predictive models for successful petroleum exploration. For me, the most interesting area towards which my research can contribute, is by using contourite morphologies to decode deep paleo-ocean circulation and better understand oceanographic processes which interact with the seafloor. This assists the prediction of lithologies in deep marine settings.

ZN: Using the Gulf of Cadiz CDS as an analog to understand the effects of bottom-current processes on past depositional environments on a margin, and its wider implications on paleoceanography and paleoclimate, we could apply this knowledge to reduce the uncertainty in the seismic-stratigraphic interpretation and the evaluation of petroleum system elements on other Atlantic margins potentially affected by similar bottom-current processes.

SC: The knowledge of deepwater sedimentation and the influence of oceanographic currents in continental margins are a valuable asset in reservoir characterization and especially in research and development for carbon capture and storage (CCS). Also, the high concentration of microplastics we find on the seafloor is still poorly understood. Bottom currents can concentrate microplastics (mainly comprised of fibers from textiles and clothing) within thick sediment accumulations, especially in contourite drifts, which researchers have termed "microplastic hotspots".

JR: That is a very interesting emerging area of research, and these are important research questions that could fill a career. The whole world wants to know….where in the world are you going next to study contourite and mixed deepwater depositional systems?

DD: I would be thrilled to continue my research on the evolution of contourite systems in different active tectonic settings. There are many possible regions to broaden the field, such as the Argentine margin transfer zones (where I could collaborate with Adam and Sara) or the collisional setting in the Bahamas, where contourites have previously been identified.

JR: Are you accepting applications for research assistants?

DD: Sure, come along!

JR: Packing my bags now.

OM: There are many places in the world where we do not know anything about the influence of bottom currents on recent sedimentation and ancient deposits. In my opinion, areas with enormous subsurface information could be the first target, such as the Gulf of Mexico, offshore Brazil, offshore Norway, and West Africa. However, it is clear that if we want to have more success in hydrocarbon exploration, we need to know the patterns and evolution of bottom currents in every basin around the world.

AK: It would be really exciting to continue my research and the next place I would like to study is in the North Atlantic, looking at contourite features in the Rockall Trough and around the Porcupine Basin. I have colleagues already working here with whom it would be great to collaborate. Beyond this it would be interesting to look at contourite features in an equatorial setting where Coriolis forces are less influential on their development.

JR: That has been a longstanding question, and I hope you find the answer.

SC: We should start looking for misinterpreted places... maybe the Annot sandstone? Haha!

JR: We should rethink our classic interpretation of the Annot Sandstone.

ZN: Given the opportunity, I would like bring this knowledge home, and to conduct similar research in Malaysia and the wider South East Asia region. Following conversations with fellow colleagues, the idea of contourites and bottom current processes is rarely discussed in the Malaysian academic context. However, the vast knowledge and resources available in the Malaysian petroleum industry could make this possible.

WW: Tricky question this. Contourites in outcrops are only scarcely recognized and as such, the location of the ones that are, seem to be quite well shielded. I would like to visit and study all these places to compare them to the outcrops I have been studying already, but my particular interest goes to the contourite outcrops identified in Angola as the outcrops have great scientific potential. Furthermore, I will be going back to Morocco shortly (if Corona related restrictions allow it) as I still have some particularly exciting projects planned there which I was not able to undertake last year.

JR: What has been (i) most challenging aspect of completing your graduate research and (ii) the most fun part of your graduate program? Can you describe what it is like to work in the field and in the lab? Perhaps an interesting story or two?

DD: When I think of challenges, my mind undoubtedly goes to the current world pandemic, which has complicated our research (and life) in the last few months. As for the fun part, there are many to point out! I have met some incredible people I now call friends and have had the change to travel to many different and beautiful places. If I had to choose favorites, I would say our group trip to the Sahara Desert (with near-death driving experiences) and also exploring Edinburgh during the British Sedimentological Research Group (BSRG) 2018 conference.

OM: The most challenging aspect has been to understand some oceanographic processes that I didn't originally know about and how they are represented in the geologic record. The most fun I believe has been sharing this experience with my colleagues. We are eight people in our office – all from different countries and with different projects from around the world. Now you can imagine that every day has been an adventure.

JR: That is amazing how your work characterizes bottom current and their deposits from some of the most remote places on Earth.

OM: In my opinion, to be able to combine lab work and field studies is the best. In this way, one can see different scales of deepwater deposits from seismic to outcrop, which is one of the best methods to understand them.

AK: Of course, Covid-19 has been a major challenge both for me and the research group, but thinking optimistically it has taught us how to adapt to difficult circumstances during our work. Overall, the PhD has provided many opportunities to meet new colleagues such as yourself, and work abroad in places such as Cyprus, Morocco and SE Spain. One experience I really enjoyed was travelling to work on seismic data in Uruguay, this not only allowed me to expand my horizons with regards to contourite interpretation, but also gave me a chance to analyze the many wonderful beaches and sandy sediments of the Uruguayan coast during their summer.

ZN: I am grateful for the opportunity given to me by my supervisors and various data providers in setting up the research project, and for the financial support in the form of a research degree college scholarship provided by Royal Holloway, University of London. The most fun part of the program is the congregation of multi-talented young researchers in tackling various problems in a common scientific topic within a 4-year period, which has helped me develop professionally and personally. I find that the most challenging aspect however is the difficulty in resource management of a project. My experiences in project management over the last few years have taught me a lot.

WW: Where to start...no, just kidding. I think overall I don't have much to complain about. Probably the most challenging aspect of my graduate research was the lack of being able to properly plan everything. I am quite organized and like to know what is about to happen where and when. During the project much of the planned trips and many of the objectives had to be changed. For one, I was to visit more outcrops in different countries. This, however, tuned out not to be possible. Furthermore, of course, there was this pandemic which significantly changed the planning of last year. Having said that, the thing I like most about going on field trips is that it is always an adventure, coming across obstacles and having to find a way to overcome those.

I think the most fun part of the graduate program is my research group, as the dynamics of research groups significantly affect the experience of the graduate program. I really love my colleagues and we shared some amazing experiences together, one of my favorites being a trip to the Moroccan desert together after the JIP meeting. A road trip from Fes to Merzouga, crossing the Atlas and experiencing four seasons in a roughly 8-hour drive. Sleeping in the desert with the most amazing night skies, spending the days crossing the dunes by car, camels and by foot to return to the office two days later where the fun, however, continued. Interesting story or two...too difficult as there are so many.

JR: We'll need a longer interview next time.

SC: Being pioneer researchers in contourite sedimentation is not easy! Especially when you have to compare your results with previous publications which are few...

JR: How can the world learn more about your research? Do you have upcoming conferences you're organizing? How does your research reach the broader scientific community?

DD: You can always find the latest news on our very active twitter account (@driftersrhul) or can find me @niobsidian. In the next few months, Covid allowing, we will be present in some conferences such as the AAPG Mixed/Hybrid Systems, next May in Lisbon, and the 4th Deep Water Circulation Research Conference in Edinburgh from the 8th–10th of September.

JR: Can we register now?

DD: Unfortunately, you cannot register yet, but visit this link to keep up-to-date with the Edinburgh Conference (https://4dwc.hw.ac.uk). You can upload an abstract to the Lisbon Conference, the webpage for which is at this link: (https://www.aapg.org/global/europe/events/workshop/articleid/56182/mixed-hybrid-systems-turbidite-mtds-and-contourites-on-continental-margins).

OM: During this year, I will publish some papers about my research in Northwest Australia. I think this is going to be an excellent way to know more about my investigation. Since I started my PhD, I have attended some congresses and meetings. I believe this is a good complement to the paper that will come.

AK: In addition to the flourishing Twitter account (@DriftersRHUL) as Debora mentioned, we attend many conferences such as BSRG and IAS, and recently held the 2019 BSRG conference at Royal Holloway.

SC: We try to be present in most of the sedimentology-related congresses as Debora and Adam mentioned. However, this year has been a bit challenging due to the current situation.

ZN: I aim to have part of my work published in the near future, and I hope these results will be helpful and beneficial for the upcoming ICDP/IODP amphibious drilling IMMAGE (Investigating Miocene Mediterranean-Atlantic Gateway Exchange) project. As for our Twitter page @DriftersRHUL, please help us in reaching the next milestone of 1000 followers!

JR: That is so awesome, congratulations Lin. And I hope all of those conferences run soon. It will be a great opportunity to collaborate and share new knowledge on deepwater depositional systems.

WW: Now I'm occupied with finalizing my PhD, and haven't signed up for any upcoming conferences yet. Besides the publications that will hopefully be out soon, I'm also collaborating on an upcoming applied geoscience textbook.

JR: What did I not ask that you'd like to tell us about? Could be research related or on another topic of interest.

ZN: While both turbidites and contourites were first recognized around 60-70 years ago, it is only recently that we have started to comprehend the significance of the latter in understanding ocean and climate systems. We can use these deposits as proxies to reconstruct paleo-circulations and -conditions, in hope to provide new perspective and answer some longstanding questions relating to ancient Earth surface dynamics.

DD: We, as a community, are facing challenging circumstances. Following a volcanic eruption, destruction can give way to fertile ground upon which we can grow as a society. Set in stone ideals can deteriorate, allowing for adaptation to new realities as we have seen in the last year. Science and prejudice-free thought should lead the way, as we learn from not only our, but also the Earth's past.

OM: In my view, geologists need to learn more about oceanographic processes. Especially where we work in deepwater environments, which I think is a fundamental arena to understanding the evolution of these environments to promote greater success in hydrocarbon exploration.

AK: To progress as a species it is important to remain open minded and challenge paradigms, as has become clear in the last few years. Whilst our research group will continue to push boundaries in Earth Science it has become evident to me that we must take individual responsibility for our impact on the World.

SC: One of the key aspects towards a successful team is supporting my colleagues to ensure that they continue to grow their skills which makes for a more collaborative environment.

JR: Thank you so much Drifters!

Paul Mann (August 2021)

"My career has been a lot of twists and turns. For you youngsters out there, always remember careers don't always need to follow linear paths – in fact they may benefit from being non-linear. My career is certainly an example of a non-linear path – partly related to the practical need to find projects that were fundable, partly related to allow curiosity to drive project selection, and partly by collaborating with others and getting pulled into their areas of interest.

Professor Paul Mann, the Robert E. Sheriff endowed professor of geology and Director of the Conjugate Basins, Tectonics and Hydrocarbons Research Group at University of Houston.

Starting off as an undergrad and grad student, I had zero interest and exposure to subsurface data mainly because the curriculum at that time was mainly focused on preparation to do field geology. But field work just doesn't work in certain situations. I recall gazing across featureless plains or lakes in places like Hispaniola or Central America and starting wonder: How could I access or collect new subsurface data to start filling in these blank areas? The featureless plain to the field geologist is a whole other world to those with subsurface data." – Professor Paul Mann

Paul Mann received a B.A. in geology from Oberlin College and a Ph.D. from the State University of New York at Albany. His main interest area is the tectonics of sedimentary basins in the Caribbean, Gulf of Mexico, circus-Atlantic margins, and southwest Pacific. He is currently the Robert E. Sheriff endowed professor of geology in the Department of Earth and Atmospheric Sciences at the University of Houston, where he directs the CBTH Project: http://cbth.uh.edu/index.php. Anyone who has met Paul or read his team's work understands his prolific understanding of rifted passive margins from the Caribbean to the Gulf of Mexico to the Atlantic and Pacific margins. I interviewed Paul Mann to learn about the Conjugate Basins, Tectonics and Hydrocarbons Research Group (which is now in its *sixth* phase) at University of Houston.

Professor Paul Mann is one of the most successful researchers of the Gulf of Mexico and conjugate margin tectonics and hydrocarbons. Mann leads a large group of researchers at University of Houston through the CBTH Research Group. The group is sponsored by dozens of energy companies, all of whom wish to know more about tectonic frameworks and sedimentary basin evolution for their exploration programs. Mann has so many projects with so many masters, doctoral, post doc and seasoned researchers from around the world. Mann's research over the years has been among the most prolific of any scientist. Many people from the outside ask, "How can one person and one research group produce so much high-quality and in-demand research?" As you'll read in this interview, it takes great vision, deep subject matter expertise, creativity, careful attention to detailed planning and time management, talented leadership and the ability to build great relationships – among many other leadership traits. It has been a great honor and privilege to get to work with Paul Mann and his hardworking and talented team at University of Houston since 2019. I have learned so much from them. Paul Mann's work has already left a deep legacy toward geoscience around the world, particularly the GOM and Caribbean and conjugate margins, and he is considered a legend by those who know his work.

Read the interview below.

Jon Rotzien (JR): Paul, I'm so thankful you had the time to visit today and share your story. Could you share your background and what led you to become a geoscientist?

Paul Mann (PM): I went to small liberal arts college and wasn't really sure what to major in. I ended up getting into archaeology, probably because our family had gone on some epic summer vacation trips to Europe, the Mediterranean, and East Africa when we were kids. Part of the curriculum for anthropology and archaeology was to take a physical geology course. In my first geology class, I immediately seized on the field and geosciences and the dynamic, fun group of people that were geology students. Fortunately for our cadre of about 10 geology majors at the time, our newly arrived structural geologist was Grant Skerlec, who was finishing up his PhD on the Villa de Cura thrust belt in Venezuela with John Suppe at Princeton (now our colleague at UH). Grant took our structure class on our first extended field trip to the Delaware Water Gap in Pennsylvania, and that was a real turning point for me in the geosciences. Grant had been there many times as part of the Princeton program and we undertook a mapping and cross section exercise of some overturned folds. I recall him patiently explaining to me, "That is not a formation – that is a bed of sandstone that forms part of the x formation."

Grant was a really critical person in my development. His first recommendation was, "You need to go to field camp between junior and senior year," – since our small college did not operate a field camp. The Indiana University (IU) field camp was a great introduction to field geology and the northern Rockies. I came out of the camp feeling like a field geologist who could figure out any area. Back in the fall, Grant asked me as we passed in the corridor: "What are your plans after graduation next spring? I think you should consider going to graduate school in geology." Grad school was a fuzzy concept to me but in the course that short interaction and later interactions he explained the process of visiting and applying for grad school. He recommended SUNY Albany as a place to consider studying structure and tectonics. He said, "You need to go out there and visit and make sure that it's a good fit for the type of project you are interested in."

I have since given that same five-minute grad school pep talk to many undergrads – especially at UH where I have had more interactions with undergrads. It has worked for some, but not all. Timing and mindset are key: *When the student is ready, the master will appear.*

You can facilitate learning and point out the many opportunities that exist but that person has to actually commit to that path.

My path began when I boarded a plane from Cleveland to Albany. Grant also told me, "You need to read up on ophiolites." While I had never heard of ophiolites, I remember flying out there with an Elsevier volume on ophiolites on my knee. During the visit, I met the faculty and many students that included Doug Nelson, Eric Rosencrantz (who I worked with for years when we were both at University of Texas), Jack Casey (a colleague now at UH), Dave Rowley (now chair at University of Chicago) who graciously toured me around Albany and the department, amongst many others. By the end, I thought, "This is where I want to go!"

Back at Ohio, I received a call from Win Means, one of the structural professors at SUNY. He said, "We'd like to offer you 3-year fellowship," that came with no TA or RA responsibilities. This was a really great opportunity as I was finally on my own and financially independent from my parents.

JR: What great guidance from many mentors in your academic training. IU's challenging field camp has produced a number of icons over the years.

I've seen you present several times and have learned so much every time, including at the AAPG Deepwater Conference in Houston in 2017, the GCAGS and GeoGulf conferences in San Antonio and Houston in 2017 & 2019 – as well as during CBTH research meetings. You're one of the foremost experts in the geology of Latin America, the Caribbean and especially the Gulf of Mexico. It's hard to read a paper on one of those regions and not see your research group's work cited.

What are some of your recent findings?

PM: For years, I worked in the Caribbean, which is a small plate with all the tectonic environments in close proximity: subduction, transpression, transtension, a small oceanic spreading center, internal plate deformation, and much more. But with our CBTH group, it's not just about me. It's about me being able to find data the students working in the group – I call it "feeding the monster" –

JR: A monster?

PM: Which another way of saying: "I've got to get them data to develop into MS and PhD projects!"

JR: Absolutely.

PM: We mostly work with subsurface geology, so that means reaching out to oil companies and service companies for mainly seismic reflection and well data. But after about a decade of doing this in the Caribbean region, the group had analyzed almost every bit of subsurface data in the Caribbean that we could lay our hands on. At that point, we had to look wider – the data-rich Gulf of Mexico to the north beckoned.

The Caribbean and the GOM, they're like twins in a conjugate margin sense. The Yucatan connects with the Texas coast to the northwest and to northern South America in the south.

We launched our research group into the Mesozoic opening of the Gulf of Mexico in 2013. We were the new kids on the block and had a steep learning curve to climb up which was facilitated by some nice data sets provided to our group by Spectrum (now TGS).

JR: Spectrum and now TGS gather and produce excellent data.

PM: The other event of 2014 was when David Sandwell at the Scripps Institution of Oceanography in San Diego made his global marine satellite gravity data available for the world. That data for the first time showed the Gulf of Mexico fracture zones and spreading centers deeply buried – but distinct. It was astounding for me to see an actual image of the deep structure of the GOM and this energized our efforts as it appeared that the Mesozoic opening history was not that complicated: let's explore the geologic ramifications of the highly curved fracture zones of the Gulf of Mexico.

JR: That's so interesting, and I remember when Pindell gave that 2019 GeoGulf talk citing your team's work. Amazing how our understanding of the deep GOM has progressed over the last decade.

PM: We also had a student work on the Mexican Ridges and he came up with good results on how that structural system evolved from an early opening transform fault that ran along the east coast of Mexico.

But soon we started to burn through the GOM data we had access to. We had to start looking bigger – again – and this time we looked to the Atlantic margins. That's when we changed the name to *Conjugate Margins*, Basins, Tectonics and Hydrocarbons Research Group. In essence, we had a bigger hunting license, and could look at conjugate margins anywhere.

We went to Brazil in collaboration with ION and the ANP, the hydrocarbon agency of Brazil, allowed access to those data. We also developed another relationship with GEOX, working with Morocco data sets. Our study area became huge compared to the original Caribbean. What I've found through these student-led studies is that these rifted passive margins seem a lot simpler than the stuff we grappled with in Caribbean. That pretty much summarizes the history of our Project.

JR: Can you tell us about some of the most unexpected finds as part of your career in research?

PM: I guess, this is a little awkward. I find with rifted margins, there are complexities. But there are a lot of simplicities to them, too. We coined the term "marginal rift" – that's when you thin continental crust and produce a necking zone, when you go from 30-40-50-km-thick continental crust to transitional crust, which can be 10-km-thick down to even 5 km and less. If you can imagine, this is a triangular zone in a 2D seismic data profile. This phenomenon occurs due to necking of that triangular wedge. That is what we call the marginal rift. There may be more than one, but usually just one. It's quite simple, this necking process. The marginal rift is usually full of salt, and it could be a half to full graben.

JR: Your students have shown great examples of marginal rifts in the GOM, Morocco, Brazil, to name just three.

PM: People have argued about what we call it. Other people interpret this area as exhumed mantle. But we find these marginal rifts to be sediment filled – and not characterized by protruding mantle. Not saying 100% of time in all areas, but this is a common theme we see in different places. It's exciting when you see the same thing in different settings. You start to think it's a fundamental process. When you know all models and can identify their variability, observing this simplicity is intriguing. So, we're making our way to a simpler model of rifted continental crust.

JR: What was your inspiration for starting CBTH?

PM: My career has been a lot of twists and turns. For you youngsters out there, always remember careers don't always need to follow linear paths – in fact they may benefit from being non-linear. My career is certainly an example of a non-linear path – partly related to the practical need to find projects that were fundable, partly related to allow curiosity to drive project selection, and partly by collaborating with others and getting pulled into their areas of interest.

Starting off as an undergrad and grad student, I had zero interest and exposure to subsurface data mainly because the curriculum at that time was mainly focused on preparation to do field geology. But field work just doesn't work in certain situations. I recall gazing across featureless plains or lakes in places like Hispaniola or Central America and starting wonder: *How could I access or collect new subsurface data to start filling in these blank areas?* The featureless plain to the field geologist is a whole other world to those with subsurface data.

Sources for data varied. While at UT and then at UH, we had a steady supply of grad students from Venezuela, and Colombia and Trinidad who would arrive with subsurface data sets from their home countries. Oil companies were always helpful in providing data sets from obscure areas. Finally, I was increasingly drawn into actual marine geophysical cruises to collect new data in the Cayman trough, the Puerto Rico trench, the Solomon Islands, and the Macquarie Ridge. These new data acquisitions were especially important for areas where there was no footprint of older industry data as for example in sediment-starved areas like the Cayman trough or Macquarie Ridge.

JR: You have used so many different methods for evaluating tectonic processes.

PM: In our group we use as many tools as we have at our disposal: seismic reflection, refraction, structural restoration, gravity modeling, burial histories, basin modeling, maps of outcrop geology, GPS geodesy. We use GIS as the merging tool to stack results on top of one another. You know are on the right track and close to a final result when all the methods are telling you the same result. The key is not to be intimidated. Everyone starts out knowing nothing about a certain method – but as you use that method more and more then you become more adept.

JR: You have used so many different methods for evaluating tectonic processes.

PM: I started my career as a field geologist and spent the late 1980s and early 90s traveling to places like the Dominican Republic, Puerto Rico, Cuba, Panama and Costa Rica for outcrop-based field work. When you have a career as long as mine (now coming up on 4 decades), one of the advantages is being able to apply new technologies and tools as they become available. For example, I was glad to be around as GPS-based geodesy evolved back in the late 80s and early 90s. I'm grateful for being able to work with GPS experts Eric Calais and Chuck DeMets along with many other experts on a regional GPS study of the northern Caribbean. Also, I was intrigued by applying fault trenching methods to the active Caribbean strike-slip faults and was able to do this by working with Carol Prentice of the USGS who had honed her skills from years of fault trenching of the San Andreas fault in California. We worked together on fault trenching for about 10 years and produced the first prehistorical records of earthquakes on faults in the northern Dominican Republic.

Above: CBTH PhD students Mei Liu (to left) and Jack Kenning (to right with blue shirt) presenting their research on the GOM at AAPG Hedburg Conference: Geology and Hydrocarbon Potential of the Circum Gulf of Mexico Pre-salt Section, Mexico City, Mexico.

PM (cont.): The more geology I worked on in different geographic areas, the more I realized the importance of the subsurface to understand the "complete picture", so by the late 90s I was increasingly involved in marine geophysical surveys and was working with various seismic reflection data sets provided by the oil industry. About 2000, our institute at UT had moved to the Pickle Campus about 10 miles north of the main UT campus in a brand new building right next to the UT Bureau of Economic Geology - which is a powerhouse of subsurface mapping. There I began working with Lesli Wood who had worked in Trinidad as part of her PhD and during her time at Amoco. We both had a shared interest in Trinidad and thought: "Why don't we start a consortium study for the Trinidad on- and offshore area?" She knew how to run a consortium so we worked collaboratively on a Trinidad consortium for 3 years.

As Lesli was more into the sedimentological aspects of the basins and I was more interested in the structure and tectonics, my postdoc, Alejandro Escalona, and I thought, "Why don't we start our own consortium?" Which we did in 2005. We built it around work we had done in Trinidad and in Venezuela and expanded the consortium to include Colombia. At that time, oil prices were high, and we had lots of interest and great sponsorship. Alejandro completed his PhD at UT in 2003 and his postdoc at UT in 2006 and took a professor job at the University of Stavanger in Norway in 2007 where he continues to lead the CBTH group at that university.

My next career turning point occurred when I left UT Austin and moved to UH in 2011. We had reached a natural break at this time with the completion of a 2011 special issue in the journal *Marine and Petroleum Geology* on the Venezuela-Trinidad projects we had been working from the early 2000s to about 2010. During the UH move, the group was pared down from graduations to myself, Rocio Bernal, a PhD student from Colombia who had started at UT, Jeff Storms who was our project manager who had started with us a UT undergrad in 2005, and two new students, a Colombian PhD student Javier Sanchez who had done his MS with Brian Horton at UT, and MS student Luis Pachon, another Colombian, whom I re-routed as an entering new student from UT to UH. We hunkered down in temporary offices while our present, spacious work area was being completed. The larger workspace allowed us to grow our UH student numbers to 21 within 3 years. Our focus remained on Colombia and that took us up to the 2015 CBTH publications in AAPG Memoir 108 on Colombia that was edited by Claudio Bartolini and myself. With the larger group and improved ties to Houston-based data companies we were able to begin student projects mainly in the southeastern Caribbean. Much of this work that includes many papers from our groups both from our CBTH group at UH and Alejandro's CBTH group in Stavanger is now in press in AAPG Memoir 123 that is edited by Claudio Bartolini. We appreciate all of his efforts in merging all of our CBTH work with many other studies from other groups into a volume that is more than 800 pages long.

JR: Your research group produces so much excellent research, and it is so collaborative – one of the most productive research groups I've ever seen. Can you describe what teamwork means to you in your research group?

PM: Thank you for that nice compliment on behalf of the CBTH group, including both present and past members! Although I am the primary supervisor of many students in the CBTH group that has included up to 21 students at one point, with such large numbers I quickly reach my limits in both my time and my skill sets. We involve many UH faculty members on the thesis committees like Dale Bird, John Suppe, Jonny Wu, Julia Wellner, Stuart Hall, Jiajia Sun, Mike Murphy, and John Castagna. I have encouraged the participation of subject matter experts like yourself, Charles Sternbach and Kurt Rudolph to become adjunct professors at UH and have a closer link to our project. But we also reach outside the pool of full-time and adjunct UH professors to people I know in the wider community and ask them "Would you mind meeting on Zoom or Teams with this student to discuss their project?" For the Houston area we have such a great pool of oil industry experts to choose from.

JR: Absolutely, it's been a great learning experience to get to work with you and your students on subsurface projects. Can you describe how you get students started on their research?

PM: I then ask the student to prepare a PowerPoint to share with the expert to test ideas and methods. These meetings are especially important for those new students starting out. I emphasize to new students the importance of not "reinventing the wheel" – i.e., starting a project that turns out to be a project someone else has already done or are currently working on with similar methods. The best way to avoid reinventing wheels is to have the student show that they have an encyclopedic knowledge of previous work on their topic and that they have also met with the leading subject matter experts in that area to gain insider knowledge of the state of the art. Also, these discussions lay a vision of what topics have not been solved and what is the best way to address those problems. I find the people we reach out to are very giving of their time, their ideas, and are happy to see this new generation following up on problems that they have thought about for a long time.

JR: The CBTH students are industrious, creative and hardworking. Their success is evident at regional and international research meetings. How do you organize your time with your students?

PM: The time I put into students comes in two phases: Phase 1 is when they enter the program with the question of what they will work on, what is the research problem, what data will they use? The sign that Phase 1 is succeeding is when the student begins to take "ownership" of his or her project. Ownership means they are now "driving their own band wagon" – so my role diminishes as their role expands as they are now fully empowered. I know ownership has taken hold when they start sending me references on their topic rather than me always sending them references. This gives me a great feeling that I have linked the right student with the right project.

As Phase 1 wraps up, I move to the sideline but remain a cheerleader who meets with them weekly to track their progress. This is where my patience comes in as students are all different. Some students are like rocket ships blasting off the launchpad – others are like old cars that will take longer to rev up. For this period, I encourage them to present their results at meetings that were in person conferences in the old days – nowadays virtual conferences. These meetings act as what I call "milestones" and I ask the students to map their grad school milestones as a Gantt chart. This graphic representation shows their entire MS (2 year) or PhD (3-4 year) timeline with all of their conference milestones indicated.

JR: That is excellent.

PM: General Eisenhower said something like: *Plans are useless but planning is indispensable* – the idea being that plans may change in during the heat of the battle – but having the baseline, long-term plan is critical.

JR: What an applicable quote. What does the next part of the phase look like?

PM: UH requires students to have their committee organized and a proposal meeting in their first or second year. This is the culmination of their Phase 1 project planning so this period is a spike both in their workload and mine in order to get ready for this meeting. I encourage them to write their first chapter/article by the time of this meeting – the bonus for them is that this submitted paper would exempt them from the UH qualifying exam – which is a general exam on all the major fields of geosciences.

JR: A very challenging exam.

PM: The other important part of this middle phase is the student becoming a good team member. So, people come in ready to go as team players – for example, they were athletes on college teams, or they led student organizations, or they had jobs where they had worked in teams. Other students arrive to us with little idea of what being on a team means in terms of their behavior or view of the world. To promote our CBTH team, we meet for two hours on Friday of each week and we all present what we have worked on that week. In these meetings, you'll often hear other students say to their peers, "Hey, you know there's a better way to do what you are working on…" which encourages collaboration. We file these hints into a "work saving tips folder" that archives them all for future use.

JR: What a brilliant method. Can you describe the inspiration for the work saving tips?

PM: The idea is that they recognize that freely sharing information benefits the group so the sum of the parts become greater than any individual. Also, I encourage the older students to help the newer students – how to set up their, layered, GIS database of their areas, for example. Over time I can see the transition in reticent, non-team type students to sharing team players. This is an important life lesson that can be applied to all aspects of their future lives.
Since we have been virtual since March 2020, I meet individually with each student for 15 minutes on Mondays and Tuesdays to get a quick update of their progress. Here I can offer up suggestions and any more focused input on what they are doing. There is an incredible amount of polishing needed to get the final product. All these virtual meetings are meant to keep them engaged and feeling that they are part of the group despite the physical isolation.

JR: Sounds like CBTH was able to efficiently shift gears quickly during the pandemic with the virtual meetings. How do students get a feel for the timeline of graduate school?

PM: I ask them to plan their grad student timeline so each thesis chapter is presented as a poster or talk at a minimum of one conference. That way their work is vetted in a public way to gain input and to polish and fine tune their message. So, this middle part of the study (Phase 2) is the heavy lifting by the student where most of their original work is happening and being reported to both me and the larger community.

My workload again spikes for the crescendo of Phase 3: that is their final year when they are completing the thesis student that usually is one chapter/article for the MS student and three articles/chapters for the PhD student (and the necessary course work of 30 credit hours). If Phase 2 goes well and they have submitted as they progressed though Phase 2 their article or articles then this final workload is lessened. The workload spike would nevertheless include the MS or PhD defense and the preparation of that final thesis document.

There you have a long-winded explanation of our student workflow – and along the way I remind the students to start think outwardly and beyond the walls of UH. UH is one of the largest geosciences departments in the western hemisphere – but it will not provide them the source of their first internship or job – nor all the expertise, data and resources that they will need to solve their thesis-related problem. Jobs are not going to happen if you're under a rock. Instead, they need to put themselves out there, reach out to industry and other institutions.

JR: What a focused and effective workflow – very impressive. How are the students achieving this today?

PM: I give new students the task of creating a Research Gate site, a Google Scholar site and LinkedIn site to expand their world beyond our physical department. Also, on Research Gate set up a project based on their thesis study that runs up the flag on what they are working on and starting assembling those with similar interests. All are important for career building and finding a job. Close to 100% of the students in our group get jobs. Most have figured out teamwork, which is important to get and to keep a job. If you're not team oriented, you're not going to survive in industry. You need to be open for change, and ready to make those changes.

JR: Great preparation for joining industry.

PM: We have Jeff Storms who as our web developer and database manager has worked diligently for years to improve our website and deliver our products via the website. The project website is our window to the world – especially during the Covid time when travel to meetings has been restricted. Anyone on the planet with an internet connection can see what the CBTH project has done in the past and the areas that we are presently working on. While Covid has been challenging, I applaud the group here since the start of the virus in March, 2020, for adapting to the new situation – especially given that the group has been as productive as the groups pre-2020.

JR: What is next for the consortium?

PM: We have several newer students who are in the pre-proposal starting phase for the Permian basin, Colombia, Gulf of Mexico, Brazil, northwest Africa, and the Red Sea. Our project footprint now takes in the Permian, GOM, and Atlantic margins. The Red Sea is out of that footprint but we would like to develop it as an analog to the Mesozoic rifts around the circum-Atlantic margins and GOM.

JR: Congratulations on your regional and world championship wins in the AAPG Imperial Barrel Award (IBA) Competition. What was it like for University of Houston to win those competitions?

PM: Thank you for that compliment. The UH IBA success we have enjoyed took many years of slow, steady effort. John Castagna and I took over the faculty leadership of the UH IBA program started in 2012. Before we started, IBA at UH was a "club activity" so was not a for-credit course. Our first action was to convert it to 3-credit course, as the program is run in most other geoscience departments. Interest lagged and in 2012 we could only recruit four students for what normally is a five-person team. From 2012 to 2016, we had three consecutive third place finishes in the Gulf Coast area and finally in 2016, we broke through with a second place finish and followed on in 2017 with our first global championship. So, there was a long learning curve in figuring out the program what a good presentation should include and look like. We also worked a lot on the Q&A session by preparing students for likely questions and making sure that they could answer those questions in a concise way. All the success made recruiting easier and we were able to expand the non-presentation teams, or those students who could take the class, but not be part of the five-person presentation team. This opened up the wonderful, IBA hands-on learning experience to a lot more UH students. All the awards in the competition were a huge boost in confidence – not just for those on the competition team but also for the entire UH geosciences program. Recruiting also got easier as more UH students thought: "If they did it, I can do it."

JR: What else drives the success of the team?

PM: A lot comes down to picking the right students and then helping them prepare. The chemistry between the students has to work. Sometimes we have to work out inter-personal differences, but that adds to the value of the experience. For most students, they have never been part of such an intensive team effort so it's no surprise of the importance that industry recruiters place on the IBA program.

JR: For universities just getting started with IBA, what are some good pointers?

PM: First priority is to find a faculty advisor who will coordinate the effort and put the time in. The time commitment can discourage many from joining.

Second priority is to maintain faculty continuity as we have maintained at UH since 2012. Because of the time and commitment, some universities will alternate advisors every second or even third years. When you rotate advisors, however, you can lose some continuity and collective knowledge that accumulates with each passing year.

Being consistent in the effort level over the eight-week period also important. Long-term planning is important to avoid any sort of last-minute crunch in getting tasks done – or equally as important to practice and polish the presentation and Q and A session. Excellence is not the result of one action, but the result of many good habits.

JR: The consistency sounds key.

PM: In the end, there is great payoff – and it's not just about winning awards. I observe that students who come out of the IBA program are supercharged and operate at a higher energy level. Their time spent working goes way up and you can see that work ethic persist, and you can see a higher confidence levels. Part of it is that they have learned a lot of new skills – including how to put together and deliver a presentation.

JR: Congratulations on your recent AAPG Distinguished Educator Award. That is a huge achievement. Can you tell us a little more about what that means to you?

PM: I greatly appreciate this award and I thank Charles Sternbach for nominating me. Charles has been a big advocate of UH Geosciences for at least 10 years and all of us at UH really appreciate his efforts along with those of his partner Linda Sternbach. Also, kudos to AAPG and the bequest by Grover E. Murray to set up the award.

JR: What do you tell students interested in getting into the energy industry? How do you prepare your students for successful careers in the energy industry? UH has a long and distinguished record of producing top energy industry professionals.

PM: That's a tough question during this era of transition between the fossil fuel-based and expansion of non-carbon-based green fuels. I get asked, "Why aren't you interested in CCUS?" Our CBTH group remains focused on conventional, deepwater exploration and the students are continuing to be employed in this sector. Their skills could be applied to the reverse problem of putting carbon back into reservoirs rather than extracting oil and gas from reservoirs – but we are not yet at that point.

JR: What is your message for oil and gas explorers today?

PM: The biggest problem facing the oil and gas industry today is the need to reduce fossil fuels and their emissions. But that said, we also need energy to get us to the promised land: a non-carbon-based world. For those of us in Texas who huddled in freezing, blacked-out homes back in February, we had a hard lesson in the consequences of losing our energy supply. But we cannot just stop using fossil fuels on a dime as the green segments of the energy spectrum are only a very minor component today. The challenge is now to increase the green component, decrease the fossil fuel component, and make the transition in a way without events like the Great Freeze of 2021.

JR: Thank you so much Professor Mann.

F. Javier Hernández-Molina (January 2022)

"The resolution of bathymetry data was so poor in 1990s. You think everything is so smooth – not too many changes in the seafloor. When you analyze the high-resolution maps, you see how complex it truly is. This was a big find for our group. To realize the complexity of the ocean from the geologic perspective. And not only the surface, but with the subsurface features, too. That is a key moment." – Professor F. Javier Hernández-Molina

Professor F. Javier Hernández-Molina pausing for a photo while exploring Antarctica on one of his many oceanographic expeditions.

Dr. Hernández-Molina is currently Professor in the Department of Earth Sciences at *Royal Holloway University of London* (RHUL). He is a specialist in sedimentary processes, seismic stratigraphy and basin analysis, and is experienced in core description and sediment structures identification. His research focuses on deep-marine sedimentation and the influence of bottom-current circulation along continental margins as well as the study of *contourites* and *hybrid depositional systems* in both low latitude (e.g. Gulf of Cadiz) and high latitude (e.g. Antarctica). He has participated in 67 national and international research projects in marine geology and geophysics. He has worked on different continental margins, and has particular expertise on the Iberian continental margin, South Atlantic and Antarctica.

F. Javier Hernández-Molina is one of the most knowledgeable and experienced contemporary scientists researching ocean and seafloor processes. It is in part because he has sailed on more oceanographic expeditions than almost any other geoscientist, exploring many continental margins around the world. His publications and research accomplishments especially in bottom current and contourite research are legendary, with over 11,000 citations of his research at the time this book was completed. Javier's focus, curiosity, enthusiasm and joy for scientific discovery attract a large number of scientists who want to be a part of Javier's community. He has charisma and has a very large scientific family as a result, a very wide network of sedimentologists, ichnologists, biostratigraphers, geophysicists, physical and chemical oceanographers and biologists and many more. Javier brings in a broad diversity of thinking to his research to get to the truth about the details of how ocean water masses and sediment combine to sculpt continental margins. Javier truly has brought together a global community, something that is very rare in any profession. Javier takes his research very seriously and takes great joy in sharing discoveries of the Earth with his students and colleagues. His humor generates smiles wherever he goes. When colleagues or students bring to him an idea about what they think is happening, he asks, "What is the evidence?" And when students pressure him into providing more information about what the answer may be on field trips to southeastern Spain, he smiles, and says, "I have never seen these rocks before," with a grin. Of course, he has seen these rocks before. This is a clever phrase I now use with my students.

I originally met Javier at a presentation at Royal Holloway followed up the next year by a short course on deepwater sedimentology to The Drifters research group. I focused on downslope processes. After all, I wasn't going to attempt to try to explain bottom currents and along-slope processes to the most knowledgeable group on the subject in the world. Since then, we've organized conferences together in Europe and the USA, taught courses, published a textbook, led field trips in Spain and France. Javier was integral in shaping the deepwater book to include observations on the key advancements that have been made in all subject areas dealing with deepwater sedimentary systems (all 21 chapters!). He also framed the importance of developing the next generation to be able to handle the demands of energy resources and understanding deep oceans' role in climate. Javier has a very high energy level and is a true team builder. I do struggle to keep up with Javier in the field, however, since he is a sub-2:45 marathoner. Along with hundreds to thousands of others from around the world, I have learned so much on marine processes from Javier and am indebted to him for teaching me so many things about the broad range and variability in deepwater sedimentary systems.

I sat down with *F. Javier Hernández-Molina* to learn about ocean processes – specifically bottom currents and mixed deepwater sedimentary systems in January 2022. Read the interview below.

Jon Rotzien (JR): Javier, I'm so thankful you had the time to visit today and share your story. How did you become a geoscientist?

F. Javier Hernández-Molina (FJHM): I've had a passion for flying and being in the mountains since I was a teenager. Don't know if I ever told you this, but I won the lottery when we were children. I spent all that money learning to fly when I was 14. Really flying is one my passions and even today, from time to time I go gliding. However, I started to doubt myself in being a pilot. I wasn't sure to do biology or geology in school. I decided on the earth science pathway, and took an optional course in geology. And it was really a change in my life. Later, from 1983 to 1988 I did my degree at University of Granada in Geology. Then I started to specialize in marine geology with my thesis, which was done between the Spanish Oceanographic Institute and the University of Granada. Later, I was working at Marine Science faculty in Cadiz and Vigo, and since 2013 at the Department of Earth Science at Royal Holloway, University of London.

JR: You have a way of presenting research as a puzzle, and how studies have led to "assembly of more and more pieces of the puzzle" and, in effect, a greater understanding of the Earth's oceans. Currently, what are some of the missing "pieces of the puzzle" toward scientific understanding of the oceans?

FJHM: Now there are not big pieces. We know the big pieces, but we don't really know the details and interaction between the pieces. I used this as an analog in a talk this year to try to convince the community that bottom currents are important to sedimentation in deep-marine settings. In the last decades only a few specialists have considered ocean circulation as an important factor in shaping continental margins and in controlling marine sedimentation. Not in general, and not for industry. "This is one of the missing pieces," I said in that talk. It is the interaction between the pieces, between gravity and bottom currents and pelagic and hemipelagic sedimentation, and so on. And the timing. We need to understand when these interactions could or couldn't happen.

JR: Can you tell us about some of the most unexpected finds so far in your career?

FJHM: Difficult, eh? Probably to the present in my career, this is when we started to work on the Gulf of Cadiz. The possibility to observe the seafloor with more and more detail, and how complex it really is. The resolution of bathymetry data was so poor in 1990s. You think everything is so smooth – not too many changes in the seafloor. When you analyze the high-resolution maps, you see how complex it truly is. This was a big find for our group. To realize the complexity of the ocean from the geologic perspective. And not only the surface, but with the subsurface features, too. That is a key moment. More key moments were in expedition Tasyo-2000 in the same area, as well as ANT94-0020 and ANT96-1001, and SCAN-2000 in Antarctica. From 1996-2000, those expeditions really changed my perspective and helped me to understand in the seismic data what we were seeing. We also switched from routine mono-channel and high-resolution seismic to deeper multi-channel seismic.

Later, in a drilling expedition, it was surprising to see when we drilled the wells how frequent the hiatuses were and how wrong we were in our previous seismic interpretations. What we saw as high-amplitude intervals we thought would be sandy came in with missing sections and were muddy. It is important to think of processes. With this drilling project we realized the important role of tectonic events in controlling deepwater sedimentation and the close link between internal and external processes even at high-resolution scales (>0.4 million years).

Another key moment was when we started to work in Antarctica, when I realized the global implications of past environmental changes. In Antarctica, the work conditions and environment are so much different than what I was used to in Europe – the difficulties due to the remote nature of the expedition, but also the friendship of the people working on cruises. Antarctic research is very different for how people collaborate in that environment.

JR: What was your inspiration for starting *The Drifters*?

FJHM: I moved to the UK in 2013, and later in 2016 I gave a talk for BG Group, the company that was acquired by Shell. BG mentioned they could be interested in funding a PhD student for 3-4 years. I had never had that experience of working with industry funding for a PhD project. By 2016-2017, I started to see the importance of contourite research in industry. Then I decided to develop a group, with a pure research side and an applied side for collaborating with industry. Then I got a grant for one student, and then another grant. Then, I started to contact other companies including BP, ExxonMobil, TOTAL (now TotalEnergies), Eni, Spectrum (now TGS), Wintershall Dea and others, and finally we developed a joint industry project (JIP) which started in 2017 and is ending this year.

In my previous years before Royal Holloway, at University of Vigo in Spain, northwest of Galicia, I didn't want to have any student or group. For 11 years, I was teaching for four to five months, and the rest of the time I had the opportunity of traveling to other counties to collaborate with many groups around world. This really helped me to establish a network for the later development of The Drifters. I worked with Argentines, Uruguayans, Brazilians, with Germans in Bremen, and in the UK at the Oceanographic Centre of Southampton and the British Antarctic Survey. All of these stages were really important for the next stage.

JR: How did you settle on the name *The Drifters*?

FJHM: This is a funny story. We were in Cyprus having dinner together, at the restaurant was named *Drifters Bar & Grill*. Later I realized this was the name of an American rhythm-and-blues vocal group. We decided to adopt that name because of the link with contourite drifts.

JR: *The Drifters* produces so much excellent research, and it is so collaborative – one of the most productive research groups I've ever seen.

Can you describe what teamwork means in your research group?

FJHM: Other groups in Manchester and in other universities in the UK or in other countries produce a lot of high-quality research in deep-marine environments, too. Perhaps, the difference is that our group is multidisciplinary but very focused on a specific topic. We have had intense years of activities with enough funding for research and analyzing data onshore and offshore. Other groups could have a similar structure, but with wider objectives or with more emphasis on gravitational processes and deposits.

We have had a productive teamwork effort in the group, where the students involved have been essential for its success. Most of the credit goes to these students. All the students have been exceptional. All of them. Very motivated, very hardworking students, which makes it easy on me to coordinate work.

In the beginning ~2017-2018, one of my aims was to have a student working in a specific topic in the ancient and another student working the same scientific problem in the modern ocean, in order for students to collaborate together over 2-3 years to find out what is common and what is uncommon in a deepwater sedimentary system. One of the important points in the future, is to compare the same facies from core logging with the seismic – from the modern day and the ancient record. And that has been working, and that provides the possibility for students to go deeper into the topic. As you know some students have been working in seismic interpretation and others in outcrops or using cores. The possibility to collaborate at the same time on a similar topic with different perspectives is helping us understand the topic better. We have had a lot of good discussions in these past four years in the research group.

JR: You've worked all over the world – by boat a lot of the time. How many cruises are you up to? How many days have you spent on boats and research vessels?

FJHM: I went through my CV earlier because I didn't know! 50 research cruises, 8 of them in Antarctica, and when I was working at University of Vigo I also collaborated in educational cruises so that students could learn how to use echosounder, sediment sampling, etc. Some of the cruises I have been the PI of the cruise, and for others I have been a researcher.

I don't know how many days. I should calculate this, but I don't know. Usually a cruise is 20-30 days, so if you do some quick math, that's about 1000 days, which is a conservative number considering drilling cruises are about two months, and some Antarctic cruises are 35-40 days. Is that exceptional? I do not think so. Normally marine geoscientists spend more time working at sea. For example, some colleagues working on the Spanish Oceanographic Institute have between two to four cruises per year. Considering how much they sail (as in other oceanographic institutions), I don't think it makes me special compared to the other researchers in marine geology.

Also, I've been on many field trips to outcrops. I am trying to combine field trips with modern marine basins as much as I can, which is something slightly different.

JR: Of all your research areas, where is your favorite?

FJHM: Onshore I really like the geology of Cyprus. Offshore in modern marine basins, there are several places, but Antarctica is really special.

JR: Where do you want to go next? What is next on your list?

FJHM: There are several places I would like to go and could go, for example we are trying to go to Angola for studying some new outcrops there.

JR: Why is *deepwater* the last frontier on Earth? How do we know more about the surface of other planets than deepwater areas (>200 m water depth) on Earth?

FJHM: Jon, you know well, to observe and analyze deepwater settings with the same resolution as we can image land, is very difficult. This challenge makes for a very different style of research. The resolution we cannot get there, and we cannot understand what we cannot see. This makes our interpretation partial and maybe wrong. In terms of knowledge, it is one of our last frontiers and every year researchers and explorers identify new things we've never seen before, because of our limitation to see the seafloor and subsurface in deep settings with good resolution. That's the point.

JR: Why is it so difficult to measure properties of Earth's oceans and their sedimentary processes?

FJHM: It is a combination of factors. Some processes are very easy to measure, but others are not. Trying to quantify sediment in suspension, or the strength of tides – that is relatively simple. But with gravitational processes, sediment gravity flows don't happen often and most of these processes are also very energetic. It is difficult to develop a technique that could work well in that energetic setting. Really it is a limitation, and a real challenge now.

It is not just our way of thinking, but now for example, let's move to the realm of the oceanographer. Many of them are interested in the surface or intermediate level of the ocean, yet very few are interested in the bottom of the ocean, the seafloor. Some, but not many. In general, physical oceanographers have not focused on what is happening just above the seafloor. Most of them consider that relief is controlling oceanic circulation, but not the other way around. Of course, there are limitations of getting to those depths, but understanding the processes on the deep seafloors has not been one of priorities yet. That is really changed now and new groups in Spain and Germany are focused on this topic. Also, other groups (as NOCS in UK) are trying to study modern turbidity currents. But still, as you know one of the missing parts is a better knowledge of modern processes and how they interact with each other.

JR: I admit it's difficult to keep up with you in the field. I was out of breath most of the time trying to keep pace on hikes with you during a field trip in the southern part of Spain. You do marathons, right? What is your PR?

FJHM: I used to run a lot (but not anymore!). Don't know how many miles I have done. Last marathon was in London in 2007, some time ago. I finished in three hours. But my best was when I much younger, when I did 2:45 in the Granada Marathon in 1988. It is a modest time compared to many others, but it was good enough for me.

JR: Those are speedy times, Javier. No doubt your fitness is one of the reasons you're so efficient in the field. On another topic, how do you prepare your students for successful careers?

FJHM: Yes, I try to prepare them for careers. Several training activities and courses were organized and also once per year we have a group field trip. I have tried to develop good courses on a high level, and try to involve students in those courses. Also, I try to push them to learn from other different groups and different perspectives.

JR: What is your message for ocean explorers today? For those in the broader energy business?

FJHM: It's not an easy answer. A quick answer should be for ocean explorers: to be open to new models and possibilities. Our knowledge and understanding of deepwater sedimentary systems has grown very rapidly and the interrelation between gravitational, hemipelagic and bottom current processes are proving to be more complex than previously thought. The reality is that there is still a lack of documented empirical data on the sedimentary processes in these environments. The monitoring and quantification of sedimentary processes, with the help of numerical models of gravity flows and bottom currents due to water mass circulation, are essential in the future to fully understand and quantify the dynamics of sediment laden water and the associated secondary oceanographic processes (eddies, deep-sea storms, deep tides, internal waves, etc.). A collaborative effort between academic and industrial partners is needed more than ever. Consequently, a symbiosis of science, environment and industry is essential for adopting new perspectives for the next generations and for coming decades.

JR: How can people learn more about deepwater depositional systems, including mixed systems – a blend of MTD, turbidite and contourite processes – in addition to the upcoming <u>AAPG GTW conference in Lisbon</u> in May 2023?

FJHM: We need more detailed work, and now is the time to work at a higher resolution for a better understanding of the facies, the processes and their timing. In contourite and mixed systems, we are just getting started and need very detailed work in seismic data, as well as from wells, bathymetry, core – basically more sedimentary analyses in different geological settings and areas. We need to identify more analogs in the field, and in the ancient record. There are a few mixed systems in the modern, yet almost none in ancient record. Some could be good candidates, yet there are still no analogs in the ancient record. No outcrops.

JR: Thank you so much Javier.

Above: Professor F. Javier Hernández-Molina discusses late Miocene bioclastic-siliciclastic deposits of the South Rifian Corridor, Rif-Betic Cordillera, Morocco. This outcrop belt is addressed more extensively in Capella et al. (2017) in *Sedimentary Geology* (https://doi.org/10.1016/j.sedgeo.2017.04.004) and in De Weger et al. (2020) in *Geology* (https://doi.org/10.1130/G47944.1) and De Weger et al. (2021) in *Sedimentology* (https://doi.org/10.1111/sed.12882). These outcrops are also featured in the modern treatise on the important and timely subject of deepwater sedimentary systems.

Entrepreneurship

Without entrepreneurship, society and humankind wouldn't make progress. Entrepreneurs build new companies to serve a human need. Entrepreneurs are met with varying levels of success. There are more failures than there are success stories. Entrepreneurship naturally aligns with The Explorer's Mindset since both explore new opportunities that didn't exist before the entrepreneur took that initial step of faith.

The word is often associated with building some new, external entity. However, entrepreneurship can be from within as well. This section dives into the entrepreneurial spirit with several key interviews highlighting important leadership traits of entrepreneurs in the geosciences and energy industry. These leaders exude the following traits in abundance, among other skills and talents that are useful in competitive industries: creativity, energy, risk tolerance, market knowledge, business savvy, salesmanship and courage.

Derek Adams shows how he takes his foundational experience in global exploration at a supermajor and uses these skills as CEO to positively change and transform the world of alternative energy, specifically geothermal energy.

Per Avseth is one of the top technical experts in seismic rock physics in the world, and, as CTO, has used his talents and thoughtful perspective on business to create one of the most successful companies in this space.

Tom Fett, a legend of the South Texas oil and gas industry, describes his journey with the largest service company in the energy industry and how he was able to innovate and sell products that helped operators achieve higher levels of success in their drilling programs.

These leaders are at the top of their fields in exploration and development, rock properties and downhole logging techniques – all skills required to analyze and understand the economic viability of subsurface resources. Their accolades and achievements are well-known and respected among their peers. They have taught their skills and passed on their knowledge at universities and to the next generation at some of the top universities and conferences around the world. Their entrepreneurial skills and experience will benefit anyone interested in putting skin in the game and creating a new business venture.

Derek Adams (November 2021)

"To develop a great team, the team needs to have common goals. They need to all be pulling in the same direction. No selfishness. That is key. You also need a diverse team. You need diversity of thought, different backgrounds, life experiences, etc. There is nothing worse than a team that all agrees with each other. That probably means you're missing something. You need disagreement, but not dysfunction. Everyone needs to feel comfortable enough to disagree, to be comfortable with being vulnerable in front of their team-mates and having the trust that that vulnerability won't be taken advantage of. It's a deeper level of teamwork." – Dr. Derek Adams

Derek Adams is the Co-Founder of EarthBridge Energy, a geothermal development company based in Houston, Texas. Previously he worked for ExxonMobil as a geoscientist for 10+ years where he took on a wide range of roles including: development and prospect appraisal work, regional exploration, seismic processing and reprocessing, petrophysics, and reservoir quality in both clastic and carbonate systems. A majority of his time was spent working in the US Gulf of Mexico and offshore Brazil salt basins where he developed a broad and diverse technical and business skillset. Derek has experience leading cross-functional and multi-cultural teams and possesses a strong entrepreneurial drive. He enjoys solving problems collaboratively to find innovative solutions to the world's current energy challenges. Derek earned his BS in Geological Sciences from New Mexico State University and his MS and PhD in Earth and Planetary Sciences from Northwestern University.

What do you do with an undergrad degree in geology? You can crush rocks. Not just any rocks, but billion-year-old carbonates collected from Australia to learn about ancient climate and ocean chemistry. The rocks I crushed were for Derek Adam's PhD thesis, so if there are any errors in the Nature Geoscience papers, I'm sorry Derek, it was probably me. That summer crushing rocks at Northwestern taught me how a research relationship works, between PI of the lab, the graduate leader of the study and lowest in rank – the rock crusher. Derek, despite being at one of the top schools in the world for geoscience, was always interested in my work and always took great care to teach the lab workers how to operate the equipment. It wasn't just so he could get great data; he enjoyed the teaching aspect and being able to grow the other person and equip them with new skills. I came away from that summer role with a new appreciation for the teamwork and setting required to do world-class research, thanks to Derek. Many years later, we're neighbors across town in the greater Houston area and collaborate frequently. Derek's leadership style has always stood out to me. He works very hard, yet is always available and approachable for those who work with him and for him. He's one of the most intelligent geologists I've ever met, yet he uses language that can be understood and appreciated by anyone in the business. His list of accomplishments is hardly humble, yet he isn't concerned about the past – only how his team's efforts can benefit the world and the next generation of energy consumers (and we're all energy consumers). While there are many other exceptional qualities of Derek and his work, his humor and self-deprecatory one-liners make working with Derek more like the boss you'd always wished you'd had. Derek is an Eagle Scout, which is not surprising considering he's cut from a similar mold as Rex Tillerson and other current and former CEOs leading major and independent companies around the world.

I spoke with Derek Adams, Co-Founder of EarthBridge Energy, in November 2021 to learn about exploration, career transition, leadership and most of all – geothermal technology and innovation. Anyone who has met Derek or read his work understands his in-depth expertise in exploration and development of energy resources.

Jon Rotzien (JR): Derek, I'm so thankful you had the time to visit today and share your story. Congratulations on EarthBridge Energy. Can you tell us more about your company?

Derek Adams (DA): Thank you for having me, Jon. A privilege and honor to be here. I think most people recognize that renewables are needed to achieve a net-zero energy future but they are currently unreliable. Also, society's demand for clean energy is ever-increasing. EarthBridge Energy solves both of these challenges by harnessing the nearly limitless energy inside the Earth. We are a Geothermal company aimed at rapidly scaling small- to medium-sized power plants to bridge the gap in intermittent renewable power generation, meeting society's current and future needs for clean energy. We do this by combining our deep knowledge of US Gulf Coast Sedimentary Reservoirs with highly-efficient drilling and completions technology developed in the oil and gas industry to harvest this underutilized resource. By integrating advanced power generation techniques, namely ORC (Organic Rankine Cycle) technology, and ubiquitous subsurface well control, EarthBridge can accelerate project timelines in order to scale geothermal adoption in a matter of years instead of decades. Our solution synergizes with regional CCUS (Carbon Capture Utilization and Storage) operations, green hydrogen production, and even wind and solar projects to magnify decarbonization efforts and expedite the energy transition.

JR: Did you know, while you were a PhD student at Northwestern, that you would be embarking on geothermal tech innovation a decade later?

DA: No, not specifically but I'm glad to have found this opportunity. I tend to focus on what's in front of me. Own a problem in the near term. As you get older, it becomes easier to have foresight, because ultimately you need hindsight to have foresight. I think they call it wisdom. I think it's ridiculous that we ask our 18-year-old selves to define what we'll do for the rest of our lives. My 18-year-old self did a decent job with the information and life experience I had at the time but there's always more you can do and learn. I honestly appreciate the path I've been able to travel.

JR: What are some of the barriers to geothermal energy, from the geosciences perspective?

DA: From a technical or scientific standpoint, geothermal shares many of the same challenges that oil and gas faces. There is indeed a lot of overlap between geothermal and oil and gas. When I say geothermal though, let me take a step back. In EarthBridge's case I'm specifically referring to utility-scale power production and/or large-scale direct use of heat. The word Geothermal encompasses a lot. There are many ways to utilize heat from the Earth. They essentially fall into 3 buckets: shallow heat pumps, electricity generation, and direct heat. Small-scale residential heat pump systems can regulate the heating and cooling in your home. Large-scale heat pumps can do the same for medium to large businesses, facilities, campuses, etc. Or in some places geothermal energy is used to heat entire cities. It depends on where you are, what the resource is like, and what type of energy is in demand. We're focusing primarily on utility-scale electricity generation, initially in the US along the Gulf Coast states. These are the same reservoirs, or the same plays if you will, that made the Gulf Coast onshore so successful in the oil and gas space.

We're different in that we're going after the hot water, brine really. There are a few different ways to extract heat energy, largely dictated by the geology and temperatures. Traditionally geothermal was focused on point sources of heat, geysers, steam coming out of the ground, volcanic areas. A challenge with that, similar to other renewables like wind and solar, hydro, etc., is that the energy resource may not be co-located with the customer or the population. Later, other methods like EGS (Enhanced Geothermal Systems) were developed where thermally induced fractures in the subsurface create a permeable pathway for hot water circulation. This method carries more overall risk because you need to explore for it, and once sufficient temperatures are found, the fractures may not connect the production and injection wells or may not provide a large enough conduit for the high rates of fluid circulation required. They also need to be careful about induced seismicity.

Our method of extracting heat is what's referred to as Sedimentary Geothermal where we use porous and permeable rock layers in the subsurface to circulate hot water. A production well sends hot water to an ORC (Organic Rankine Cycle) power plant at the surface, then cold water is returned underground in an injection well to be reheated again and again, creating endless energy. ORC is a type of binary power plant where the hot water from the reservoir flows through a heat exchanger with a fluid that has a lower boiling point than water, like isopentane or a refrigerant for example. This working fluid then boils and the vapor drives a turbine, which spins an electrical generator, is condensed back to a liquid, and returned to the heat exchanger to repeat the cycle. It's a completely closed system, so no emissions or waste and it pairs well with what are called low enthalpy, or low T, geothermal systems in the 100C to 200C range. In the end you need to get to high enough temperatures to be able to extract enough energy to generate this electricity. You also need good porosity, a large enough aquifer to draw upon such that you don't deplete the T over time and good enough permeability to achieve high enough flow rates. It's all about mass of heat energy per unit time. So, in a sedimentary basin, you need to drill deep enough for high temperatures and you also need your reservoir to be at that depth and have good RQ. Here along the Gulf Coast, we have over 20,000 feet of sedimentary fill to work with.

What are barriers? RQ, resource deliverability. Poro-perm and flow. I worked a lot at ExxonMobil on RQ, learned from some of the best experts in the field, and that passion has carried over to the geothermal world. With high temperatures though comes diagenesis. Your temperatures and RQ are at odds with each other. Typically, the deeper you go, the poorer the RQ, but that's often where you need to go for sufficient temperatures. We are very lucky to have the happy circumstance of moderate geothermal gradients and plenty of stacked reservoirs to choose from. In this sense, if you want to do Sedimentary Geothermal around the world, you need to be an explorer just like in oil and gas. The Gulf Coast is low hanging fruit because of the 10s of thousands of wells that have largely de-risked the resource but there aren't many places that have this kind of subsurface control. You're going to need seismic, wells, petrophysics, stratigraphy, reservoir engineering...almost all the same stuff, except you don't have to worry much about source, migration, or even a trap which is kind of nice. In a lot of ways, it's a simpler system than a hydrocarbon system but it's more challenging in other ways. It's harder in the flow rates for instance. From an energy density standpoint, hot water has less energy per unit volume or mass than that of oil or gas. You have to move more mass per time to get an equivalent commercial amount of energy out of the ground. Orders of magnitude higher flow rates ...10s of thousands of BPD. But it does work. There's a series of plants in Turkey flowing over 400K BPD!

JR: Gushers.

DA: Yep! So, you may need a lot of wells, or really good rocks, or you need really powerful pumps. Likely a combination, it's an optimization game. Just like oil and gas, front-end CapEx is high but there's thinner margins. You need to optimize to make a development as efficient as possible. The fewest number of wells with the highest temp waters, at the right flow rates.

JR: Where in the world is geothermal on the cutting edge of technology development?

DA: Here's the classic geoscience answer: it depends. It depends on what you're trying to do. The big up and coming thing that attracts a lot of press and a decent amount of VC money is 'geothermal anywhere'. Traditionally, where you can do geothermal has been limited in geographic extent. That's still true for the most part but is beginning to change, witness Gulf Coast Sedimentary Geothermal. But the idea of doing it everywhere has people excited, and for good reason. One way to do it is Closed-loop or AGS (Advanced Geothermal Systems). This is where the working fluid, the fluid used to drive the turbines and spin the generators, remains in the wellbore in a long heat exchanger that connects to the power plant system. There are some who are testing this now but it remains commercially unproven at this stage. This method relies on conduction for transferring heat energy which is not as efficient as convection, so it's a challenge from an efficiency standpoint. Sedimentary geothermal uses convection to transfer the heat which is more efficient, of course we need the injection well to talk to the producing well, which, if you've done your feasibility study right, shouldn't be a problem but it still remains a small risk. I say that but as an aside, you don't necessarily have to reinject back into the same reservoir. Let's say you're using a geopressured reservoir/aquifer. You could produce from that high pressure reservoir and reinject into a shallower or deeper reservoir assuming you're confident the aquifer you're producing from is very large or acts in an infinite sense. Remember, because of the stacked reservoirs, the Gulf Coast gives us that optionality. That being said, I honestly think that the technology needed to do geothermal everywhere, the thermodynamics, the drilling tech, etc. is a ways out but that's the holy grail. It's good that folks are working on it.

At EarthBridge we have a fast-to-market strategy. Use off-the-shelf but state-of-the-art technology to get projects up and running fast, to be able to make a difference now, not in 10-15 years. Our technology marries advanced drilling and completions techniques with ORC power generation, which hasn't been done before. We of course monitor the developments and if other designs become a better way to do things, integrate them down the line. Lastly, there is a lot of opportunity to improve efficiencies in operation with things like downhole sensors to optimize the system in real time. Applying tech like that can make existing systems that much better. Traditionally there hasn't been much tech transfer from oil and gas to geothermal. That's changing now and we plan to be first-movers in this space. We think there's a big opportunity here for geothermal to take a large step forward in market penetration and provide a renewable baseload power source in the near term.

JR: You studied oceanic anoxia under some famous scientists at NU, Sageman ("The Dude"), Hurtgen, Jacobsen. In fact, your research published in *Nature Geoscience* on carbonate associated sulfur isotopes is used in petroleum geosciences classes at UT Austin and South Dakota School of Mines. How has your experience and training in analytical geochemistry helped you along your career pathway?

DA: I'm humbled and honored that my research work in school is useful. Jon, I think the answer lies within the question. The analytical part. Doing any kind of chemistry or geochemistry, or geophysics where you're worried that your code is up to snuff... In the lab, you need to be very careful. From the physical day to day work, to make sure contamination doesn't happen. Following the proper methods, you need to be meticulous. You have to write everything down, etc. That, I think, is how an analytical mindset has carried me through much of what I've done in my career. Sometimes, even to a fault. In grad school, you're trained to find the right answer, the whole answer. You can work for years on one problem but often in industry, you need the 80% right answer, not the 99%. You need to know when to stop working a problem. You develop the wisdom to know what to work, what moves the needle in a big way. You can always cross all t's, dot all the i's but focusing on what is really critical in order to answer the business question at hand is what's needed.

Patience, also, is another one. Being able to plan fieldwork, go to the field, measure sections, be careful about sampling, labeling samples, preparing the samples in the rock lab, cutting, crushing them, powdering them, cleaning the machines, labeling bottles, then moving into the chem lab and, at least in my case, dissolving them all away, filtering, cleaning, more cleaning, then going to another even cleaner lab to work with a mass spec or other high-end piece of machinery, etc. etc. The whole thing is almost like you are a huge supply chain you need to figure out. Grad school taught me how to take ownership of a project. When something went wrong, that failure was all on you. Need to learn from those failures. Ultimately that's how we learn.

So yeah, starting with a hand sample, I ended up with a number spit out of mass spectrometer. The sheer amount of care needed to get accurate and precise results helped me get into industry. Subconsciously it helped me when I got there because of that experience. I knew there would be a long road to get to the answer. It really instilled a project management mindset. You see where you need to get, maybe you don't know exactly how to get there but you start planning out the steps. And sometimes some of those steps don't work and you need to adapt to get at the answer. The biggest difference between my academic career and my professional career is that in academia, you were your own team whereas in industry, it is literally impossible to achieve the things we needed to do alone, collaboration and teamwork is key. Oftentimes, a grad degree can be isolating. You're an individual doing your thing. Not the case in industry. One of the most important lessons I learned over the years in industry is collaboration. You succeed when you work well together with other people.

JR: You're an exploration and appraisal and development geoscientist by training, having worked at one of the best companies that rivaled BP for many years for best exploration company. Now, ExxonMobil is in a league of its own with incredible success offshore South America. How does your experience in finding and assessing oil and gas fields help with your new role at EarthBridge?

DA: I think part of that answer I just discussed. A big one is teamwork. Finding the right people to complement my skills and fill in gaps is key. It's definitely been key in our startup. Some of the most fun I had at ExxonMobil, was working the Gulf of Mexico (GOM) for a lot of my career. The GOM was a challenging place to work in the company because ExxonMobil has projects all over the world, so we had to compete within a global portfolio. Often the GOM didn't compete on paper compared to a lot of other plays. We had to be that much more rigorous and creative in the work we did. We were a little company inside of a company. It was there that I learned a lot about business.

I've heard from some within my network that their roles within their respective companies can be fairly well-defined and specific. At ExxonMobil, and in particular in my experience, I had to be very broad in the roles and experiences I had in order to be successful. I took every opportunity to learn and talk to other functions and groups. I think this likely had a lot to do with my personality. I'm super curious and love to learn and I also don't enjoy the monotony of doing the same thing over and over. So, I would go talk to the land teams, dig into the commercial side of things, the development planning. Try to really understand the whole picture and why decisions were made. Then I could guide our technical work to be the most useful, to inform the business decisions the best. "Work what matters" is the simplest way of saying that. And to work collaboratively as a team. You have to play to the group's strengths. Allow team members to do what they do well. Let everyone be their whole selves on the team, because they're going to bring life and professional experience to the team that's unique to them. They'll have unique perspectives that can help solve the problem or solve it faster or in a new way, a better way. Right now, understanding commercial and technical risk is central to my current role. Being extroverted by necessity – you need to do a lot of bridge building. ExxonMobil is a huge company, we had to do business within our group and do business with other groups within the company. Get to know them on a personal level, so you could arrive at your answer efficiently and to bring in perspectives beyond the technical considerations. Those networking skills, business development skills, are one of the biggest things I'm relying on now as a co-founder.

JR: I just reviewed the list of presentations from 2019-2021 for the Houston Explorers Club. You've had some impressive oil finders and upstream leaders speak at your luncheons, including Cindy Yeilding, Matt Furin, Susan Morrice, Carter Overton, Erik Oswald, Vicki Hollub on everything from the Explorer's Mindset to the Pikka-Horseshoe discoveries, to Pathways to Net-Zero. What's next for the Houston Explorers Club?

DA: Well, we've been around for 3 years now. We continue to bring in great folks to learn from. I think that is a key 'leg of the stool' of the club. I see the speakers as a catalyst for building relationships with other members of the club. I think the future of the club is to have a really great group of explorers that are genuinely interested in finding energy resources – many types of energy resources. It is no doubt the members will be building lasting relationships to create new exploration business ventures (from oil to geothermal).

Being inside a large corporate bubble, networking is key. Building an actual relationship with folks is so important. Important for an individual, but also the companies they work for. Often we think we can't or shouldn't engage with other players. And some companies are large enough that they might think they have all the answers. Inspiration can come from many places. Having an outside perspective on a technical or commercial problem can be crucial for success.

Going forward, we'll see more partnerships grow from the HEC, not only oil and gas, but also other forms of exploration in renewables. I think collaboration between oil and gas and renewables would be amazing. We can learn so much together to provide energy for the future. We can't go it alone.

JR: Leadership is an important theme, and has always been important in the geosciences and in the energy industry. How did your unique style of leadership develop? Did you gain insight from peers and mentors? Was it from your experiences in Scouting as an Eagle Scout?

DA: Yes. I think now that you bring that up…Scouts did build the foundation. It was extremely formative for me, just growing up. Honesty, integrity, courage, perseverance, the experiences I had and the people I had them with. Later, in my professional career, observing leaders and seeing how your boss leads in a company – how they lead both positively and negatively. There is a lot to be learned from leadership failure. Over the years, I tried to take the good bits I saw from some of the good leaders and mentors. The ones that I respected the most were probably the humblest. They were people that listened to others before giving an opinion on something. My own success and failure taught me a lot too. Failure is learning. I became a much better leader from things I did wrong and integrating all things that went well. Oftentimes you learn more from things that don't go well than from the things that do go well or you learn what works for that project, that team, in the moment, and you have to adapt quickly to a changing business environment.

In summary, I try to practice Servant leadership. The failure of a company is not because a leader didn't have an answer. The leader thought they had the answer, but they likely didn't empower their team to help them arrive at the right answer. Having a lot of trust between the team and whoever is calling the shots is so important. The foundation upon which all successful teams are built is trust. Trust between the team members and trust between the leaders and the team. A leader can't have a big head. Maybe that's part of the definition of integrity…being a leader that is willing to see the team succeed over any personal gain they might get out of it. If the team succeeds, the project succeeds, and the company succeeds. This is where my core motivation comes from. That's how I work.

JR: What are your perspectives on how to develop a great team?

DA: To develop a great team, the team needs to have common goals. They need to all be pulling in the same direction. No selfishness. That is key. You also need a diverse team. You need diversity of thought, different backgrounds, life experiences, etc. There is nothing worse than a team that all agrees with each other. That probably means you're missing something. You need disagreement, but not dysfunction. Everyone needs to feel comfortable enough to disagree, to be comfortable with being vulnerable in front of their team-mates and having the trust that that vulnerability won't be taken advantage of. It's a deeper level of teamwork. So, team building is important, early on in the relationship. There's no magic secret sauce for the actual thing you're doing to team build like going to ride go carts or something (though that sounds fun). You need to get your team to be – ultimately – friends. Maybe not 'outside-of-work' friends but professional friendship. Everyone respects and trusts each other and treats each other how they want to be treated. You'd be surprised how many people need to go back to being a child to re-learn how to integrate well with others. A leader needs to recognize the value of everyone on the team. From the people doing the not so fun grunt work, to the more senior person applying their wisdom to the problem. Everyone's opinion should be heard, valued and considered. Of course, you can't have a committee to decide everything but if you've built the team correctly, including the leadership, there should be a natural flow to things and you shouldn't need a whole lot of process to succeed.

JR: What is your message to students pursuing exploration geoscience as an area of study, or a career?

DA: There is a bright future for exploration geoscience, in oil and gas, renewables, academia, and government agencies. Geoscience is not going away. My message is if you enjoy geoscience, and you can channel that enthusiasm into what you're doing, you're in the right place.

As a student, if I could give myself advice, it would be to consider where what you're doing now is taking you. There are a lot of places you can go to with your degree. Maybe 5 main areas you could be working on. Of those 5, there are so many subdivisions or niches that need to be filled. Think about what is exciting you, not the actual action or work but the higher-level thing, analytics, communication, writing, critical thinking, teamwork, leadership, etc. You need to be motivated. Reach out to folks on LinkedIn, at a company you might want to work for. Maybe just look into the work that person is doing. Say, "Hey, I'm a student and I'd like to learn a little about what you do. Can I get 10 min of your time to ask you a few questions?" Don't worry too much about the questions. People are usually more than happy to tell you about what they do if they enjoy doing it. 90% of those people will give you an email back or have a conversation. I understand that it's hard to know what you want to do until you try it. While someone else's experience isn't necessarily going to be the same as yours might be, it will give you a chance to see how the work goes from day to day. What are pros, what are cons? Ask them if you "could go back in time and give advice to someone starting out?" Also, keep in mind that I'm but one voice, but there is a lot of wisdom and hindsight out there to help you get to where you want to go. Remember: you're not locked in to doing the same thing for the rest of your life. It's a big decision to get a job somewhere. If it's not for you, you can change. I'm living proof of that. You need to stay flexible and not get stuck in a rut because it's comfortable. Always challenge yourself.

JR: Thank you so much Derek.

Above: Gulf Coast reservoir intervals may be ideally suited to serve the sedimentary geothermal industry. This is a select cored interval of the Paleogene Wilcox Group, a classic felspathic litharenite sandstone commonly targeted for oil and gas.

Per Avseth (April 2022)

"I really think science is a lot about being creative, and exploring the unknown. Gantt charts are needed to some degree in many projects, but Gantt charts can kill creativity. You need to be able to make detours and new directions during research projects; this is what I refer to as "creative space" – which can last quite some time. Before you get to that, you need to load data, assess quality, have a feel for the data. This is the exploratory analysis. Then one should think outside the box, and be allowed to become a bit wild. And a team should brainstorm. I try to convey that to others – this mindset of the creative process. You can't always plan to get new bright ideas, but having that space opens up the possibility for new ways of thinking about the solution." – Dr. Per Avseth

Per Avseth is a geophysical advisor and CTO of Dig Science in Oslo, Norway, and a part-time researcher at the Department of Electronic Systems at the Norwegian University of Science and Technology (NTNU) in Trondheim. Per received his M.Sc. in Applied Petroleum Geosciences from NTNU in 1993, and his Ph.D. in Geophysics from Stanford University, California, in 2000. Per has more than 20 years of experience in the oil industry, and he was the SEG Honorary Lecturer for Europe in 2009. He is a co-author of the book Quantitative Seismic Interpretation (Cambridge University Press, 2005), and has published extensively in the fields of rock physics and AVO analysis. His current research focuses on basin-scale rock physics and integration of basin modeling, sedimentology and rock physics.

Per Avseth's leadership spans academic research, technology and business. His achievements across these disciplines are one-of-a-kind because he is so talented at integrating different aspects of technology and geoscience to provide solutions in very challenging subsurface scenarios. Avseth is one of the top researchers in quantitative seismic interpretation, and he applies his expertise across the upstream value chain. In fact, he wrote the book on the subject that is soon to be in its second edition. With such a command of a subject that enables petroleum exploration companies a better understanding on subsurface reservoir quality and fluid types, it was only fitting that he become an entrepreneur and build his own company, DIG Science, to provide solutions to the industry with a team of explorers and consultants, where Avseth serves as Chief Technology Officer. He is also a natural teacher, having co-advised over 30 MS and PhD university students, and he explains why it is valuable to remain active in the academic community. Avseth talks fluidly about seismic rock physics and is an award-winning keynote or invited speaker at applied geoscience conferences in Europe and around the world. He has a unique and creative approach of exploratory analysis that is used to solve difficult problems involving subsurface geology that he describes in the interview, making his methods among the most successful when dealing with exploration, in which many scenarios don't have readily available analogs. Avseth is very well-known and well-liked by the global energy and scientific community for his significant and valuable contributions to geophysics and basin analysis as well as his engaging and friendly personality. He made an immediate impact on writing the deepwater volume and was instrumental in completing a significant portion of the geophysics sections. While the high-level math and physics he applies can only be understood by a fraction of the energy industry, he makes the computation look so easy as he explains the solutions with his charismatic smile.

In April 2022, I sat down with Per Avseth to learn about quantitative seismic interpretation and what it takes to lead in the industry in technical results with DIG Science. Read the interview below.

Jon Rotzien (JR): Per, I'm so thankful you had the time to visit today. How did you get started in geophysics?

Per Avseth (PA): I think I have to go all the way back to my childhood. My father worked as a stonecutter and used to bring home rock samples from work. I was very fascinated by the different minerals and rock types. Then, a teacher in high school was very enthusiastic when he taught us how the mountains around us were made, first from the Caledonian orogeny, and much more recently by glacial erosion (I grew up in a small village with fjords and mountains all around). I was very curious about how the mountains and fjords had been generated over geological time. That's why I ended up studying geoscience at NTNU. Since Norway is a large oil and gas nation, petroleum geoscience was a natural choice, and during my studies I also learned about geophysics. In fact, the program was tailored for the industry, so I had a lot of geology and geophysics. My favorite class was in fact sedimentology, but I was also very fascinated by seismic wave theory. In my third year (1992), I had a project where I tested out one of the first versions of Hampson-Russell software, and learned about AVO. That I found very fascinating. This led me into an awareness of rock physics, and I found out about the Stanford Rock Physics group at Stanford University. I wasn't too keen on starting work after my undergraduate studies in Norway, so I applied for graduate studies at Stanford, and was very happy to be admitted to the Geophysics Department there in 1994, first in a Masters program, and later as a PhD student.

JR: Why did you choose Stanford to pursue your PhD?

PA: I was on a geology field trip to USA in the summer of 1993 (Utah, Colorado, Arizona, Texas), and was very impressed. In the same trip, I visited San Francisco and California, and fell in love with the area. The fall of '93 I completed my Master of Engineering degree at NTNU with an external Diploma Thesis at Norsk Hydro in Oslo. The thesis topic was on seismic interpretation, basin analysis and sequence stratigraphy of Lower Cretaceous rocks in the North Sea. I had a desire to learn more geophysics, and at this time Norsk Hydro performed some of the first ever 4D studies at Oseberg field in the North Sea, and they were a member of the Stanford Rock Physics Laboratory (J.P. Blangy was then working on data from Oseberg as part of his PhD thesis). When I learnt about this, and started reading rock physics papers from SRB, I was very fascinated, and started thinking that this could be very relevant for seismic interpretation. Hence, I was tempted to apply for a Master of Science program in Geophysics at Stanford University, and I was very happy to be admitted. Then, after I arrived at Stanford, I was convinced and encouraged by Professor Amos Nur to pursue with a PhD, and I was not too difficult to convince. I enjoyed Stanford very much, I loved the Bay Area, and I really liked the rock physics science I was diving into. Also, I was very enthusiastic about all the new doors that opened when I started to combine knowledge from sedimentology with rock physics, as I had one leg in the SPODDS (Stanford Project on Deepwater Depositional Systems) consortium, and one at SRB (Stanford Rock Physics and Borehole Geophysics laboratory) during my PhD. I was really at the right place, at the right time.

JR: And you chose to focus on geophysics – not something more meaningful like law, business – or deepwater sedimentology?

PA: I would say that my favorite topic is sedimentology, and I love going on sedimentology field trips. However, I also really like the more quantitative aspects of geophysics, and in particular I was very fascinated with AVO analysis. I realized that AVO is really an integrated methodology that requires both good geologic understanding and good geophysics/rock physics understanding. Hence, I wanted to strengthen my "geophysics leg" (after I had focused more on sedimentology during my undergraduate in Norway). I really wanted to become a jack of two trades (which is reflected in the title of my PhD thesis: "Combining Rock Physics and Sedimentology for Seismic Reservoir Characterization of North Sea Turbidite Systems"), and that served me well during my PhD, but also in my professional career later, it has been a great advantage.

JR: You've written the book on quantitative seismic interpretation with Cambridge, a global best seller, with Tapan Mukerji and Gary Mavko. What was your inspiration for creating the book? A monumental effort. It's in its third edition, right?

PA: It's actually only in its first edition still (2005), but we had a small update in 2010 (paperback), where we did some corrections. Tapan and I are currently working on the next edition. Hopefully it will be out in a couple of years. The book was inspired by a compendium Tapan and I put together for a graduate course at Stanford on something like "Quantitative Interpretation using Rock Physics", based partly on my thesis and on statistical rock physics research by Tapan. Cambridge University Press had a local office next to our Geophysics building, so we got the idea that the compendium could be made into a published book.

JR: How and when do you decide when the next edition will come out? Do you decide? Does the publisher decide?

PA: It's a little bit of both. Cambridge approached us around 2014-2015, which was about 10 years since it came out. They'll contact us proactively after so many years that it's time to do an update. Either the sales go down, or the info needs updating. Now it's 18 years since our book first came out. Time flies! The thing is, the book is quite popular, but sales I've imagined have gone down. I still get emails like, "I'm reading your book, it's very helpful." Regarding the timing of the book, it came out almost ahead of its time. When we were making the paperback edition original in 2010, it was just after I did an SEG Honorary Lecture tour in 2009. Attendees saw the book alongside my name, and it was good PR for the book – that lecture tour. The tour essentially gave it another boost. It prolonged the sales period of the book for more years.

I am trying to find time to work on the book updating, but time is precious and it is hard to find the spare time needed. I have 4-5 projects going on at the same time now and pretty much need to prepare for status meetings every week. I can't rewire mind to do chapter edits during the week. I'll see if I can put in some weeks at Stanford with Tapan and get the work done. We also hope that the next edition of the book can be used in more generic sense, in CCUS, geohazards, hydrogeophysics. In these topics, there should also be a market for good book sales. A lot of things still need to be updated. On shale rock physics, for instance, there has been a lot of research progress over the last 10-15 years. Also, we need to get the references updated, of course. Recently, there have been a lot of new studies in ML and DL – Tapan has done a lot on that too. I have the motivation to get these edits done, but it is hard to find the time. Time is the most precious resource.

JR: How has the field of quantitative seismic interpretation evolved over your 20+ year career?

PA: The foundation for quantitative seismic interpretation was already made by pioneering work by Han, Marion, Yin, Blangy, Doyen, and other graduate students in the rock physics group at Stanford University. Concurrent work at other universities, and the groundbreaking work in AVO for lithology prediction by Castagna, Hilterman and others, also played an important role. Standing on the shoulders of these giants, we took a step further by integrating rock physics, sedimentology, statistics and AVO into what we referred to as "Quantitative Seismic Interpretation". This integrated approach was picked up by the industry and further developed by several companies, into commercial software.

JR: Where is the science and tech headed today?

PA: Today we see even more integration of geology, basin analysis, with rock physics and computation statistics. Professor Henning Omre at NTNU embraced the use of AVO data and rock physics models together with Bayesian inversion techniques, and several of his students over the last 20 years have contributed with great advances in QI/QSI. Today we also see a big move towards using machine learning/deep learning in QI workflows, where rock physics and geology are integrated in highly non-linear ways, beyond what is possible for the human brain to analyze and to interpret.

JR: Did you know that you'd one day be the CTO of DIG? Did you grow up saying, "I'm going to one day be the CTO of DIG Science," or something to that effect?

PA: No, before I became a PhD student, I said to myself I will never do a PhD. Before I started my own company, I considered myself absolutely not a person with an entrepreneur's mindset. But I am always curious and open to testing out new things. I don't like to follow pre-defined strict rules, and I think when I realized that being a PhD student gives room and time to be free and creative, then I realized this was something I wanted to pursue. And a bit the same with running my own company (together with a handful of other great colleagues), it gives a lot of freedom to think and work in a creative space.

JR: You co-founded DIG Science four years ago and have consulted companies mostly in Norway, but also in other areas of the world, in prospect hunting, reservoir prediction and reservoir performance studies. How were you able to recruit and retain the expertise required for big projects at DIG Science?

PA: This is a tricky part. Over the past 4-5 years, we have experienced an oil-price crisis and COVID-19 crisis. Hence, we have had low ambitions for growth, and just been running the company as a small entity with a few projects. The last couple of years ('21-'22) we have seen an increasing interest, and we are now in a position where we need to think more about growth and upscaling. But we are still in a mode of "stone-by-stone" more than expansive growth. We'll see where we are in a couple of years.

JR: You're an active leader in the scientific community – you're invited to give many talks, courses and panel discussions every year with EAGE, SEG, CSEG and other industry organizations – including the Honorary Lecture tour. Why is it important to pursue these opportunities?

PA: I really enjoy keeping in touch with academia, and being in contact with fellow researchers in rock physics. Also, it is important to reach out and convey a message about the importance of rock physics during seismic interpretation and subsurface characterization. I enjoy teaching, and I also learn a lot from others when I teach or give talks to a wider audience with different perspectives. It's a win-win situation, I guess.

JR: You've held a number of leadership roles as an academic, too. Can you tell us more about your role at NTNU?

PA: I held an adjunct Professorship position from 2008-2020 in the Department of Petroleum and Geoscience, and I was the advisor of close to 30 master and PhD students during this period. This was a very fruitful position, and again a win-win situation. The students got to work with fresh data and relevant problems from the industry, whereas I got a chance to look at relevant problems that I didn't have time to investigate in detail myself. Now, I have a visiting researcher position at NTNU, in the Depth of Electronic Systems (Acoustics

Group), where I still co-advise some students, but also contribute with some relevant research.

JR: What are some of the current projects with the acoustics group?

PA: In the center for Geophysical Forecasting, there are all sorts of projects from geohazards, to CCUS, to earthquake research and many others. But the consortium directed toward oil and gas companies (GANES) solves issues related to the integration of geophysics, computational sciences, machine learning and much more. My research position is sponsored by this consortium since my adjunct position ended in 2020. My role is to co-advise PhD students, and work on projects including quantitative interpretation, inversion, computational statistics, rock physics and more specific geological projects – like one I'm working on in the Barents Sea on uplift and tectonics. There is a wide range of big-scale tectonic problems, geophysics physics to reservoir prediction. Martin Landrø is the PI, who is well-known for his work in 4D seismic monitoring.

JR: What is your favorite part of your job?

PA: Solving new problems, and seeing happy costumers that get their problems solved.

JR: Worst part?

PA: Bureaucracy, all the formal things that need to be taken care of, bad quality data that need to be handled before one enters the creative space of any data analysis, and time-consuming reporting, traveling and meetings.

JR: When you think about leadership styles in the industry, what are some of the most important traits of leaders – like those who lead companies like DIG Science?

PA: We have a very flat structure, but I lead the technology development. The most important thing, I think it is to give a lot of freedom, be open to alternative solutions suggested by the others, and stay away from detailed Gantt charts that can kill both ideas and creativity. At the same time, it is important to have a good strategy, a road map, where one finds time to focus on deliverables and customers need (i.e. balance between doing fun work in the creative space, and sometimes less fun work in the focusing/delivery phase of projects).

JR: How do you make time for the creative space? Many people think science is so much by the book and regimented – and boring.

PA: I really think science is a lot about being creative, and exploring the unknown. Gantt charts are needed to some degree in many projects, but Gantt charts can kill creativity. You need to be able to make detours and new directions during research projects; this is what I refer to as "creative space" – which can last quite some time. Before you get to that, you need to load data, assess quality, have a feel for the data. This is the exploratory analysis. Then one should think outside the box, and be allowed to become a bit wild. And a team should brainstorm. I try to convey that to others – this mindset of the creative process. You can't always plan to get new bright ideas, but having that space opens up the possibility for new ways of thinking about the solution. Or you go for running trip, or you wake up in the middle of night with a solution to a problem. You have to have time to do that. If you are in PowerPoint mode or working your butt off to finish a project, you don't have time to do that. And at the end, you have to get back to the real world and plug all the pieces together to make everything fit. So, you have these divergent views on things, and then you need to arrive at the convergent view. You need to connect the dots at the end. But you need to be able to draw crazy cartoons at first, and then finally bring it all together at the end.

I missed this feeling at university when we had exams. That way of working is often neglected. I found at Stanford much more room for being able to think of ideas and work creatively on projects. Maybe this is just acceptable in a PhD setting. But in courses also, you should work with other people. In courses the problems are often predefined. But in real life, you also need to explore what is the problem. So, your role as a scientist, whether you work in the industry or in academia, is not only to find the solution, but also define what's the problem.

JR: Norway has a rich history of oil and gas E&P as you mentioned. One of my favorite cities in Norway is Stavanger – with that excellent oil museum that has many of the original pieces of hardware from Ekofisk, Edvard Grieg, Troll, Valhall. I'm sure you've been.

PA: Yes, indeed. I like Stavanger, but I spend more time in Trondheim which is the technology capitol of Norway. Trondheim also usually has nicer weather than Stavanger.

JR: I always thought it was just either rainy and temperate or cold in all of Norway all the time.

PA: Well, Trondheim is inside a fjord, and commonly you get wind from the southwest, but Trondheim is hidden behind mountains. Hence, you end up with more sunny days actually. It is milder and warmer than Stavanger.

I have a cabin not far from Trondheim, so I often combine work trips to Trondheim with some leisure time at my cabin. I've never lived in Stavanger, but I have a lot of friends there. I also lived in Bergen for 12 years. Bergen is less windy, but rainier than Stavanger and Trondheim. Now I'm based in Oslo, where weather is even nicer.

JR: How is the offshore E&P industry changing in Norway when it comes to the next 10, 20, 30 years of offshore activity? How about for the broader energy business offshore – not just for oil and gas E&P?

PA: There is a change happening as we speak. There is less focus on exploration in new areas, more near field exploration and improved oil recovery. There have been several mergers lately (Spirit-Sval and Lundin-AkerBP), and we will likely see more consolidation. We still have at least 20-30 years with the petroleum industry in Norway, and it will be important for our welfare, jobs, and for the energy security in Europe during the transition age to the renewable society. I see today's situation as a springboard into the future, both economically and technologically, and not least in terms of improved sustainability and for a cleaner environment. I disagree with those who see the oil industry today as a threat and a sleeping pillow when it comes to the climate challenges we are facing.

JR: Did you have a favorite class at Stanford while you were a student? What is your favorite class you teach now at NTNU?

PA: My favorite class was "Sedimentary Basins" by Steve Graham. He is the best teacher I ever had, and thanks to him I really got a good understanding of the greater picture. Don Lowe's class on "Sedimentary Processes" I also enjoyed very much, and helped me better understand the small-scale details. And then of course "Rock Physics" taught by Gary Mavko was just so enlightening and eye-opening, and really these three courses today defined my "mixed" expertise in Quantitative Seismic Interpretation. But at Stanford we could also select some "obscure" volunteer classes. For instance, I enrolled in a class called "Urban Plunge" where part of the curriculum was to spend 2 days and nights as a homeless person in San Francisco. That was also a very eye-opening experience. At NTNU, I only taught a course on Reservoir Geophysics during my time as Adjunct Professor. Now, I do some guest lectures every now and then.

JR: The urban plunge?

PA: It was a class of mostly undergrads, but it was also open to graduate students. I think there were two grad students, overall, 15-20 took the course. It was an older guy who was running course, and he actually had been homeless himself. He had been living in the street, and now he was a lecturer. It was part of the course on social injustice, focusing on *why are people homeless*? There were quite a few homeless people living in Palo Alto at that time. The class discussed *Why are so many homeless in San Francisco and Bay Area*? And there are many reasons, but overall, it is a place where they're treated with some dignity compared to other places. So, they escape more hostile places and come to San Francisco. Also, the climate is better. Part of the course discussed that if one is unlucky, anyone could end up in the streets. Part of the course was to spend two days in the streets in San Francisco. That year, it was medio May I remember, and it was a record warm day – above 100 degrees in downtown San Francisco! The week leading up to the two days, we were told, "Don't shower, don't shave." So, we actually looked like homeless people. We were able to walk around and sleep in the street. During the night, police came and kicked us, told us we were not allowed to sleep in the street. We practiced panhandling, asking for money. Some of the other stuff we did was we would stop people along the sidewalk, and ask something simple – like directions. And the citizens would just raise their hands kind of telling us, "Stop, don't get near me." They might have assumed we'd knife them or something. It was a common reaction to homeless people. It was the most interesting experience..

There were one or two homeless sleeping with us, showing us around. Suddenly, and within a few hours, the outside world we had just come from was the people walking streets. And we were part of the insiders group. I had always been on the other side looking at poor people, and now we were actually seeing it from that side. It forces you to see it from that perspective. It makes you become empathetic with that side. I also met people who went to shelters and food stations. Some came in suit and tie and looked nice. But they were homeless. They were in a suit because they didn't want to look homeless. The only thing that revealed their homeless status was their shoes. Because when you are homeless you walk a lot, and your shoes tend to look tattered. Several women, also homeless, looked well dressed. They probably had been divorced, and perhaps the husband took everything. They too were out on the streets. They had been living successful lives, but one incident had changed their life. It is difficult to become homeless in Norway because of our welfare system. Another thing is that everyone in the US has a car, so many of the homeless would live out of their car. They went to work, but they were still homeless. It's a big problem in San Francisco, and a big problem in the US. This is one of the bad sides of the US, though there's lots of good things. This course I took was something very different, and I appreciate the experience.

JR: How do you prepare students and mentees for successful careers?

PA: I tell them about the situation in the industry, and that there will be plenty of need for their competence in the years to come. I also warn them about the volatility, but regardless the knowledge in petroleum geoscience is generic, and can be applied to CCS, geohazards, ocean bottom mineral exploration, etc. So, there will be work for them regardless of what happens to the oil industry in the years to come.

JR: And now oil is bouncing around with supply and demand forces out of balance.

The Explorer's Mindset

PA: The volatility in the energy market is not sustainable over longer periods. Indeed, we need to change something, but petroleum is still very important in a transitional period to a future energy market dominated by renewables. I know students studying petroleum, and they are ashamed to talk about their own degree. When asked, they choose not to say it's about petroleum. But the world need energy. A lot of people take it for granted. And we see it now in Europe and over the world. There's an energy crisis. Everyone has to pay a lot more for oil, gas, products that use petroleum, etc. and the critics are saying, "What's happening! We should have cheaper energy!" They're shouting. And it's all about supply and demand. Now demand is bigger than supply. Regardless of COVID and the war in Ukraine, China and India are still on the rise. Millions of people are getting out of poverty and energy poverty. Millions more people are able to afford a car and fridge and good medical care, and a good life, which requires energy. It's taking a toll.

JR: What is your message for oil and gas explorers today? For those in the broader energy business?

PA: Be open for change. Think outside the box, because there is no box. The digital revolution is over us, so get familiarized with new digital technology, machine learning aspects, etc. Also be open for a move or change to topics beyond oil, where your competence can be very valuable.

JR: What would you like the energy community to know about Per Avseth?

PA: I am mostly motivated by the passion for science and knowing the truth, and always curious to expand my knowledge, and explore the unknown. I have a creative mind, and find a lot of creative space in the border areas between established disciplines. That's why I love cross-disciplinary work. Also, I have a passion for people, and working for the greater good. That's why the energy need in the world is part of the bigger picture that motivates me every day. Poor people are lifted out of poverty due to access to energy, and oil and gas have played a very important role in reducing poverty around the world over the last 50-100 years. However, I also hate exploitation, narrow-mindedness, selfishness. Unfortunately, oil has also been a source of war, conflict, and exploitation around the world, and now we also have the climate crisis that is partly caused by humans increasing consumption of fossil fuels. I have strong opinions around these challenges, but I am also positive that technology, science and enough people thinking about the greater good will help us to avoid catastrophe. At the end, the good will always win over the bad and evil, I think. I'm an optimist.

JR: Thank you so much Dr. Avseth.

Tom Fett (July 2020)

"Interestingly in those early days, there was great debate over whether turbidite reservoir quality rocks were to be found along the Texas Gulf Coast. Bob Berg of Texas A&M was finding turbidites in cores from the McAllen Ranch in the south, to the Hackberry in the north and in between in the "canyons" in Lavaca County. He based his interpretations on a powerful analysis of sedimentary structures, texture, grain size, composition and sequences. Most Texas geologists were not familiar with turbidites – and many refused to describe the reservoirs as such. To side-step these issues, I developed a purely descriptive system and just described generic "channels, fans and bars," which allowed me to predict sand body type, orientation, shape – and even size and scale using my dipmeter data without getting involved in the great turbidite debate. Later developments in 3-D seismic acquisition and interpretation by Pete Vail and Henry Posamentier and others have nicely supported this approach." – Tom Fett

Tom Fett graduated from Trinity University in 1966 with a degree in Engineering Science and went to work for Schlumberger Wireline Services as an Open Hole Field Engineer in South Texas. Tom was promoted to District Manager in North Texas and then transferred to Corpus Christi as the Sales Development Engineer for Dipmeter Applications. While in South Texas, Tom taught graduate-level courses in log analysis for 10 years as an Adjunct Professor at Texas A& I University in Kingsville, TX. Tom is a registered Professional Engineer in Texas. He has been active in various industry societies, including the AAPG, SEPM, SIPES, SPE and SPWLA. With SPWLA he served two terms on the National Board of Directors. He has always been active in local societies and has led and attended numerous geological conventions, short courses, and field trips. He recently served as President of the San Antonio Geological Society and as Chairman of the local SIPES Chapter. Tom authored several papers on log analysis and the geological applications of wireline measurements, especially those of various diameter and imaging devices. Tom's early career was primarily in Texas, where he was directly involved with the introduction of the first digitally recorded Dipmeters, the Formation MicroScanner (FMS), and the Formation MicroImager (FMI). During this time, Tom was involved with the early delineation of fracturing. He analyzed the first commercially acquired FMS acquired in a horizontal well. This led directly to the horizontal drilling boom in the Austin Chalk. With the introduction of borehole imaging devices, significantly improved stratigraphic interpretations became possible. In 1992, Tom transferred to the international staff as Division Geologist in Australia and then to Saudi Arabia. He has worked on projects on six continents. In 2000 Tom retired from Schlumberger and began a career as a Geological Consultant where he developed a special interest in deepwater sedimentation. He authored a section on "Borehole Imaging" in Chapter 16 in the recently published *Deepwater Sedimentary Systems: Science, Discovery and Applications.*

Tom Fett is an icon of South Texas oil and gas drilling. I first met him during a visit to the San Antonio Petroleum Club.

"Now this is how you want to start the buffet, Jonathan," Tom told me with a smile, as he handed me a plate. There were salads, there were crudites, there were pastas, there were soups, there were so many different proteins. It was overwhelming. No doubt you need someone to guide you through this veritable pantheon of food, and Tom's gregarious nature and willingness to welcome a new guest to town are part of his winning attitude. You can't say no to Tom's enthusiasm and charisma. With the endorsement from Tom on the high-quality lunch options, my eyes were bigger than my stomach. And then there were the desserts. Packed up on stage to give the talk, I'd wish I'd worn my Thanksgiving sweatpants. Welcome to San Antonio! I was in San Antonio that day at the Petroleum Club to deliver a presentation. Like any other petroleum club, there was great food, but the San Antonio Petroleum Club has the *best* buffet of any petroleum club in North America. It was my first time to San Antonio in a long time, and a first time to the Club. After that buffet, and meeting Tom, I couldn't wait to get back to *San Anton'*.

Tom's blessing is a blessing you want. If Tom likes you, you feel like you're supercharged with his unmitigated enthusiasm and hard-charging kindness. Tom creates one of the most positive atmospheres in a meeting. This charisma is an exceptionally rare attribute, and no doubt, is one of the reasons Tom has been so successful in all his endeavors – from the industry to family to inspiring others to achieve great things in energy.

Since that first meeting in San Antonio in 2017, Tom and I made fast friends for our equally curious attitude toward deepwater sedimentation. Tom was part of the original crew of Texan turbidite specialists who worked to characterize deepwater reservoirs vs. all the other types of reservoirs found in the subsurface along the Texas coast. Tom is among the most well-known and well-connected industry professionals I know. If he didn't have the answer himself, he'd find a way to get in touch with the top specialists and leaders in the broad field of geoscience – Coleman, Fisher, Boyd, Gilreath, Weimer, Galloway, Scott, Suter, Snedden, Tinker, Kerans, Berg, LeBlanc, Bouma, Slatt, Hays, Nilsen, Vail, Posamentier, Selley, Serra – legends in their own right. Just as I admire Tom's assessment of anything petroleum related, these legends likely feel and felt the same way about Tom. That's just part of how Tom makes everyone feel as if they're the most important person in the room. It's a joy to be around him, and to learn from him. His perspective is never shy; his answers are always clear and direct; it is the person you wish you'd had as a boss or colleague on your team your entire life. And if not a teammate, you wish you'd had his advice before, during and after drilling any well.

In this interview Tom Fett shares with us his fascinating experiences on all oil-producing continents. Mr. Fett spent 32 years with Schlumberger, including serving as Dipmeter Champion for the Texas Gulf Coast, and is one of the leading authorities on logging tools and geological interpretation. Anyone who knows Mr. Fett understands he has made numerous contributions to understanding the petroleum geology of the Gulf Coast and around the world, and continues to inspire the next generation of oil finders to new heights as a consultant, upstream industry leader and instructor for oil and gas industry technical courses. You'll learn about Gulf Coast oil and gas basins, the merits and limitations of various logging tools, and the importance of collaboration in applied geosciences to develop new technology.

Read the interview below from June 2020.

Jon Rotzien (JR): Mr. Fett, I'm so thankful you had the time to visit today and share some of your experience in the global energy industry. You have 50+ years of experience (32 of them with Schlumberger), a background in petroleum engineering, and have contributed to oil and gas studies on all oil-producing continents. Could you share more on your background, and what led you through your various roles?

Tom Fett (TF): I graduated from Trinity University in 1966 with a BS in Engineering Science and went to Schlumberger and worked for them for 32 years. When the Schlumberger recruiter came to Trinity, he mentioned that no two days with Schlumberger would ever be the same! He was right! I enjoyed every day with Schlumberger. Great people from all over the world.

While I started my career as an engineer, I received world-class training as a petrophysicist. I got to spend time every year with the top log interpreters in the world including Tixier and Alger. Early on I realized that geology provided the framework on which you can hang all the various parameters needed for oil and gas evaluation. I found myself more and more getting into geology. I have always enjoyed it, and still do.

JR: It's an enjoyable field for sure. Did you spend time in the field early in your career?

TF: I spent six years in the field, mainly in South Texas. After six months I was managing a crew of my own. I made hundreds of jobs in that six-year period and learned about the oil and gas industry as well as log analysis and geology.

Fortunately for me the induction and density logs were being introduced and log analysis became more of an exact science. The dipmeter tools were being improved at a rapid pace. Even as a young engineer, I was often consulted on whether to set pipe and where to perforate.

In 1972, I was asked if I wanted to go to Graham in North Texas as a manager. I accepted and in three years, I was able to take it from a one-truck location to a six-truck district.

JR: That's incredible growth! How did that happen?

TF: While there we introduced the first fully computerized trucks and used dipmeters to define Mississippian reef systems and to chase Atoka channel systems, while continuing to learn new geology in a new area (for me) of Texas. Which is good because after six years in South Texas, I was starting to think I knew the geology! While in Graham, I put together in-house papers with water saturation, porosity and permeability cut off values for geological formations, as well as other useful items to have in a database. I was on another steep learning curve and remember always carrying a glossary of geological terms. I enjoyed always hearing the precise, colorful nature of geological descriptions and enjoyed my conversations with the mainly independent operators.

In 1975 Schlumberger offered me a position in Corpus Christi to work in sales. I was asked *who could be a good candidate for a dipmeter champion*. It sounded pretty good to me, so I became the Dipmeter Champion for the Texas Gulf Coast, and occasionally for West Texas and parts of Louisiana. That's really what I've been doing ever since, even in my consulting days. After about 15 years in Corpus, and 25 years with the company, I had a chance to go international and moved to Melbourne, Australia.

JR: Down under! How did you continue to grow as a geologist during this time?

TF: All this time I was attending short courses, going on field trips, attending conventions, seminars, etc. No one complained because we were making a good money with dipmeters and I was going to these education events on weekends and after hours. It was a great learning process. Best of all, I got to hang out with a whole lot of world-class geologists – including Jim Coleman, Bill Fisher, Don Boyd, Al Gilreath, Paul Weimer, Bill Galloway, Al Scott, John Suter,

John Snedden, Scott Tinker, Charlie Kerans, Bob Berg, Rufus LeBlanc, Arnold Bouma, Roger Slatt, Miles Hays, Tor Nilsen, Pete Vail, Henry Posamentier, Dick Selley, Oberto Serra, – and remain friends with and an admirer of all of them. Recently the many great scientists at the BEG (Bureau of Economic Geology) have helped me continue my learning curve. And of course, you Jon – my go-to guy about deepwater sedimentation!

JR: Tom, that's way too nice of you. They've truly made leaps in our understanding of geology and the subsurface.

TF: I got to work with lot of fine independents, and the majors such as Exxon and Shell. Shell has always been good about publishing, Exxon not so much; but while working with the more senior geologists at Exxon, I had access to the Exxon knowledge base. They shared information on growth faulting and really helped me with my understanding of coastal and deepwater systems.

Interestingly in those early days, there was great debate over whether turbidite reservoir quality rocks were to be found along the Texas Gulf Coast. Bob Berg of Texas A&M was finding turbidites in cores from the McAllen Ranch in the south, to the Hackberry in the north and in between in the "canyons" in Lavaca County. He based his interpretations on a powerful analysis of sedimentary structures, texture, grain size, composition and sequences. Most Texas geologists were not familiar with turbidites – and many refused to describe the reservoirs as such. To side-step these issues, I developed a purely descriptive system and just described generic "channels, fans and bars," which allowed me to predict *sand body type, orientation, shape – and even size and scale* using my dipmeter data without getting involved in the great turbidite debate. Later developments in 3-D seismic acquisition and interpretation by Pete Vail and Henry Posamentier and others have nicely supported this approach.

Somewhere along there, I started writing papers about practical dipmeter information, stratigraphy, fractures, etc. At that time the Austin Chalk was booming, but I got in on the ground floor of that, and there was a lot of demand for papers on that. In the stratigraphy paper I wrote in my early days, I naively thought there would be indicators that always could be found in alluvial fans, rivers, deltas, barrier bars, deepwater depositional systems – and things you'd never see. I decided to poll several people including Galloway, Fisher, Selley and others. I sent them a questionnaire regarding what they thought they *would* and *would not* see in each of those depositional systems.

JR: Those are multi-million-dollar questions. What did they say?

TF: They all kindly responded, and to my surprise there were no magic bullets for that! And exceptions to most of those rules. Nevertheless, it was an interesting experience.

JR: Very nice, and we continue to pursue those key truths.

TF: In 1979 I wrote a paper on log interpretation. And I have to say the trick to having a successful paper is having right title! I named this one *Log Evaluation of the Tight Rocks of South Texas*. Another hint is to always put *practical* in there! This GCAGS paper was picked up by Oil and Gas Journal and World Oil, so I got a lot of mileage out of that paper. And it is still pretty much a basis for my rules of thumb on log interpretation.

At that time, the Austin Chalk deal was going strong, I was lucky enough to be involved in the first horizontal FMS in the Pearsall Field. This was the first horizontal FMS run in the world and set the stage for the first "unconventional resource play" in the Austin Chalk. When you're suddenly producing 3,000-4,000 barrels of oil per day, you naturally want to try to keep it tight.

JR: Can't let the word out.

TF: We put the logs on a 25"/100' scale paper scale. On weekends, when no one was around, we'd lay it out in the office hall. In fact, it was so secret that the management would not even let their own employees see it for a while.

This was the FMS which started as a 2-pad device, and is now a 4-pad dipmeter device. It was tailor-made for delineating fractured reservoirs.

JR: Those are used all over the world now. Any unusual parts of the job you'd like to share?

TF: One fun part of my job was that every year Schlumberger we had a meeting in Paris. The aim was to figure out what we needed in software, processing, presentation, etc. For 10 years, I got to go to Paris once a year, spending a week there. Of course, my wife had to come with me. These meetings were filled with very smart people – almost too smart. The field guys like me often needed to steer them in a practical direction.

Oil-based mud (OBM) at that time was becoming extremely popular in South Texas. Unfortunately, the dipmeter tools didn't work well in OBM. We designed knife blades on the sensors to cut through the OBM mud cake. This innovation was developed in South Texas. Since much of our area was prone to High Temperature (and High Pressure) and the dipmeter tool was only rated at 350°F during a good day, we had to develop a flasking system that would work up to 400°F. We would cool the flask, and then rush it into the hole. Now, the industry employs a whole suite of high temperature tools, but the first ones were developed in South Texas at this time.

From my field engineer days on, I was lucky to see many things from the ground level up and to help develop the practical application of these advances. With the induction and density logs, you can come up with accurate water saturation and porosity values. That was a big development. When I went to work, we were still running the ES logs. These new measurements were a major step forward in log analysis – and the same was happening with dipmeters.

JR: No industry employee can really imagine a world without that technology today. You mentioned earlier in your career you had a thesis to write. Can you explain that?

TF: Back then Schlumberger had a European-style system of advancement. You wrote a "thesis or GFE paper" early in your career and had to defend it to upper management. I did mine on the *Geology of Webb County*. It was timely as it came right before a big boom in the Wilcox, which included the Lobo in Webb County. It was another big step in my transition to becoming a geologist.

Over the years I worked all over the world, mainly in North America, the Middle East, Australasia, but also some in Europe, Africa and South America – six continents in the end. I elected to retire from Schlumberger in 1999.

JR: All the oil-producing continents. You really can't beat that. Could you elaborate more on the development of dipmeter and borehole imaging services in the industry?

TF: As I mentioned, I was lucky enough to be in on ground floor of many early developments of the dipmeter family of tools. All dipmeters are oriented and it takes three points to define a plane. With dipmeter data, structure can be determined with a single well – a longtime dream of geologists everywhere.

I was able to witness the development of the dipmeter family – from the 3-arm CDM (with 3 oriented curves), to the 4-arm HDT, to the 6 sensor SHDT (stratigraphic high-resolution dipmeter tool), and then the multi-sensor FMS and FMI as well as the acoustical imaging tools. The SHDT for the first time allowed us to do detailed stratigraphic work. The FMS allowed us to "see" sedimentary features and fractures, and FMI made it even better.

Very precise orientation and computer processing allowed better computations and greatly improved the presentations. The advantages of these multiple pad tools allowed computational redundancy and speed corrections.

JR: But oil-based mud still presents a problem, as you've mentioned.

TF: The oil-based mud problem is still with us. New tools designed especially for OBM have proven worthwhile for structure and tectonics, but still have a problem detecting fractures since we lose the high resistivity contrast between the fluids in the fractures and the surrounding rock.

Let me tell you about an interesting piece of history when we first started doing fracture analysis with the HDT tool. We had observed that in fractured reservoirs the natural rotation of the tool resulted in different activity on orthogonal sides of the borehole. We realized we could take the dipmeter curves and by overlaying orthogonal pads, we could deduce that this was due to fracturing. We could also orient these fractures. The technique worked great in the Austin Chalk. We called the new log the *Fracture Identification Log* or FIL. The FMS and FMI tools greatly improved fracture detection and delineation.

JR: What do you think are the next big developments in subsurface evaluation and imaging techniques? What technology do we need to better grasp in order to achieve these goals?

TF: Well Jon, that's the $64,000 question isn't it! I have been fortunate enough to see major improvements in basic petrophysical evaluation. We have many new and improved high-tech tools including nuclear magnetic resonance and dielectric measurements, spectral gamma rays, lithology scanners, borehole rotary coring tools and greatly improved formation testing. Major strides have been made in all these areas and these new tools are very useful, but more must be done.

The age-old problem in petrophysical evaluation has been permeability and lithology. Though we have gone from rather rough estimates to quite precise and easily determined values and have made great strides all the while; we are not there yet. If there are to be new major developments, they will likely be in two areas. One is better vertical resolution. Most logs have a nominal one- to two-foot vertical resolution. One clear advantage of the dipmeter tools is good vertical resolution. For instance, the nominal resolution for FMS is one cm, but for high contrast events, we can see things down to a millimeter! In the right cases, and as you get familiar with the formation and lithology as we did with the Austin chalk, we can even detect features of less under one millimeter. But we still cannot see micro fracturing, so there's work to be done.

Some of the existing improvements include getting a really good value of porosity from density. With the newer sonic tool, you see the effects from the shale and improve your evaluation of rock properties. The neutron logs let us understand gas effects and lithology. The density and neutron combination lets you determine lithology and porosity on the run, as in complex lithologies where you are often going from limestone to dolostone, limestone to chert, etc.
We have developed mechanic rotary coring tools. These tools greatly reduce the shattering the rock which can create fractures and alter porosity. With these tools we can get exceptionally good values of

porosity and permeability. Permeability has been a long-term problem, and these mechanical coring devices are especially useful.

Evaluating the role of fractures is critical to understanding both conventional and unconventional reservoirs, and the image logs have provided a tool that allows us to evaluate fractures down to 1 millimeter in width. Still more needs to be done. Fractures are important; both the natural and drilling-induced ones, but also the hydraulically induced ones produced in the massive frac jobs that are now the norm. The past and present-day stress systems are also very important, and can be understood using imaging devices.

There have been lots of improvements in formation testing as well. We used to only get one try per trip in the hole. Now we can do multiple with one trip in hole and even monitor the fluid types in real time. We can even do it while drilling with LWD tools.

OBM is still very popular. The engineers love it and will keep using it. With OBM you lose the SP and some imaging details which are an important tool for basic log analysis. On the other hand, OBM does create much better hole conditions, which allows better measurements for many borehole tools. One thing I personally really would like to see is improved measurements in OBM for dipmeters where fracture detection is still a major problem. The latest developments in 3-D seismic analysis are very exciting, but that's not really my area of expertise.

JR: With these source rock reservoirs and tight sandstone plays, known to many as unconventional plays, our subsurface logging tools in some cases cannot adequately assess the rock and fluids they hold. It always seems like a tricky game the teams have to play to get the tool data to match the rock and fluid data – very different from most conventional reservoir intervals. It seems like our tools are failing us. How can we better determine rock characteristics (porosity, rock type, fluid type and saturation) in plays like the Wolfcamp, Bone Spring and Avalon?

TF: The operators, particularly in horizontal wells, always want more. They need it to make better business decisions, especially in these trying times. They need better coring and testing. This can be done in horizontal holes, but it is complicated and expensive. Fortunately, in highly deviated holes, the unidirectional density tool does a good job on porosity. Other new omnidirectional and oriented tools, as in the scanner family of tools, are helping. New measurements are routinely being developed, but their application remains a challenge. Then, there's the problem of scale. We usually make measurements with roughly one- to two-foot vertical resolution, but operators want and need inch-by-inch information. Much can change in a foot. What one value is representative of that interval? And you may not even be able to establish a good value from core or outcrop.

You need to know where to pick your core sample (plug). It very much matters where you take your measurements. The answer everyone tends to use is computer processing and statistical analysis, but can we really trust that? I would rather have you look at it, analyze it, use your judgement, move it up or down a little, rather than have that computer make the judgement. Note that the method takes time and experienced judgement.

Engineers always want specific numbers for their model. They tend to believe the measurement down to several decimal places. My experiences as an acquirer and utilizer of these measurements make me pretty nervous. The best way you could resolve it is really having people who know what they are doing. You need someone who truly understands the rocks and can quality control the data. What we often get is someone who sits down at a computer and upon getting the numbers and pretty colors just presses the print button. We need to *both* get these answers and provide judgement for using them.

"Where oil is first found, in the final analysis, is in the minds of men" (Pratt, 1952).

In these days with the internet, it is much easier to review the thoughts and achievements of those who preceded us. Have you noticed lately, however, that it is getting harder and harder to ask the right question to get you past the many pages of Google searches which are only trying to sell you something? I have found that the best thing is to add limiting phrases like "geology" to your search. Even then you will probably need to access the actual publications of the various societies (AAPG, SPE, SEPM, SPWLA, etc. and my personal favorite – the GCAGS *Transactions*) to get the good stuff. For me, the most productive way of assimilating this knowledge has always been to attend society meetings, short courses, field trips, seminars and conventions. Not only that, but these meetings are also a lot more fun.

We live in a time where we are literally in the midst of huge clouds of data and information. Computers are indeed necessary to access and organize the ever-growing number of facts, but computers cannot think. My early experience with Artificial Intelligence (AI) in some early day attempts to pick Schlumberger's Al Gilreath's brain about dipmeter interpretation, convinced me that the final answer was a long way off. I still feel the same.

If we are to utilize the principle of *uniformitarianism* to understand the present and to predict the future, we need to know how to use all this newly "easily accessible" information. That to me is where the real future of our industry lies, still "in the minds of men."

JR: Certainly, AI can be a useful tool, and I agree that the creativity and collaboration part is certainly more of a unique human trait.

TF: Back in my career, in the 70s and 80s I taught a graduate-level course on log evaluation at Texas A&M Kingsville (with particularly good and practical Natural Gas Engineering and Geology departments). I taught for 10 years and probably learned as much from the students as I taught them. I certainly learned a lot about what I did not really know as well as I thought! The students were mainly young and eager, though some just there to get a stamp and move on. It was a good experience, and I learned a lot. In later years more than one student said my course was the "most practical course they had while in school." That kind of compliment makes it all worthwhile.

JR: High praise, Tom, that's very nice.

TF: The issues of getting better resolution (both vertically and radially) and the ever-increasing number of new measurements and the ability to integrate all this data will probably always be with us. Computer solutions with sophisticated statistical and "neural" analyses offer major computational improvements, but must be tempered with an understanding of the real world. This is usually the responsibility of the geologist on the team.

JR: To help with what is realistic and out of the realm of reality?

TF: And seismic applications are a major part of the future formation evaluations – especially in unconventional reservoirs. It can be a powerful tool that provides the long-desired lateral dimension. Sometimes, however, I get the feeling that you will not get the answer if you don't already know what the answer is. Iteration is powerful but can be misleading. Again, the problem of comparing different scales of information is critical. It is very encouraging to see improvements in seismic resolution. That is where we need go to get big picture.

The Archie Equation which began as an empirical approximation has become gospel. There have been many new and sophisticated models, but the proof is usually that the equations reduce to Archie's Equation. It sometimes seems like we are going around in circles, but truth be known, the first calculation I always make is a simple Archie solution, and then I try to take all the available information and arrive at the best possible answer. As additional information comes in, I try to learn from it and improve my answer the next time. One good thing about having grey hair is that you learn it does not ruin your reputation to admit that you were occasionally wrong. For instance, while training my engineers in North Texas, I taught them that the Barnett Shale was for making pool tables. It was not until it made a TCF of gas that I realized my mistake.

In the early days of "delta versus turbidite", I was a firm believer in the idea that most onshore Gulf Coast reservoir quality rocks had to be "coastal" in nature. Over the years, I learned that both environments produced tremendous reservoir rocks. In fact, I now believe that much of the disagreement stemmed from that fact that many of the Gulf Coast fields contained both types of deposits, especially in the growth faulted areas which represented a large part of our exploration targets. It was handy that the dipmeter provided vital information about growth faults prior to the arrival of 3-D seismic technology.

The Austin Chalk was the perfect play for the development of interpretation of all the dipmeter tools, especially the borehole imaging devices, such as the FMS and FMI and the acoustical imaging tools. We developed new applications for fracturing, borehole stresses, borehole mechanics and formation bedding by real day-to-day experience. Fortunately, the Chalk was very consistent in terms of fracturing and present-day stress. This let us focus on the next level of subtlety. As it turned out, the Austin Chalk was not just one monolithic formation. There were different types of oil (black, blue, heavy, light) that had different pressures from one horizontal layer to another and from one lateral section to another. All these variations are obviously important. We literally learned how to evaluate horizontal wells and unconventional reservoirs in the Chalk. We were ready for the next boom in the geologically similar, but lithologically different, Eagle Ford Group. Fortunately for us we had good outcrop exposures of both formations, and I became a true believer in field trips to the outcrop. I even got to be an "expert" on the lecture circuit. Talk about a good way to get educated.

JR: An excellent way, for sure. As we discuss this, I'm looking at some of our Eagle Ford samples from Lozier Canyon. Onto some of your many awards, Tom…I understand that you were the first recipient of the Distinguished Service Award with GCSSEPM, nearly 40 years ago. Can you tell us about this, and also, why you think it is important to build industry connections through professional societies like GCAGS, STGS and SIPES?

TF: I was quite active in Society (CC Geological Society, SPWLA, and SPE) work in Corpus Christi. In 1978 and 1981 I served as Vice Chairman of the GCAGS / GCS Conventions in Corpus. They were kind enough to recognize my contributions with the DSA. As Tony D'Agostino once said, it should be called the *I can't say no* award. In 1982 I chaired the SPWLA National Convention in Corpus.

JR: What a great contribution – that takes significant organization to deliver just one of those major events.

TF: Additionally, along the way I became Professional Engineer. I was a National Director-at- Large and then Secretary of the SPWLA. I am an emeritus member of the AAPG, STGS (South Texas Geological Society) and the Houston Geological Society. Recently, I served as Chairman of our local SIPES Chapter and as the President of our local Geological Society. I am particularly proud of our very successful AAPG Convention which was held in San Antonio during my presidency.

JR: That was an excellent convention. Tom, you have the most inspiring presentations. This summer I'm working with some McCombs students on sedimentary geology, and they have a big final presentation on a play of their choice. Some of them are working on the Wolfcamp, another on the Barnett, Niobrara, Bakken-Three Forks and Haynesville. What advice do you have for them on delivering a high-quality energy industry presentation to management? Also quite interestingly, you met Red McCombs one time, is that true?

TF: Enthusiasm is a big factor, and be sure to know your subject. Try not to make talks about something you do not enjoy. I am personally big on illustrations. A good paper or talk must have good figures. Half of what you retain is usually in the figures.

When you start a talk, be sure you get their attention. In Australia, I learned that for the first 2-3 minutes of a talk, many in the audience are not really paying attention to you, but are thinking, "Where's he from, what is that accent?" Always try to find people in the audience who seem interested in the talk. Make eye contact and talk to them. In terms of a presentation, stress the important points. You may want to repeat them in a slightly different way, especially if there may be language or terminology issues. Try to hold back on unfamiliar jargon. Explain your abbreviations and acronyms at least at first usage.

Tell them what you want to get across, emphasize what is most important, and then summarize succinctly.

As far as my top 10 suggestions:
1. Know your subject and if you do not know the answer just own up to it. Never get caught making things up.
2. Use lots of illustrations.
3. Do not waste your audience's time.
4. Try to make it interesting and entertaining.
5. Try to avoid jargon and abbreviations.
6. Encourage questions but do not allow them to bog down the presentation. Hold until the end if necessary.
7. Try to read your audience's interest.
8. Do not get caught in a lie; nothing can be worse.
9. Try to think before you answer. A pause does not hurt anything and can win back their attention.
10. Finally, be sure what you say is right.

JR: Sage advice – and on meeting Red McCombs for our UT students?

TF: Regarding Red McCombs, yes, I met this fine gentleman. I was asked to give several sessions on the oil and gas business to his oil and gas department which included his daughter and grandson. Afterwards, I got to meet him and even got a free sample of his special line of tequilas.

JR: Fantastic, and what a nice experience, too. We had an interview with Professor Roger Slatt last September and he mentioned the time they borrowed the Schlumberger drilling rig from KL to drill and log a behind-the-outcrop well into the Upper Mt Messenger Formation at Pukearuhe Beach, New Zealand. Did you have a part in this?

TF: I had a small part in the early days of dreaming this project. Schlumberger had a district there in New Zealand. While in New Zealand for a geological convention, a friend took me down to see the Mount Messenger Formation. When I saw it I thought, "Wow, I wonder if we could get FMS over this." About that time, I transferred to Houston and Bob Davis of Schlumberger Indonesia picked it up. Together Bob and Roger made it happen. Roger put the results together, and it became a seminal study of behind-outcrop turbidites with imaging logging.

Roger was great geologist, teacher and mentor. He was an all-round good person, always smiling and happy to see you. He obviously loved what he was doing. He was a true gentleman, a good friend and an excellent geologist. I was fortunate enough to be around him several times over the years, both on field trips and in short courses and at conventions.

Interestingly, I had the opportunity to go to the Hollywood Quarry and DeGray Spillway with Shell's premier sedimentologist, Rufus LeBlanc. Later I studied Roger's work in Arkansas. It was interesting to compare the two approaches to the same outcrops.

JR: Yes, LeBlanc made some great contributions to the Jackfork Group as well. His Shell guidebooks were concise and thoughtfully prepared. Tom, your leadership across the various roles in the industry – *as well as outside the industry* – is impressive. You also serve on the several leadership boards including SIPES and the South Texas Geological Society. Can you share some of your key leadership and philanthropic principles?

TF: After retiring, I was elected to our regional water board. So, I dabbled in public service, but in the end I found it much more rewarding in the industry as a volunteer and as a paid consultant.

I have always been a big believer in giving back. I remember all the people who helped me out, taking time and sharing with me. Not to mention, I just enjoy the teaching, mentoring and learning.

JR: What would be your message to students at university interested in making a career in the energy industry? Also – I'd like to share your message, if that's ok, with our business students this summer.

TF: It is tough out there, and it is even tougher if you are currently trying to find a position. Perhaps I can provide a bit of perspective.

When I first went to work in 1966, the oil and gas industry was in the doldrums, but lucky for me, Shell was developing the McAllen Ranch and being a field engineer in South Texas was great. Later when I was a manager in North Texas, the price of gas sold interstate was $0.10 per mcf but intrastate it was $1.00 per mcf. I was fortunate enough to arrive when one operator (Dallas Production) figured out that they could produce and sell gas intrastate for 10 times the price. They were soon drilling with twelve rigs. They used Schlumberger at every opportunity, and we took the location from a one-truck location to a six-truck district.

Then came the frenzied search for oil and gas resulting from the Arab-Israeli Wars and the Embargo. We were hiring as fast as we could, and I even did some recruiting. (I learned you better have a great GPA to get hired even in good times). This is followed by the collapse in the 1980s and hard times came to the industry. I saw my A students go from multiple offers to being lucky to get even one. As for me, again I was fortunate and transferred to Australia where things were still going well. From Australia I transferred to Houston where the industry seems to always be strong.

The Explorer's Mindset

In 1997, I transferred to Saudi Arabia where things were going well. Schlumberger was doing all the exploration work. Aramco was developing the Shaybah Field. We were running an excellent suite of logs (triple combo and FMS) on every other well in these horizontal holes. It was a great opportunity to work on some of the biggest fields in the world with expats and Saudis. Another big step on the learning curve.

After my time with Schlumberger, I just decided I wanted to be my own boss and retired as planned after my time in Saudi Arabia. In 2000, I retired from Schlumberger after 32 years and moved to San Antonio and became a geological consultant. Originally, I was planning to do it only part time but soon I was doing it nearly full time.

As you can see the years have seen their ups and downs, but I can honestly say there has never been a dull moment. I have got to say that I loved almost every assignment. It wasn't always easy. We worked hard and played hard.

If you land a job, try always to be useful. Volunteer for things. Be there when they need you. I took only 2 days of sick leave in 32 years. When you need to, keep your head down. You can always outwait a bad boss. He will either be fired or promoted. It also never hurts when your product sales are strong.

JR: Amen.

TF: This business is not for the faint of heart. Part of the key to success is to be at the right place at the right time. It is kind of like riding the big waves. It's best to catch it early and ride it until it crashes and wait for the next wave. I have seen numerous ups and downs and they're all part of being in this business. Personally, I've always been fortunate to come through the downturns and enjoy the upturns.

This latest downturn in business will probably see my actual retirement, but I'm confident that the business will pick up again. I just wish I knew when and how.

JR: That's the big question.

TF: The fact is the world needs oil and gas even if just for the natural raw materials, so we are going to need oil and gas well into the future. There is really no substitute for oil and gas as a primary source of energy. If you watch Scott Tinker's films *Switch* and *Switch On*, you'll understand.

JR: Yes! Our students watch and discuss both of those, thanks to Dr. Tinker and his team.

TF: If you can suffer through the downturns and catch the next wave, you'll be in a good position. Many of the older generation will be retiring for good. The young professionals coming along will be well positioned to take their place. Do what it takes to get a start. Be a mud logger if that is what it takes. I know many successful professionals who started their careers that way. You "got to do what you got to do" to stay in this industry.

JR: It takes tenacity, perseverance, and grit. Tom, I'd like to switch gears to your "retirement" – can you tell us about that?

TF: Continuing the story of my time in the industry let us reflect on my experiences as a consultant after my retirement in 2000 after 32 years from Schlumberger.

Upon returning to the US from my assignment in Saudi Arabia we commenced building our dream house at Medina Lake. This was quite an experience as it was a steel frame house and completely covered with Hill Country fieldstone from the area. I was able to incorporate my several hundred pounds (including a nice Bouma Sequence) of rocks collected over the years into the house.

JR: Really, some Bouma Ta or Te?

TF: Well, when we hold our short course on deepwater systems, we will have to ask our participants to check them out! Unfortunately, Te is missing.

JR: Better from a compartmentalization standpoint.

TF: In the early days of retirement and in the spirit of "Murphy's Law"; at just the time we were due to receive the three truckloads of steel for the new house, Schlumberger asked me to finish up a project in Colombia evaluating a block that they intended to sell to the industry. While in Colombia the steel arrived down our caliche road, but my amazing wife of 55 years (Kris) was able to *get 'er done*.

Not long after that, old associates began asking if I was interested in doing some consulting, which I did, and have enjoyed doing for the past 20 years.

JR: Where was your first role as a consultant?

TF: Ironically some of the first work I did is near my home base here in Bandera County. The operator was drilling in the Glen Rose Formation, a Cretaceous rudist reef system. As it turns out, this was equivalent to a similar reef that I was already familiar with from the Pipe Creek outcrop near my home. I had worked on this famous outcrop with the Bureau of Economic Geology, especially Charlie Kerans. I had also worked on the equivalent rudist reef systems in Saudi Arabia in the Shaybah Field. The reefs in Maverick County have extremely high (>30%) porosity. This porosity was greatly enhanced by paleo and present-day stress systems. These were nicely evaluated using imaging devices.

Of special interest to me was the fact that these formations produced water fresh enough that cattle could drink. The Glen Rose Formation was my first encounter with fresh water at depth. When I was a young field engineer it made an impression on me. If you are off on your value for formation water, you're going to be off on your calculation of water saturation. I never forgot the lesson. It was at this point that I began to understand the importance of knowing what geological formation you are trying to evaluate. The Glen Rose tends to have fresh water at depth in older rocks. I'm still not quite sure why this happens but as Rufus LeBlanc liked to say, just because, "You don't understand it doesn't mean you can't believe it." At any rate, this was a big step in my conversion from an engineer-petrophysicist to a geological consultant.

JR: Sounds similar to a Rich Sears comment, "I wouldn't have seen it if I hadn't believed it." That calibration is so important.

TF: Not long after that I worked on a series of jobs in the Wilcox Formation where I oversaw many 24-hr-plus wellsite jobs doing multiple formation testing and rotary coring jobs using the latest technology. In 2007 I was asked to help quality control the manufacturing, calibration and deployment of Schlumberger's latest "measurement while drilling" (MD) and "logging while drilling" (LWD) tools for BHP in the deepwater Gulf of Mexico. These wells were being drilled in 4600-feet-plus of water. These Miocene reservoirs were clearly deepwater by both the physical and geological sense! Unfortunately, the BP Deepwater Horizon blowout severely curtailed drilling in the GOM, and that was the end of my work for BHP. An interesting aside, a few years later I served on the Bandera County River Authority with CR Luig after whom the BHP rig was named. Small world.

JR: What a small world, that's amazing.

TF: As always, one door closed and another opened and I began working in West Texas in the development of a 40-mile-wide Wolfcamp unconventional turbidite play. We logged numerous horizontal and vertical holes and evaluated the rocks with all the latest technology including a lot of imaging logs. Not only did we look at the Wolfcamp but we also evaluated many interesting formations above and below that formation all the way down to the Ellenberger. These were logged with all the latest techniques as well as using various "through pipe" and other new horizontal logging technologies. One interesting aspect was a study of the DNA found in the Wolfcamp organisms from a vertical well that was then used to evaluate the exact part of the Wolfcamp when it was drilled horizontally. Several times I had the experience of coring these formations. On one job we recovered over 500 feet of core in one trip using the latest in sleeved coring tools. The formation's lithology, porosity, saturations and mechanical properties were fully evaluated. Fracturing as well as past and present-day stress systems were routinely evaluated.

Once again as this project tailed off, a new opportunity arose. I got to help to evaluate saltwater disposal wells in the STACK play in central Oklahoma. These formations included the Mississippian and the Woodford Shale.

All along the way I had the chance to work hand-in-hand with several forward-thinking independent operators working on the latest cutting-edge new technology in both clastics and carbonates. I worked with all the major service companies. I worked on all types of rigs from modern top-drive rigs, including Ronan's "largest land rig" to "single" rigs where the hands wore flip flops and did not even bother with hard hats.

JR: That would never happen today, my goodness.

TF: All of which brings us to the present, where I am currently enjoying my retirement while waiting for the next adventure.

JR: That adventure continues onwards. You have been around a lot of oil and gas explorers for decades and you have seen some succeed, and others fail. What is your message for oil and gas explorers today?

TF: I've had the pleasure of working with oil and gas finders – both independent and majors, and I have learned from all of them. Two of the more interesting examples were successful independents.

JR: Who?

TF: The first one was Dan Hughes of Hughes and Hughes. He was a soft-spoken, quiet gentleman who has found literally billions worth of oil and gas. He was active in South Texas, Australia and South America. Every time I ran into him for over 45 years; he would always recognize you, remember your name, and be genuinely interested in how you were doing. He assembled an organization that was hugely successful in finding oil and gas. I did not find out until later that he was a self-made billionaire. He was always gracious and interested in you. I find these are common characteristics of people who are real successes in business and in life.

The second was Aubrey McClendon. I did not really know him personally all that well but knew of his work. He was active in the Austin Chalk in the early days, and I had a lot of admiration for him. He was a fierce competitor, and a lot of people did not like him very much, but he was in my opinion a consummate and true wildcatter. Unfortunately for his company, Chesapeake, he almost single-handedly glutted the gas market! He was nevertheless always a great benefactor of Oklahoma City. The many things he did for the community were truly awesome.

These are examples of successful people I knew; both were intensively competitive in business, but often very generous with their fellow man.

JR: Thank you so much for your time and conversation Mr. Fett.

Business Success

This section is informally termed "Markets, Finance and Oil" since it deals with how geoscientists, engineers and financial experts create value in the exploration and production of oil and gas. This is not as dramatic as scenes from "There Will Be Blood" yet the desire for success in the oil and gas sector is a major force. *What does it take to succeed in this business – and to win?* It certainly takes disciplined leadership. This section is devoted to describing the traits of leaders in the exploration and production business.

Many people think it takes an MBA to succeed in oil and gas at the highest level. Many of them do have an MBA, but many don't. This section also shows how technical experts learned how to master finance to make sound investment decisions for their companies. One thing is true: all of these successful leaders keep in mind what it takes for a business venture to be financially successful. This is one key difference from pure technical experts who don't deal with balance sheets and these business leaders who must create a profitable business for their employees and investors.

Cheryl Collarini, Billy Quinn and Peter Lellis focus on Lower 48 oil and gas deals with special attention to the private equity business. These industrious and talented individuals have risen to some of the highest levels in geoscience, finance and eventually the C-suite. They turn difficult assets into gems.

Lori Fremin describes what it takes to lead one of the most successful companies in deepwater surface engineering operations in the Gulf of Mexico.

Elijah White shows how hard work, responsibility and a team mentality can help business units achieve great success and prosperity at one of the biggest supermajors in the world.

Alex Cranberg describes how one company was able to identify opportunities using new technology in a mature basin. He demonstrates how a strong understanding of geopolitics, basin analysis and prospecting skills can enable new discoveries in a region that might be considered quite difficult to access for most companies.

Benjamin Kirkland and Ryan Weber demonstrate how leadership takes the form of deep technical expertise. Deep technical expertise solves problems and inspires and influences success in a company drilling portfolio.

The Explorer's Mindset

Cheryl Collarini, Billy Quinn, Peter Lellis (April 2020)

"The energy industry is broader than most people think – it's not just oil and gas. Though that's a big part. Clean air, coal, nuclear, solar, wind – it's about using science and engineering and using all the available energy globally to make the world a better place. It's bringing water to places without drinking water. It's bringing electricity to build lives and grow things. Energy markets are doing much more to help the world than you think. For people getting started in energy careers, I'd tell them to understand what they like, dislike, and to examine their strengths and weaknesses when they choose their careers. They must choose a path with flexibility while feeding their own passion." – Cheryl Collarini

Cheryl Collarini is a licensed petroleum engineer specializing in reserve estimation, asset evaluation and due diligence. Cheryl has years of experience working for private and public upstream companies as a distinguished advisor and consultant in reservoir analysis, reports and valuations to private equity firms, banks and upstream companies. Cheryl also serves as EVP Engineering of Tanglewood Energy Partners, Chairman of Collarini Energy Experts and Collarini Energy Staffing. She previously served as CEO of ETROA Resources and Vice President of Engineering for Explore Enterprises, both E&P companies. Prior to Explore Enterprises, she was the founder of Collarini Engineering, Inc., a preeminent petroleum engineering consulting firm conducting reserve appraisals, and authoring and instructing courses in Petroleum Economics and Risk Analysis. She began her career at Mobil Oil, where she spent 11 years in engineering and supervision. Cheryl earned a Bachelor of Science degree in Civil Engineering from the Massachusetts Institute of Technology (M.I.T.) and an MBA from the University of New Orleans.

"I think the simple answer is to find what you love to do, and go do it. Don't go chase money. If you follow what you love to do, you'll be happy, you'll be good at it, and everything will fall into place. One other thing we preach internally is openness, fairness and transparency. In the long run, this seems to work really well." – Billy Quinn

William "Billy" J. Quinn is the founder and Managing Partner of Pearl Energy Investments. Prior to founding Pearl, Billy served as Managing Partner of Natural Gas Partners (NGP). In his capacity as Managing Partner, he co-managed NGP's investment portfolio and played an active role in the full range of NGP's investment process, from transaction sourcing through analysis, execution, and exit. Billy was also a key element in the firm's business development activities given his extensive industry contacts in the U.S. and Canada. Billy gained valuable investment experience working for Rainwater, Inc. and Hicks, Muse, Tate and Furst, Inc. He also worked as an analyst in the investment banking divisions of Bear Stearns & Co. and BT Securities Corporation. In addition to his investing activities, Billy serves as a guest lecturer on private equity investing at Stanford University's Graduate School of Business and the Wharton School of the University of Pennsylvania. He also sits on the Wharton School Board of Overseers. Billy received a B.S.E. in Finance, with honors, from the Wharton School of the University of Pennsylvania, and an M.B.A. from the Stanford University Graduate School of Business.

"You need to react to what the market presents to you. If the market is receptive to IPOs, and there is a value arbitrage between IPO and a sale, then you'll pursue an IPO. If the market is favorable to selling to a public company, you'll adjust your strategy to go that direction. Now if the market isn't favorable to either, if the IPO opportunity is closed, or if selling to another company is problematic, it's a bit more difficult. You need to be flexible, to react quickly, and you need to pursue what the market is providing." – Peter Lellis

Peter Lellis has 38 years of experience in upstream E&P projects spanning exploration, development and production optimization in the US and International locations. Mr. Lellis started his career as a geophysicist with Conoco and progressed to subsurface and asset management positions. Prior to founding Advance Energy Partners with his partners, Mr. Lellis was President of CHR Energy Partners, LLC, a Private Equity and advisory firm. As President of CHR Energy, his primary responsibilities included sourcing, evaluating, and operating Oil and Gas portfolio investments. In this role, Mr. Lellis developed extensive knowledge of the US and Canadian Mergers and Acquisitions markets. Previously, Mr. Lellis spent 29 years at ConocoPhillips in various E&P technical and managerial roles. His areas of expertise included exploration, geophysics, economics, risking, production optimization, development planning, and asset management. Mr. Lellis was Chief Geophysicist for US onshore for five years. He managed large international development projects in Iraq, Venezuela and the Caspian Sea. Other projects worked were in US onshore, Alaska, GOM, Venezuela, Iraq, Russia, Caspian, Kuwait, North Sea, Brazil, Columbia, Peru, Uzbekistan, and Egypt. While on assignment in Moscow, Mr. Lellis developed a corporate Production Optimization process for Lukoil Overseas. Additionally, Mr. Lellis was Senior Vice President of International Exploration and Production for SK E&P

Company. He oversaw a variety of projects including defining and executing the upstream M&A strategy and managing exploration activities in the Americas. Mr. Lellis was also responsible for building and managing a global technical center of excellence composed of 35 exploration, production, drilling and commercial professionals. Mr. Lellis received his Bachelor of Science in Earth Sciences from State University of New York. He also studied Geophysics at Stanford University. Mr. Lellis is a Chairman of the Stanford Petroleum Investment Fund and was a committee member of the Houston Angel Network Energy Group, which leads investments in early stage O&G technology companies.

Cheryl Collarini, William "Billy" Quinn and Peter Lellis share important leadership traits that have enabled them to be very successful in the energy business. They possess deep knowledge across the value chain. They have had the opportunity to perform multiple valuable roles in a company. Cheryl, Billy and Peter are dedicated and disciplined as CEOs and are world-class critical thinkers in terms of assessing value and investing with conviction in winning opportunities. They are patient and listen intently to their teams. After I had a chance to meet them and get to know them, it became apparent their talents would be best highlighted in a group interview.

I sat down with Cheryl Collarini (Tanglewood Energy Partners), Billy Quinn (Pearly Energy Investments) and Peter Lellis (Advance Energy Partners) to learn about leadership in the energy industry and North American energy markets. Below are excerpts from the interview, conducted mid-November 2019.

By the time of this book's publication, Peter Lellis had sadly passed away. Family, friends, colleagues and those who were close to Peter gathered for his funeral services in January 2022. About a year later, his former company, Advance Energy Partners, LLC, sold to Matador Resources for $1.6 billion.

Jon Rotzien (JR): Ms. Collarini, Mr. Lellis and Mr. Quinn, I'm so thankful you had the time to visit today and share some of your recent achievements. You all have different technical and business backgrounds, yet you've each found an important niche in the energy industry – from consulting and exploration, to private equity management, to development in the Permian Basin. Could you share more on your background, and what led you to your current roles?

Cheryl Collarini (CC): I graduated in civil engineering from MIT and was fortunate to land a job at Mobil Oil in my home city of New Orleans. It was at an exciting technological time (for then) of emerging computer structural design of offshore platforms. I was assigned to learn and use the FORTRAN based program on a main frame to design platforms. At that time, we used keypunch cards for input. The main benefit of those was that the used ones could be used to make Christmas wreaths! In a two-and-one-half-year period, I designed seven offshore jackets and pilings, including buoyancy tanks for an especially heavy one. At that time, deep water was 300 feet! It became clear that advancement in the company required a knowledge of its fundamental business, that of oil extraction. By pursuing an MBA, I demonstrated to management that I was serious about advancing. I was allowed to move from civil engineering to production engineering and eventually to my current field of expertise, reservoir engineering.

I resigned from my position at Mobil as a reservoir engineering supervisor in order to stay in New Orleans (my family needed me) and started a business as a consulting reservoir engineer. Getting business was not easy, especially in the horrific downturn that occurred in the middle 1980s. However, I left Mobil on good terms, and they asked me to return as an instructor of petroleum economics only three months after I left. Thankfully, that turned into an 18-year engagement and allowed me to travel and learn reservoir and economic situations all over the world. I was fortunate to build a consultancy that grew. In 1995, our clients began asking for in-house support, and we started a staffing company for oil and gas professionals. It still exists today. In 2003, when one of my clients offered me a partnership in his startup company, I joined as the VP of Engineering of Explore Enterprises. Since then, I have been a partner in several small E&P companies where I have been the head of reserves and engineering, and in most cases the CEO. I am currently the CEO of Tanglewood Energy Partners, an acquire and exploit company looking to invest where others do not want to go and take advantage of a market that has become illiquid and needs to shed assets that are or can be made profitable.

I have so much fun in the oil and gas business. It is technologically amazing and extremely satisfying from a money-making and business perspective.

Peter Lellis (PL): I majored in earth science at Stony Brook in New York, and I went down the path of geophysics. I spent a year of grad school at Stanford in geophysics, and I left Stanford, took a leave of absence from my PhD and went into industry. I left for personal reasons and joined Conoco in '82, working exploration in the GOM. I liked it so much that I had no desire to return to complete my PhD. I spent 29 years with Conoco and ConocoPhillips and had a great career in exploration and development there, working multiple basins in the US and international. In the early years it was all technical work in exploration, and over time, I took on different roles ultimately as Chief Geophysicist for the Lower 48 for a number of years. Then I progressed to asset and technical management in different locations. I took early retirement and in 2014 formed Advance Energy Partners with 3 other COP exploration employees I had worked with for years. We sought backing from private equity and quickly got on with EnCap. We got funded by EnCap for an initial $300M commitment in the fall of 2014 with a strategy to find a position in the core of an unconventional basin, which we were able to achieve after a few intense years of business development. We secured acreage in the Delaware Basin, and we are currently drilling wells, operating the assets and growing the company.

Billy Quinn (BQ): As you know, much of my background is heavy finance, pretty much my entire career. I started out investing in a lot of things, then in oil and as where we concentrate our activities.

JR: When I emerged from grad school several years ago, energy stocks took up a significant (double-digit) part of the S&P 500, yet now that percentage is low single digits. Why is investing in North American exploration and development critical today? How do privately owned companies and private equity create a successful role in this market?

BQ: That is a really tough question, and I could probably spend 30 minutes on that question alone. The last five or six years the industry has destroyed a ton of capital. You need to be tolerant of market conditions and be patient in business. Once you do that, you'll see returns.

CC: I think that it's clear oil is out of favor in the marketplace, and part of the reason was the rush to shale plays. We've observed a lot of capital destruction due to the extensive manufacturing process and how and where returns are being invested. Companies are wanting more of a yield on their money, so they're seeking other ways to get that. Probably there will be opportunities in energy in the US, maybe going back to conventional, and there will be less intensive continued development in shales. That will eventually attract capital needed to keep the US energy independent.

PL: There's opportunity now as there always is, and I believe it's a good time to invest. We find our company in an interesting period. We were built as a traditional PE company to acquire acreage, consolidate, drill appraisal wells to prove reserves, then sell to larger entity. We achieved that goal, except for the goal of selling it to larger entity, because the market changed dramatically. The market for PE-owned assets is very weak, even if you have good quality assets. We have transformed from a "buy and flip" company into a longer-term operating company. We built the company with a high level of technical expertise and operational capability – and were originally designed to run one rig. But now we've undergone a transformation so we can *run four rigs*. We operate a much larger production base than we've ever anticipated. We're in that transition right now. As a private company in this market, we definitely have advantages over public companies. We're not under investor pressure to live within our cash flow.

The economics of $50 per barrel are good, so we have the green light from our sponsor to invest beyond our cash flow. We can grow our company with cash flow and bank debt (not free cash flow) to take advantage of a soft services market and grow company production significantly. If we were a public company, we would be under pressure to scale back and return money to investors.

Also, I think at this time for us, we see opportunities to acquire acreage at prices that are below what they were a year ago. That's another incentive for us to further invest in the business.

JR: Cheryl and Billy, I understand that you have completed your MBA in addition to technical engineering, finance and science degrees. Peter, I'd also like to get your take on this. Numerous WSJ and Barron's articles have been evaluating the market upon graduation for MBA grads. Can you explain what is the importance of an MBA for achieving results in the energy industry?

CC: I think a lot of people are very successful managing oil and gas companies without MBAs. Studying topics like finance, personal management, law and other disciplines gives you a strong foundation – along with experience – to build confidence in the ability to do those things. One of the things the MBA did for me was Mobil Oil recognized I was serious about advancing in the company. They recognized my strength in finance, which was where my major study was, and I began teaching petroleum economics at Mobil and eventually ExxonMobil for nearly 20 years. It has been extremely important to my success – in addition to running a company – having this broader understanding and basic concepts in business. Small companies can't afford to employ a lot of outside experts in law and accounting when getting started, so having the knowledge in one person can be very valuable.

BQ: These are simple answers. Getting an MBA isn't necessary. There are a lot of benefits from it – from the basic academic exercises, the network and the contacts you meet while there.

PL: I think having an MBA is useful, having the education. But it's not a requirement to be successful in this industry. We have a strong preference for people in our finance group to have an MBA and relevant experience in banking and financial markets, but honestly to be CEO, you don't need an MBA. You need an overall understanding of the business, which you basically get from experience. What I've gotten in my career has been instrumental to be able to gain the trust of financial backers and to understand how business works as a whole.

Now if I had an MBA, would I have some sort of advantage? Maybe. But any kind of area of finance area I may not completely understand, I have MBAs in our company to talk to.

JR: Cheryl, congratulations on your new venture with Tanglewood Energy Partners. What was your team's inspiration? This is a new venture for you and your team, though you and your partners possess decades of experience in these types of transactions.

CC: Our team is a little bit different from most management teams who have been starting up, like private equity groups. Our team started with two investment bankers, and they brought on the rest of the technical people like us after it was formed. Their interpretation looking at the current state of the energy industry is derived from experience. They observe a downturn and a need for what they call yield instruments, which provide cash returns for shareholders, rather than asset growth like private equity does. We also provide opportunities in the $10-100M dollar range not readily available to smaller banks and investment banks. We're expecting, due to the downturn, more investments will be available outside of the unconventional arena, and assets to be up for sale.

JR: Peter, as I've learned from you and others with the Petroleum Investment Committee, a successful company is built with a vision, correct implementation of a strategy, adequate deal flow, deep subject matter knowledge – and probably a bit of luck – among other things. At the end of PE-backed company's journey, there are a variety of scenarios to realize value from all the hard work and smart investment. Can you describe the various scenarios companies like yours envision in the PE market? From my perspective, I've observed some companies sell, others IPO, still others choose to continue to grow the company.

PL: What I'll add to what I've already said is that you need to react to what the market presents to you. If the market is receptive to IPOs, and there is a value arbitrage between IPO and a sale, then you'll pursue an IPO. If the market is favorable to selling to a public company, you'll adjust your strategy to go that direction. Now if the market isn't favorable to either, if the IPO opportunity is closed, or if selling to another company is problematic, it's a bit more difficult. You need to be flexible, to react quickly, and you need to pursue what the market is providing. Right now, for our company, our path has switched and we are going down path to develop the asset – more fully than we ever imagined. We have four rigs now. We had planned to develop only a small percentage of the asset; now we are looking at ~40% or more into development. We imagined selling to a large company, and this is still part of the strategy, but if it turns out not to be there, we'll turn this company into a dividend paying entity and find a way to return capital to investors.

And being a small company, it really does give you an advantage for changing strategy and making decisions. We're very flexible and our financial partners are very adept at reassessing situations, making pivots, moving into different directions fluidly.

JR: Billy, if I remember correctly your original fund was hard-capped at $500M. Is that correct? Now, your group is managing well over a billion in capital. How do you plan and assess your growth with Pearl Energy? Can you tell us what is keeping your teams motivated in the current market?

BQ: That's correct. I think first off it's different how we deploy capital. If you look at the companies we own today, they're managed very well. Our management teams have been patient with market cycles. We've been able to keep the companies going, and these companies are generating returns at a company level. And we keep on looking for opportunities in the market.

JR: Your leadership across the various roles in the industry is impressive. Can you share some of your key leadership or management principles?

In fact, I remember when you – Cheryl and Billy – visited University of Louisiana in 2017, and shared with our hardworking students some key tips. Several of them have mentioned how much they appreciate your candid advice and review of the North American industry, by the way.

BQ: I think the simple answer is to find what you love to do, and go do it. Don't go chase money. If you follow what you love to do, you'll be happy, you'll be good at it, and everything will fall into place. One other thing we preach internally is openness, fairness and transparency. In the long run, this seems to work really well.

PL: How would I describe my leadership style…I stay on top of what's going on in our company, without trying to be intrusive. First and foremost, having top quality managers to run the different business segments is absolutely key to success. Beyond that, I stay in constant communication with my VPs regarding their business areas. It's important to have a firm understanding of what is going on, on the drilling side, production and operations, geoscience, finance, land, reservoir, planning side. When things are going well, I'm not that involved with the day-to-day events. When things aren't going so well, or when there are opportunities, I can get very involved. My involvement across the disciplines waxes and wanes. Regular communication is very important, and I put a lot of stress on that. I formally meet with VPs once a week for 3 hours, go through the entire set of business opportunities and their status, and also have informal conversations with VPs several times a day.

And another key part of the communication aspect is with our Board of Directors. I keep a regular open line of communication with the Board to discuss what kinds of proposals we'll bring to them, and that's very helpful to gain trust in the company. Having the trust of your major shareholder is critically important to the health and well-being of your company.

CC: My best secrets I believe are in servant leadership. It's a whole area of study, but I believe in getting down and *doing* all the different parts of a company, especially if it's your own. So, from the beginning – it's programing, accounting, tax returns, payroll, office leasing, stopping for office supplies – and many other things you must do. But it also makes you appreciate the people that work with you. It gives you the ability to teach and bring them along. Also, it teaches you to believe and practice that every person in a company is important. And the receptionist can be the most important of all, since he or she is the first contact with customers. In my business, everyone represents an important part of the company, and I hope they remember me fondly because of that.

I also believe in being as close to perfect as possible and working harder than people around you.

JR: You've attended some great colleges and universities, including MIT, Rice and Stanford. What would be your message to students at these universities interested in making a career in the energy industry? You may have seen YouTube videos from professors that encourage students to take career paths outside of the energy industry.

PL: If you want to make a career in the energy industry, don't spend it in academia. Spend it on the job. If you spend too much time in academia, when you come out to join industry, you will be viewed as narrow specialist. That's been my observation. I'd recommend getting out after a Master's degree and diving head-first into whatever part of industry attracts you.

BQ: This answer is similar to the last question: find what you love to do, and pursue it. If your passion is in engineering or geology, pursue it. Don't go chasing something just because it's the hottest new trend. Make sure you have love and passion for it.

CC: The energy industry is broader than most people think – it's not just oil and gas. Though that's a big part. Clean air, coal, nuclear, solar, wind – it's about using science and engineering and using all the available energy globally to make the world a better place. It's bringing water to places without drinking water. It's bringing electricity to build lives and grow things. Energy markets are doing much more to help the world than you think. For people getting started in energy careers, I'd tell them to understand what they like, dislike, and to examine their strengths and weaknesses when they choose their careers. They must choose a path with flexibility while feeding their own passion.

The energy industry has always been fascinating to me, even though I started in construction, and the energy industry's technology is actually second to none.

JR: You've been around a lot of oil and gas explorers for decades…you've seen some succeed, and some fail. What is your message for oil and gas explorers today?

CC: The first well I participated in was a dry hole. And I think that I would tell explorers not to quit. But probably most important is to embrace the technology of the present. And respect experience of the past. That while the digital age has afforded us opportunities to do more, there is the opportunity for spectacular failure by not knowing the fundamentals. Think about combining well logs from

1920 with seismic technology today to create some spectacular successes.

I'd just say I've been around the business for 45 years and I'm still having fun. I still get excited when I see the problem in a reservoir and find an interesting economic opportunity. And I still do my own analysis and operations, because I enjoy it.

PL: For explorers and someone who wanted to enter on the upstream side, is to, over time, diversify their experiences and don't become locked into a particular basin, a particular narrow discipline. That is if you really want to experience the fullness of the industry, you should work different basins, work different countries and work outside of the academic discipline. I've found it to be a satisfactory career path. Now a lot of people get satisfaction from doing something narrow and becoming an expert in one area, but I have not found that to be the case with my career.

BQ: Be patient and disciplined. There are two key points on this: you can't rush it, and you can't get too aggressive. If you can be patient and disciplined throughout the cycles, you'll fare well.

JR: Thank you so much Cheryl, Billy and Peter.

Lori Fremin (July 2023)

"For me I had not always thought I wanted to be a leader. After 10 years with my head down, someone asked me to lead. I thought, "I see some of the leaders out there. I can do what they're doing, and maybe, I can do it better?" Once you get into those roles, you realize corporate leadership roles are not for the faint of heart. You need to care for people, care for their development. It means you must do things that are not a lot of fun. If you get through all the requirements, the leadership is fundamentally straightforward. Learn, Do, Care - you need to know all about where the person is coming from. How can I help that person? How can we get them aligned to help themselves and also get the company to where we want to go? If you don't know the path of the person or their journey, you don't know how to get them on the right path." – Lori Fremin

Lori Fremin is the President and General Manager for HC Manvel, Inc and Haltermann Carless. In her current role, she is accountable for delivering strategic value and manufacturing results in the US. She is also the Chairman Emeritus and Interim Executive Director (Volunteer) for the Board of Directors of the Energy Education Foundation. This is a nonprofit that promotes energy awareness, provides energy-based STEM education to schools, teachers, and students across the US, recognizes "Hall of Fame" technology and seeks out to honor the pioneers of the energy industry.

Prior to her current roles, she was the General Manager of Disruptive Thinking for Global Deep Water (DW). Her remit was to research to understand how DW will thrive through the energy transition. In her previous role, Ms. Fremin was the General Manager of Surface Engineering in the Gulf of Mexico. She was responsible for safely and sustainably delivering the surface technical and operational engineering needs for all of Shell's DW Gulf of Mexico Assets.

Throughout her over 29 years in Shell, she has held technical, commercial, and operational leadership roles, worked short-term assignments in Aberdeen, Rijswijk, Perth, and a long-term one in Calgary, and held roles that covered Brazil, Venezuela, Argentina, Nigeria and Malaysia. She worked in the DW, shale gas and unconventional oil businesses for over 25 years after spending her first 4+ years in Shell Chemicals. She is married and proud of their two engineering college students and their oldest, who is now working as an engineer.

Over the past three decades, Lori Fremin has set an international example of bridging the gap and leading the conversation between geoscientists and a variety of engineering roles to deliver reliable, cleaner and safer energy both onshore and offshore, domestic and international. Throughout her career, Ms. Fremin has led efforts to sustain and grow production in some of the world's most prolific fields, including Mars in the deepwater Gulf of Mexico. She is one of the few industry leaders who has pioneered efforts across an entire supermajor company to increase success in deepwater basins, as well as work to inspire and train the energy workforce of the future through the Energy Education Foundation (EEF). Her ability to communicate facts on the energy industry reaches audiences of all ages, from executive management to K-12 students. One of the most impressive aspects of her career is that she has spent significant time offshore providing solutions to complex challenges involving multi-billion-dollar production projects. As a result of her many leadership roles throughout her career, she has a highly nuanced understanding of the global energy industry, markets and the complexity of tasks required to get petroleum (in its many forms) to the consumer. In this interview, Lori also explains the importance of knowing your colleagues, the company objectives, and how to remain focused in working hard toward adding value with the "learn, do, care" motto. I first met Lori through mutual colleagues while preparing the book

Deepwater Sedimentary Systems. Since then, we've developed and delivered seminars and training courses on topics from deepwater technical capabilities to exploration leadership. I've learned so much from her, especially in the areas of problem solving with large teams and dealing positively with unforeseen and unexpected circumstances in business settings using the "learner's mindset" approach.

Read the interview below from July 2023.

Jon Rotzien (JR): Lori, I'm so thankful you had the time to visit today and share your story. Your background in deepwater and offshore surface engineering enabled you to contribute significantly to the global energy industry. Your teams throughout the years invested meaningfully in Super Basins such as the Gulf of Mexico since the mid-1990s.

Could you share your background, and what led you to your current role with HC Manvel Inc?

Lori Fremin (LF): I've had technical staff and service roles offshore and onshore. When I first started, I actually lived offshore to learn from and work with operations, though I started in chemicals where I could really get my feet on the ground. I lived offshore Monday through Thursday on a shelf platform. Then, I worked through major developments, project startups or reconstructions after Katrina. I lived offshore with the very experienced team at Mars to get through the precommissioning and actual startup. The folks who work offshore are extremely resourceful and I deeply respect their knowledge and expertise. Learning and living offshore helped me lead organizations in the offshore world.

JR: Energy stocks took up about ~12% of the S&P 500 about a decade ago, now it's lower. Yet humanity still uses about 100 mmboe per day globally, and 20 mmboe in the USA. How does the oil and gas industry navigate these constantly changing market conditions?

LF: Here's my thinking on this. This is my thinking, not any corporations' view. My opinion is that fossil fuel energy is needed as part of the energy mix and supply for the next 50 to 100 years. In my simple view, the world around us is continuously changing. For me to say, "Let's predict a strategic direction and go," would be wrong. Oil and gas and all the energy industry and its partners need to create a world where we're always looking for the safest and most energy efficient path forward. That's just how we live. Whether we're 1% or 100% of the stock market, it shouldn't matter to anyone working in the industry. I believe that the world is always changing and I really believe in the "power of and" mindset. We need all forms of energy and we need to be smarter consumers. For instance, I just walked into my study and turned on the light. I have 15-ft windows, and I don't absolutely need the light on. Ten years ago, I wouldn't have thought anything about it. Now I think about it. We are on a treadmill now and energy resources are decreasing. This treadmill needs good people on it. How can we do things differently? How can we work or study differently? How can I help the church down the street differently?

And if I work in industry, I need to ask myself, "How can I produce what I'm producing a little more efficiently every day?" If we're not conscious about it, it will be our kids' problem. It could be a dire world.

JR: Congratulations on your recent move to becoming Chairman Emeritus for the Board of Directors of the Energy Education Foundation. What inspired you to lead the Energy Education Foundation?

LF: The Chairman Emeritus status is natural. Once you're Chairman of the Board and then your term ends, you're Emeritus forever. However, now I'm sitting in as Vice Chair of Personnel and Administration and volunteering, as Interim Executive Director. I'm not getting paid a penny. I do care about sharing the concept of energy awareness to all ages. The EEF is set up to increase energy awareness from kindergarten to college-age students. It does have two types of curricula, one for 5th grade for standardized testing in regards to earth sciences and the 8th grade program which is focused in and around STEM. The program helps structure K-12 as well as college students produce public awareness. By volunteering, I'm giving back to society a little. Every day, I hope that we wake one person up to join the energy industry or to change how they use energy, or if they can, to improve the energy system around us. I want folks to ask themselves, "What or how can I enhance energy resources that we have?" People don't like it when you say there is a lifespan to energy resources. To a geoscientist, we're but a blip in the history of Earth. Renewables have a lifespan, too. This fact is not abundantly clear to everyone.

JR: Can you describe what it takes to grow *within a company* like you did for 29 years at a supermajor?

LF: I don't know if I know the secret to that. The people are incredible. I have been fortunate to work with some amazing people. I'll tell you what I think made 29 years enjoyable to me. What made 29 years enjoyable, including the last years at my petrochemical company, is that every day I center myself. I ask, "What do I need to get done today? How will what I do fit into my future, my kids' future, and the future generation?" When I think about this, I get energized that I'm adding value, and not just for the here and now. That said, there are good days and bad days in any company. I'm blessed to have worked for these companies. You need to be able to sit back and be flexible and adaptable. You need to be able to put the "learner mindset" on in all situations.

The other day, I had a very bad day.

JR: Oh no, what happened?

LF: Not just for me but it was a bad day for everyone. It was bad because we were receivers of bad information. Even though it was very stressful, I sat back with my team and asked, "What can we learn from this?" We don't control and can't control other people, but to respond to these situations, you need to have mitigations in place. People can do or say anything they want. That's why we like it here in the US. But you need to be able to take all good and bad situations and make them into learning situations. And that way, you can improve the mitigation process for situations like the one we had three weeks ago.

There are good ways of resolving situations like this. We're going to have bad days. What can we do to shorten the bad part of the bad day? When I look back, I ask, "How do you step into the problem with a learner's mindset?" First, break down the problem into its core parts. The knowns, the givens, the assumptions, the tests, risks, opportunities, right? For 29 years – and I wasn't great at first – there were boring days and great days, and really bad days and super good days. "How can I adapt, change, and never make this type of mistake again?" In hindsight, I learned when I messed up more than when I was doing things right. You need to take the good with the bad and take every situation as a potential problem to solve. You can last forever in most companies, as long as you stay focused, work hard and deliver results safely. Strive to deliver more than what was asked, always. And you appreciate the people around you.

JR: That is such a positive mindset on providing solutions for industry challenges. Can you tell us what it takes to "be disruptive" with your previous role as GM of Disruptive Thinking for Global Deep Water?

LF: This was a once in a lifetime opportunity. I learned two things: 1) people have incredible ideas – and getting them out with an open mind in a structured fashion – can add tremendous value; and 2) structure and discipline with focus can ensure great ideas can be implemented quickly. Failing fast adds value. This creates a learning opportunity and ensures that resources can move to the next great idea.

I say serendipity to your original question. When you ask about 29 years, a lot of people stay up to 40 years. It's hard work. You have to work super hard. So, your results are safe, sustainable and you're delivering value with the team. Stay focused on working within strategy or planned direction of the company. And also, I believe I was really lucky. Hard work, staying focused and a little luck will take you a long way – with a positive and stick-to-itiveness attitude.

JR: As some might say, "The better you are, the luckier you get."

LF: Every team I worked in or worked for was composed of just incredible people. I was at the right place at the right time. There are about five examples of where I had landed in roles right before or after a significant event happened, simply by coincidence. As an example, before Katrina, I had just moved to Houston. I saw the hurricane sit over the Mars TLP during the hurricane. I was called to lead all initial offshore investigations of the platforms. It worked because I was high and dry in Houston. Right place at the right time.

JR: Your leadership across the various roles in the industry – *as well as outside the industry* – is impressive. Can you share some of your key leadership and philanthropic principles?

LF: For me I had not always thought I wanted to be a leader. After 10 years with my head down, someone asked me to lead. I thought, "I see some of the leaders out there. I can do what they're doing, and maybe, I can do it better?" Once you get into those roles, you realize corporate leadership roles are not for the faint of heart. You need to care for people, care for their development. It means you must do things that are not a lot of fun. If you get through all the requirements, the leadership is fundamentally straightforward. Learn, do, care – you need to know all about where the person is coming from. How can I help that person? How can we get them aligned to help themselves and also get the company to where we want to go? If you don't know the path of the person or their journey, you don't know how to get them on the right path.

JR: It's all about getting to know your colleagues.

LF: This works well and happens when the person and company are reasonably well aligned. It's difficult to lead when employees are closed or don't want to share. In these instances, they don't trust me, so I don't know their experiences. I do what I can do today to show that I care and that I'm listening. Sometimes for leadership, you have to go slow to go fast.

Before today, I wrote down on a sheet, "Learn, do, care." In any leadership role in the 21st century, you need to learn about work and learn about the person. You need to learn about the strategy, environment, role and risks. Do. Very few leaders can sustainably lead without doing anything. Where out of the work, can I as a leader, pick up some of that workload? Workload includes everything that needs to get done to mitigate risk, seize opportunity and deliver value. And this needs to come from the point of care. For me, "learn, do, care" has helped me over the last decade. I usually say 33% learn,

33% do, 33% care, which is all your time. You're not going to be a leader the organization needs if you can't give 100%.

JR: Amen. Congratulations on your recent book chapter: *Chapter 19: Technical (engineering) advancements enabling deepwater exploration and production.* What was your inspiration for designing that chapter?

LF: Rich did the work! Charlie and I did our parts. We all shared in the edits, but Rich was the lead. Charlie was a big mentor to me. Rich left a legacy. It was an honor to capture some of the information in the chapter with Rich and Charlie. The work was a lot of fun. After we lined out the case studies and timelines, I booked the meetings and divvied up the case studies. Rich and Charlie were hilarious to work with. We had a lot of fun. We had more case studies than we could put in the chapter. In total, we had 20 options and only put in 5-6 of those. We had a hard time picking which case studies to put in there. Three of us could write a whole book! Problem is no one would buy it!

JR: Please put me down for two copies of your new book with Rich and Charlie.

LF: It's fun if you think about energy awareness education. For people to read, how learning in class, how it applies to reality. It generates the energy that got them to university that day.

JR: Great point!

LF: Of course, I have three engineering kids. None of them read the chapter! I think my oldest read it. I have two mechanicals, and one electrical.

JR: You've attended some great colleges and universities, and now your kids are excelling at top universities and beyond. What was it like being a student in engineering then? What would be your message to students at these universities interested in making a career in the energy industry?

LF: I remember college being really fun and a lot of work. I remember college for sitting in lab all night, then going home, changing clothes, going back to class, turning in homework. You had to get your homework to a printer that still had ink. We had no online stuff. I remember college being fun and not necessarily hard, but the homework and studying taking a ton of time. I breezed through high school. I realized in college you need to be the best. I wanted to do very well in college.

If I had to sit back – and I've done it with three kids – why should kids be interested in the energy business? One piece of advice is that college is your time to shine, to prove to yourself you can do the things the professors are asking you to do. The professors sometimes don't have corporate experience. The homework may not have practical application from the perspective of an engineer in the energy industry. As a student, you need to figure out why they're asking you to do the assignment. If you can't figure it out, do it anyway and be the best you can be. Two is try to get them to work in the energy industry. There are stats that show the number of students with degrees going into core industries like energy are shrinking. And we don't know why. I have to bring someone along, all three engineers if I can – or at least bring one along. We need to at least be replacing ourselves.

JR: Why?

LF: A career in energy has the potential provide significant reward and by working in this industry, the worker is helping out the community in which they live. I've failed if I can't get anyone recruited into energy industry.

JR: As a developer of offshore oil fields, what is your perspective on the teamwork it takes for exploration and development teams to succeed?

LF: That's an easy answer. Honestly, the closer that offshore and onshore teams can work together, the faster you can turnaround projects with truly integrated discussions, and in the end, the safer the delivery will be of results and value. The offshore industry has to continuously evolve and change. How the work gets done needs to change. The opportunities we have offshore are going to become harder and harder to get to, to drill and to produce. Plus, the volumes of the reservoirs seem to be smaller and more difficult to develop.

JR: True, yet the deepwater resource curve continues to grow, as shown in the first chapter of our deepwater book. Thanks to Jon Minken for that.

LF: We need to think hard how to come back and sweep reservoir for the 80% of the petroleum we left behind. Today is a world of scarcer resources and people to get the job done. You can't do these important jobs without strong teamwork.

JR: Favorite part of your job in the energy industry?

LF: That has been working with people, both with folks off and onshore. Working with people is incredible to me. The technical roles I've been involved in show that I'm an introvert. But I'm a very extroverted introvert. It's fun to watch and work with people and see how things can be delivered and teams can grow. Working with people is the best part.

If you ever get a chance to participate in the mobile energy units, or energy education foundation when they take it to schools around here in Houston…

JR: I haven't yet.

LF: The most amazing thing is to sit back, listen to the facilitator and listen to the kids talk about energy activities at each station. You would just be amazed for every class to watch their eyes light up when they finally get something. Like, "That's what a well does." Or, "That's an oil platform. That's a drilling rig."

JR: I bet it's an eye-opening experience for those students to learn how petroleum is discovered and produced.

LF: There are activities at all six MELU stations that keep the students engaged. Robotics, Earth Sciences, Petrochemical and Refining activities to name a four. There are examples that help students understand how energy impacts them daily. I'm helping the Energy Foundation with how kids come through learning about energy systems. It's just amazing. We bring in items to show how petroleum is used today. A Barbie doll. A Diet Coke bottle. You and I know those are made with hydrocarbons, but kids don't. It's just plain fun to watch them make these discoveries.

JR: Least favorite part of your job in the energy industry?

LF: Right now, the very frustrating problem is getting the next generation prepared to be successful in the energy industry. The attraction to the energy industry is a problem. People don't know it's a problem, yet it's a problem we should all care about. There is competition for talent.

JR: You've been around a lot of oil and gas specialists for decades…you've seen some succeed, and some fail. What is your message for oil and gas professionals today?

LF: I've taken a different view to the word "fail." I think I've gone full circle. I started my career working hard to avoid failures. If you take the learner's mindset to the challenging situation, failures are part of the process. So, in that regard, I've haven't really seen people fail. It's like the scientific method. You try things, some work, others don't. So, I cannot say I've known someone in the energy industry who was a failure.

We're going to have energy problems requiring solutions on Earth in the next 50–100 years. Those people that can solve them are people in the energy industry, today and into the future. These professionals need to have thick skin, and they have to have the strength to work through problems. These people know how to solve problems. For me success looks like the IMAGE conference if it grows by 1000 participants per year.

JR: IMAGE is coming up soon in Houston. I hope we get 1000 more professionals and students this year.

LF: More people need to be joining the industry through the IMAGE conference. Not just the same people year after year. In practice, everyone next year would bring someone along. Like Charlie has done, like you've done with the people for the deepwater book effort. People that will contribute for 25–40 years. People like those bring resilience. The future needs people with resilience and stick-to-itiveness.

JR: Thank you so much Lori. Is there anything else you'd like the world to know about Lori Fremin?

LF: I just hope that all readers find something in themselves that sparks. Something that causes them to have extreme passion. We need good people to keep finding, developing, producing precious resources through secondary, tertiary or primary recovery. I'm hoping they find and create passion so future generations can have energy on the planet. Most people haven't done the math that deals with supply and demand for energy now and into the future. The data is out there. We need energy and energy is scarce.

JR: Thank you so much President Fremin.

Elijah White, Jr. (February 2022)

"You need to push your thinking when you change roles. It's not a different skillset. It's a different mindset. And it's different if you're a researcher vs. a production geologist vs. an explorer. In research, you're studying how to predict where there's oil and gas. You need to understand depositional environments. You're developing tools to get people better at doing their jobs. Your job in exploration is to find something new. In production, your job is to get the most oil from fewest amount of wells." – Elijah White, Jr.

Elijah White, Jr.

Elijah White, Jr. retired March 1, 2019 after a 36 year career with ExxonMobil. A native of Wilson, North Carolina, Mr. White earned his Bachelor of Science in Geology from Elizabeth City State University in 1981 and a Master's of Science in Geology from The University of North Carolina in 1984 before joining the company in Houston as a research geoscientist.

After an original assignment in the Research Company, Elijah moved to Exxon's Exploration Company where he served as the technical team lead in the Asia Pacific Project. Since then he has served in ExxonMobil's Exploration Company, Development Company, Production Company and Upstream Research Center in a variety of individual contributor and leadership roles, including Exploration Vice- President for the Africa Region, Geoscience Vice-President of the Production Company and most recently as the Geoscience Vice-President for the Upstream Research Company.

As geoscience vice president of ExxonMobil Upstream Research Company, Elijah lead the Corporation's worldwide geoscience research function and the application of differentiating and proprietary technology in support of ExxonMobil's global upstream operations.

Elijah is a member of the Geological Society of America, the National Association of Black Geoscientist, the Executive Leadership Council, and Sigma Pi Phi Fraternity. He currently serves on the board of Inspiration Ranch and is the Co-Chair of a Board Advisory Committee for the School of Arts and Sciences at the University of North Carolina. He most recently served on the UNC Arts and Sciences Foundation Advisory Board, The Texas A&M Energy Institute External Advisory Board, as well as a Trustee of the ExxonMobil Foundation. Within ExxonMobil he is a past president of the Black Employee Success Team. He also was a board member for 3 years for the United Cerebral Palsy of Greater Houston.

During his career at ExxonMobil in addition to technical and management responsibilities he also served as a formal and informal mentor and advocate for Employee Resource Groups. Elijah has presented technical and Keynote speeches at many national and international conferences (Africa Oil Week, Libyan Gas Conference, Global Women's Leadership Conference, Congressional Black Caucus Panel on Energy, Stephen F. Austin University Women's Conference, and the National Association of Black Geoscientist, etc.) Elijah is married to Dr. Diana Wandix-White and is the proud father of three daughters and one son, and has one grandson and one granddaughter (so far).

Elijah's leadership roles with ExxonMobil took him all over the world and allowed him to work with and inspire very successful teams in exploration, development, production and research. Elijah describes what it is like to take an education and then learn on the job. While many people probably think that part of leadership is being one of the smartest "in the room" Elijah discusses the other more important facets of leadership in the applied geosciences and energy industry. Elijah's describes specific circumstances and vivid memories of when key principles became apparent in his career – from the importance of producing petroleum for the advancement of humankind, to honest conversations with higher ups in the business. Elijah's ability to lead at the highest levels of the business particularly resonates with his teammates and former employees. As a leader embodying the principles of servant leadership, he states that the success of a leader can be evaluated simply by the success of the team. It's no secret that Elijah was one of the most celebrated, exceptionally rare and successful leaders during his career. Whenever he goes anywhere in the Houston area, he's usually stopped by a former colleague or friend who just wants to say hello to their former boss and current friend. In February 2022, I sat down with Elijah White, Jr. to discuss the energy industry. Enjoy the interview below.

Jon Rotzien (JR): VP White, thank you for your time to visit today and share your story. Could you share your background and how you became a geoscientist?

Elijah White (EW): I always go by Elijah. But thanks for asking. In different countries and cultures titles are very important and should be used properly. But you can call me Elijah.

JR: Thank you Elijah.

EW: For those who don't know, I grew up in Wilson, North Carolina, a tobacco town. It sits on the boundary of the coastal plain and the piedmont of North Carolina. Being there I had almost no exposure to geology. Luckily, the main railroad track through town was bedded by granite. So, I had lots of rocks to throw and to study.

I always knew I had a love of rocks. I attended Elizabeth City State University in hopes of becoming a professional football player. That didn't work out too well. But I got an amazing education at a Historically Black University. One of the amazing things about Elizabeth City State University is that when you show up as a freshman, you don't have any say in schedule for the first semester. As part of that schedule, you will be placed in a science class, either biology or geology. Well, I got put into geology, and I fell in love with it. So, I signed up for another class, and another. Before long, the Chairman of the department approached me and said, "You're doing great in geology – have you thought about majoring in geology?" I almost laughed because I didn't even know there was a major in geology. The Chairman continued telling me about the program, and then he told me that oil and gas companies recruit from our program. Then he started telling me how much money oil and gas companies will pay for a geology grad, and I said, "Sign me up!"

Then I moved onto UNC for my masters. I had an amazing time with John Dennison at UNC. He was my principal advisor, my mentor, and became a dear friend. I majored in sed/strat. In addition to my B.S at

Elizabeth City State I also got a minor in geography. Didn't really know how I found myself in so many classes in geography, but it all came together at the end. During my time in undergrad and graduate school, I had many internships: Mammoth Cave National Park, Woods Hole Oceanographic Institute. Then I had three straight internships with Exxon.

JR: You obviously enjoy being a geoscientist – from your beginning analyzing granites along the railroad track to your days at the Research Center. How did you develop your specialty in geology?

EW: In any geology class, you get to work outdoors and travel. I love being active in the outdoors, so it was easy to fall in love with geology since we were always outside. At Elizabeth City State University, we did a field trip to the Western United States and many other field trips. As you know, you get the basics of an education in college. The real learning takes place on the job.

As a permanent employee when I joined Exxon, they put me right back into school. These were classes ranging from 1, 2, – even 3 weeks in length. And I did the calculation. If you're in class eight hours a day for a full week, that one-week school at Exxon is equivalent to a full semester in college! My first three-week class was in the Book Cliffs. I spent so much time studying in the class, learning how to interpret the rocks and how to learn and apply sequence stratigraphy. I told my instructors how interesting it was to be able to be out here, and how much I was learning. My instructors replied, "Well good, because you'd better be learning the material since you're going to be teaching the next one." As you know, to learn something is the easy part. It's when you have to understand something from every angle to be able to teach it. In that way, you learn the material that much more in depth than if you were just to learn it as if you were a student. You definitely learn a lot more when you teach it.

The best part was learning side by side with the most brilliant geologists I've ever come across. When I first started, some of the people were the authors of the famous AAPG Memoir 26.

JR: Yes, of course. Memoir 26 is still used in modern sequence stratigraphy courses globally.

EW: Those people included Vail, Mitchum, Todd and Haq. In addition to those legends were also some people you've mentioned like Kurt Rudolph and Art Donovan. Kurt was still teaching those classes until the day he walked out into retirement.

Then the younger breed came in, and they're so interesting to learn from as well, having completed superb research before joining the company. I enjoy learning from the new team members, and I'm still learning from those younger people as the science and technology advance.

One of my key moments in mentorship and mentoring was on a trip to Libya. During a discussion about the topic of mentoring and having mentors; the most senior person there, an engineer, commented he didn't have anyone as a mentor. So, I asked him, "How much do you know about geology? See these five people here – all geologists? I guarantee you can learn from all these people." The most important lesson is that you can learn from everybody and anybody. You cannot be a master of all workflows and techniques. You need to have mentors and you need to mentor others to share knowledge and succeed as a team.

JR: Many people in the world probably don't even know what a company like ExxonMobil does, or any of the supermajor integrated oil companies, more recently rebranded to *energy companies*. Maybe just provide gasoline to put in our tanks at the local gas station.

EW: This is a sore subject with me. The oil and gas industry – we – we do a horrible job of explaining who we are. I'll tell you a story about that.

Obviously we do a lot of in-house learning and training, training in the geosciences as well as leadership training. There's a place out in Glendale, Arizona. The American Graduate School of International Management (a.k.a. Thunderbird).

JR: Sure, a well-known program for executives.

EW: Thunderbird does a lot of management and leadership courses. We were there for a leadership course in oil and gas management. If you know anything about Thunderbird, it's a one-year program if you're proficient at two languages. But the program takes two years if you only know one coming in, so it takes that extra year to prove you're proficient at a second language.

The university holds a networking event to encourage the students to meet with visiting executives. I was talking with some of those students. There was one man, who had spent 15 years at IBM and decided to leave IBM. I had told him I was currently at ExxonMobil. I asked him why he chose Thunderbird. He had done the research to find out that many companies hire from Thunderbird (~5 of their 6 companies he contacted). That made a lot of sense, but I'd never thought to do that. And then the man continued, "I'm going to put you out of business."

I replied, "Well how do you plan to do that?"

"First, I sold my car," he replied.

"How do you get around?" I asked.

"I ride my bike or take the public transportation including the bus or train," he said. Now my smile got bigger.

"Where do you live?" I asked.

"In an apartment," he replied.

"Do you have electricity in your apartment?" I asked.

"Well, yes," he replied.

"Do you have lights that turn on and off in your apartment?"

"Of course," he said.

"Well, do you drink milk? How do you get your food?"

"I shop for my food and milk at the grocery – yes it comes in containers. Why do you ask?" he replied.

"Well do you wear shoes when you go shopping for your groceries? Or do you go barefoot?" I asked.

"Yes, I wear shoes," he said.

"What kind of soles?" I asked.

"Rubber soled – I think?" he replied.

I was trying to teach him that many things he uses and depends on comes from those companies he wanted to put out of business!

I continued, if those companies go out of business, you're going to have to run around butt naked and live in a teepee. Not one of those teepees you'll buy at Target or Walmart, but a real authentic teepee made of animal hide. You're going to have to go into the woods and kill a deer to get your hide for your sans petroleum teepee. Then I told him, "Then you're going to have a whole other set of problems – wait till you get those animal rights people get after you!"

After all of this he mentioned to me, "I'm going to go buy myself another car."

JR: I wonder what car he bought that time – maybe an F150?

EW: But it wasn't just him. In Washington, I was asked to sit on a panel for a congressional black caucus forum on energy. While normal people who have to work for a living were being accused by powerful leaders of excessive use of energy and petroleum products, it was those same powerful people polluting Earth. They own their own planes and fly all around the Earth.

JR: Guess they never questioned their own use of petroleum products and fuel.

EW: What most people don't know about the oil and gas business is that many geologists, engineers, etc. are really into the outdoors and outdoor activities – hiking, climbing, biking, camping, fishing, golf – you name it. Most of the people go into our business because they love the Earth. The true environmentalists. No one knows about that.

When you look at the energy outlook – and many entities publish an energy outlook. Companies like ExxonMobil, BP, even government organizations. When you look at the needs and demands of society around the world, there is this term used in the reports – non-OECD (Organization for Economic Cooperation and Development) also called *underdeveloped countries*. These reports talk about the percentage of the world population that does not have access to clean water or electricity. People around the world want access to the same types of energy we have here in the US. And the energy is not just coming from oil and gas. Society uses all energy forms – wood, coal, oil, gas, wind, solar, and water. This is an energy supply and demand issue. And for populations to grow in a healthy way, they need energy. Energy builds economies.

JR: How else can this message make its way to the public?

EW: We need to lobby our neighbors and relatives. A lot of people don't understand. People think, "ExxonMobil is a gas company, and they just put gas in my car." This is so far from the truth.

JR: How did you find yourself in the ExxonMobil research division?

EW: There are two ways to tell that story. I'll tell the funny way.

I eventually got hired by Exxon Production Research Company. There were a lot of geniuses in the research center, but I only had a masters. Because of my internships they figured they could get just as much work from a MS candidate and pay me less. I was happy to accommodate them. That's how I got hired to the Exxon Research Center without having a PhD.

There were great people in the lab, really the most brilliant geoscientists. In addition to Vail and Mitchum and Todd were the likes of Bilal Haq, John Van Wagoner, Rod Erskine, Kevin Bohacs, Ann Reeckmann, Wendy Burgis, Todd Harding, Henry Posamentier and so many others.

Any way you look at it, people hired at ExxonMobil are really smart. Other companies, too, I'm sure, but my experience was with one company. When new hires arrive at the company their first question is often, "Wait, you're going to put me back into classes? Back into school?" We called it the Exxon University, and now it's the ExxonMobil University, to help new hires learn the skills required to do their jobs at the company. There was a time when only the PhDs were allowed into the lab, but then Exxon got smarter and realized. "Hey, we have all this talent internally, and we can teach them what they don't know."

JR: Great strategy.

EW: Well, as I mentioned I had three consecutive internships with Exxon, starting in the summer of 1980. Exxon came after people like me who had done the internships because that means we were familiar with the company and could be put to work and help the business right away. I had many assignments at the Company during my 36 years. Research in the early part of my career, I left research, did exploration, production, and development then came back as division manager. Then back to exploration and production, then back to research where I finished my career. Now the company is back to hiring PhDs for the lab. If I was coming out of school today, I wouldn't get hired.

JR: Good timing!

EW: I learned so much at the research lab. I got to take so many classes, but also teach so many classes. I was considered an expert at seismic sequence stratigraphy. Now I've never called myself an expert at anything, including seismic sequence stratigraphy – but I did really enjoy it.

JR: Back in the day, it was all by paper and hand?

EW: Back then it was big paper copies interpreting seismic by hand.

JR: Many of the research papers authored by members or former members of the XOM lab are still among the most cited in the area of deepwater depositional systems – for instance the paper on lateral accretion packages authored by Vitor plus Kurt, Morgan, David, Carlos – they were all coauthors, too, before they went on to lead deepwater efforts at other companies ~2000.

EW: And that is just a small amount of the published research. Many papers and books – on *everything* from shallow marine to sequence stratigraphy to biostratigraphy – are still considered to be proprietary. People like Bill Devlin who did a great portfolio on parasequences, and understanding their boundaries And not only for geology, but also engineering and other fields in the earth sciences including geochemistry and paleontology. That changed at a specific time in the 1980s.

Exxon used to be a place you worked for a lifetime. 1986 changed everything. All of sudden during Exxon's first layoff they lost talent to other companies. They were not only losing talent but expertise. They thought, "If we don't start releasing things, the company won't get credit for the things we've done." I'm not sure those words were spoken but that's how everyone felt.

When I came in 1984, I guess the hard work had been done. When sequence stratigraphy first came out in the AAPG Memoir, there were these big conferences on the subject. The room was filled by doubters, and there was a lot of skepticism about its usage and applicability to exploration. It was really a war with people who thought it wasn't correct. Today, the concept is still tried and true. But it wasn't easy. There was a tremendous amount of work that was done and it was in the integration of that work that made the difference.

JR: I thought John Van Wagoner got the credit for defining the parasequence in the early to mid-1990s in a few key papers.

EW: I can't believe I forgot about John Van Wagoner! He was awesome, one of my best mentors and friends. Let me tell you a story about him.

We were about to embark on a 3-week training program in the field. I had just gone to a GSA conference in New Orleans. There were nine geology students from UNC I was traveling with, and all nine of us piled into a room to save on expenses. One guy was on the floor, one on the couch, one was in the bathtub. We made it work.

But on this training trip, they almost cancelled the trip. It was a trip that included Wyoming, South Dakota and Colorado. Two nights we were going to be in South Dakota out of the three-week trip, and we needed four rooms. We could only get three rooms. Everyone needed a separate room by unwritten rule. Having just had to share a room with eight others at GSA, I thought this was ridiculous to have to cancel the trip for such a small reason.

John told me, "It's ok, I'll share a room with you." It was as if it was an act of God to even think of sharing a room. A completely unreasonable request! Unthinkable. But in the end it worked out. They let us run the trip. John told me, "If it hadn't been for us willing to share, we would've had to pull the whole trip." And I get privacy is one thing, that's important. But another issue is that the type of people we work with, the day never ends. We come in from the field, eat dinner, and then at night we're working in our field books, and planning for the next day. These creative field geology types need that working session in the evening, and they need that creative space.

Every day you're working. You gotta give creative people time to be creative.

John is awesome. He was retired by the time I'd gone back to the lab for my last assignment. Though at one time, he was a senior scientist who worked for me. There were some people who don't understand men like John. He's a great Christian. He's all business. In my time at ExxonMobil, he was the most misunderstood person in the world. He had a mentality about him of *let's get to work*.

JR: Work demonstrates faithfulness. I can imagine others don't know how to approach people that are all business. What skills do you think are important for a career in the energy industry today?

EW: Oh boy, it's changed so much. It used to be that you could come in with one set of skills and learn many things in the in-house training programs. Now with advent of all this new tech, you'd better be able to use all the different tools we have for mapping and interpreting the subsurface. But you will always need to have a strong base of geology fundamentals. It is going to be that skillset and what else. UNC has a program called *Synergies Unleashed*. At ExxonMobil, we simply called it integration. This was the integration of geology and geophysics, and these themes are done better when they are not done separately. It's even more important for geologists and engineers. Every day, geologists and engineers should be handcuffed together and never leave the table!

JR: There could be worse ways to work.

EW: And you've got to be great communicators and willing to work really hard. Soft skills are becoming much more important as you're forced today to work across boundaries. Actually, they have always been important. One person can't have it all, so you need to be able to work well with others. The basics are key. And then you need to be able to collaborate, integrate and keep learning.

So many people are very good at teaching themselves new skillsets. We're fortunate to have had so many in-house experts in the geosciences at ExxonMobil. In fact, among the many classes I took, geological modeling was the first thing I took at ExxonMobil. And I became decent at using those skills. Certainly not as good as other experts, but I had a good understanding of it and how it works. In my last assignment I had a few bright young people trying to reteach me geologic modeling. I think I failed.

But what underpins success at a company will always be a good fundamental understanding of the basics.

JR: Probably a little more advanced than just understanding the basics, like the law of superposition, to be considered for a role at one of the supermajors.

EW: At one time, 95% of the people hired to ExxonMobil were summer interns. Internships are a cheap way of evaluating talent and a willingness to learn. But with a good background in geology, smart and willing students can learn anything.

I graduated with a degree in stratigraphy, yet I learned most of what I know when I started to work full time. My understanding of the principles changed.

Today, workers need to be well versed in data analytics, to take the maximum amount of various types of data into a model and learn from it. We didn't have this scale back then. Today, you're doing all this with super computers.

JR: You had a long and distinguished career at Exxon and ExxonMobil – 36 years. Can you describe what it takes to grow *within a company* like you did at ExxonMobil? Some people think the *grass is greener* and jump from company to company. You didn't.

EW: When I graduated from college, I had four offers: Dowell, Arco, Mobil – you've probably heard of them, too – and Exxon. Exxon made me the lowest offer. Mobil made second lowest offer. But I had had three summers with Exxon, and I loved the people I worked with. They knew me and had confidence in me. I developed many friendships and essentially built a family there.

Art and I worked together. I was best man in Art and Cindy's wedding. They're Godparents to my kids. That's family. That's what ExxonMobil continues to be for me. I've been retired for three years now, but I'm contacted on a daily basis by friends and colleagues – and many of them are from ExxonMobil. And they're not the same people every day. I made good money, but you can make good money anywhere. A job is a job, and you do your daily work. But my career was about the relationships I built which continued as family.

JR: That's wonderful.

EW: My wife jokes that it takes us forever to go anywhere since we always see people I know, and we stop to chat.

JR: In recent years, your leadership across the various roles in the industry – *as well as outside the industry* – has grown. Can you share some of your key leadership and philanthropic principles?

EW: I'm going to go way back to when I began at Exxon. My goal was to be the best geologist that Exxon ever had. And if my career was based on that goal, I'd be considered a miserable failure! I got to work with many brilliant geologists.

In the beginning, I told my managers I have no desire to be anyone's supervisor. I came here to be a geologist, and to do geology. That's all I wanted to do. I'd come into the office in the morning, work all day, go to the gym, have dinner, and come back and work in the evening.

When I was working one time on a long seismic line, Bob Todd came in and said, "I'm making you a team lead." I asked, "How long do I have to decide?" He replied, "About half an hour, that's when the new org sheet goes to the printer."

So, the office had this big announcement the next day, and Bob Todd announced, "And Elijah White has graciously agreed to take on the role of Team Lead…"

JR: Wasn't that nice of Bob.

EW: But I never turn down what my boss wants me to do. My boss tells me what my job is and that's what I going to do to the best of my ability. While in Norway working on a short project with a very diverse team I got a call from my boss. He told me, "We're going to make you supervisor of the seismic stratigraphy team." And in fact, they were going to fax me the new org chart to share with the team. I asked, "Couldn't you have told me this earlier?" My boss responded, "I'm telling you this now." My principle has always been, "If you tell me what my job is, I'm going to do it, and do this job the best I can." I did that job for about 3 years.

Then I transferred to Exploration to become a technical team lead of the Asia–Australia project. To this day, I still don't know what that role really was for, or what we did. But I did know I had a lot of fun.

After more assignments in Exploration, Production and Development I went back to research as the division manager, did that job for three years. Then I became area manager for the Middle East. And that was an amazing job.

But let me talk about a key leadership principle if you will.

JR: Sure.

EW: As area manager for any region, your main job is to add resource to the resource base. You need to bring resources onto the fold through drilling wells, acquiring assets – any number of means – but you need to add resource to the resource base. So, at my first review, I was sitting down with the VP for the Middle East, and he told me, "You're the first area manager who has not added resource to the resource base in over six years."

JR: Not a good sign.

EW: My fiancée at that time gave me a call, "So how'd your review go today?" And of course, I'm thinking this woman has a vested interest in my ability to be gainfully employed. I told her it didn't go so well.

"Are you going to get fired?" she asked.

"No, I don't think so, I just might not get any promotion anytime soon," I replied.

Now if you know anything about the Middle East, you know it takes time to build relationships. Nothing happens overnight. I was only in the job for 18 months. We did some good things, tested some concepts but made no discoveries.

Then I get a call from the EVP: "We're going to make you Exploration VP of the Africa region." This was unexpected news. When my fiancée called back and we talked, I said, "Hey, I got a promotion." She replied, "I thought you were getting fired!"

JR: Well done.

EW: And that brings me to my point, the VP was just stating a fact. He never told me I was getting fired or that I had not done a good job. But there were many questions that could have been discussed during that first conversation. For instance, I wondered, "What does this mean about future opportunities at ExxonMobil?" and "What could I have done differently or what would you have done differently?" and many other questions.

The principle is: Never walk out of a room or discussion about you with questions. You need to stay in that conversation, in person, and discuss all that needs to be discussed right then. Do not leave the room with questions or doubt in your mind.

With that position, I started out in Sub-Saharan Africa, then all of Africa. This included Nigeria, Angola, Equatorial Guinea, Libya, Madagascar, Mozambique, Tanzania, and eventually we picked up South Africa acreage. You constantly need to be bringing in new acreage to explore. And it hit me that this little simple-minded geologist from Wilson, North Carolina was able to work at such a scale in places I thought I'd never get to visit in my lifetime.

JR: Amazing.

EW: I met the heads of state for Ghana, Liberia, Madagascar, Mozambique, South Sudan. And Energy Ministers and Ambassadors of many others. My higher ups at ExxonMobil had the faith in me and put the trust in me to have meaningful relations and negotiations with these very important figures.

No, I didn't meet the man running Libya at the time. But I did meet nearly all the people that surrounded him on his leadership team. My philosophy during this time I was in Africa was to communicate, communicate, communicate. And answer the questions needing answers while in the room.

My other philosophy on leadership is to hire right, train right, give them the tools they need, and set clear goals and objectives – and then get the hell out of way and let them go.

I love dogs. Let me tell you about a dog show I once saw. I was at this dog show where dogs were to be ranked on their agility. There was this new handler that owned one of the fastest dogs on record. These dogs were to race around a circuit. So, the dog and owner got in the ring and they ran this course together. The dog ran a flawless race and came in last place.
The dog that won, his owner was not running with the dog. He was merely pointing to where the dog should go. The dog was allowed to run at the dog's speed, and won the race.

If all in the organization can only move as fast as me, we're not going to get very far. Sure you need periodic check-ins, but you can't micromanage. You can't keep employees at a pace that only you can keep up with. You can't lead that way if you're going to be successful at all.

At the end of my career, I'll be judged on the success of people that I worked with, which is a subtle difference from how some people measure success.

JR: Do you keep in touch with them and their success?

EW: 90% of my Facebook conversations are about life, and this includes many of my former ExxonMobil colleagues. I play golf with them, too. At least they'll always know they've got someone to beat when they play me.

A lot of it is just catching up, and very little business. This makes me feel ten times more important. What is the success in my opinion from my career, is that people at ExxonMobil still want to talk to me.

JR: I think 100% of the time we've spoken recently, you've either been on your way to the golf course or at the golf course. Do you think golf played a role in your success in the energy industry? If new students coming out of school want to become VP, maybe they should take up golf?

EW: I play with a group every Wednesday. Usually, it's a shotgun start at 8:30, sometimes a rolling start. It was canceled today because of the weather. I started playing at 55, and retired at 60. My wife bought me golf lessons a few times during my career, but I never made arrangements to actually take the lessons.

This last time my wife bought me lessons, she said, "Don't waste my damn money again." And that convinced me I should take those lessons. My four kids are all athletic; three were athletes in college. And I didn't have any hobbies because for years, I was following all my kids in sports.

I may have bad knees, but I love swinging a golf club. I told myself when I retire, I'm going to play three to four days a week. That's what I'll do. And that's what I do now.

JR: But not really during your career.

The Explorer's Mindset

EW: In my career? No. I played in several ExxonMobil United Way tournaments and was recently invited back to play with Morgan Stanley and one of the EM presidents. And most of my friends in San Antonio I've met them on the golf course. It is a community building sport.

Back as the Africa VP, we were trying to get a rig into Nigeria. The issue was Nigeria only wanted vessels with Nigerian ownership. We didn't own any vessels. We always contracted 3rd party rigs. The Nigerian guy in charge was going to be in Houston for OTC. I told him I wanted to talk for 15 minutes. When I showed up to meet him, the line of people wanting to talk to him was 200 people long! It was at the Hilton of the Americas downtown. So somehow I managed to get on his schedule. I was sitting at Starbucks for the meeting. The first question out of this guy's mouth was, "Do you play golf?"

He wanted to play a round or two, at a good club. He told me, "We can spend 4-5 hours tomorrow golfing." But I told him I didn't play, and I basically had 15 minutes to make sure this rig could get in and out. But I almost missed an opportunity because the interest was all business. I almost lost a deal because he was thinking, "This guy doesn't play the sport."

JR: No one has ever asked me, "Hey do you want to do an Xterra triathlon and we'll talk about a prospect deal?"

EW: The message is, if you birdwatch, go watch birds. If you love rocks, be a geologist. If you love to play the piano, go make music. Follow your passion. But please don't get into something just because of the money. You gotta follow your passion.

JR: So, you've always been very serious about personal fitness?

EW: I used to be an exercise buff. I was in the gym at 5am. We had a great gym in Spring at the new campus. I even had a personal trainer. Twice a week I'd have personal training sessions. I was pretty regular. A few times though, my trainer would say, "I haven't seen you in three months." Sometimes the business gets very busy. I'd travel a lot. Most of my workouts now include yoga via facetime if you believe that. The mental and physical aspects of life all go together.

I communicate with folks that being physically fit is very important. Especially in a leadership position. And you know what, sitting in a meeting for eight hours takes stamina. You need an outlet.

So, we have this beautiful gym on the Spring campus. However, only 30% of the people were using the gym on campus. I think we had people following this mantra: When at work, you're supposed to be at work. But I thought maybe if they see the leaders in the gym, they'll go to the gym. If I have free time – and it doesn't have to be over lunch. It could be 10am, 1pm, anytime. I made a point of going to the gym. The work is going to get done. We want people to use the gym. I've had meetings where I say, "Hey, let's go get on the treadmill." We talked business the whole time on the treadmill. You need to look for innovative ways to stay in shape and still get work done.

JR: A very efficient day. You've attended some great colleges and universities. What was it like being a student in geology then? What would be your message to students at these universities interested in making a career in the energy industry?

EW: It was intimidating going from Elizabeth City – a historically Black college and a very small school at that – to the much bigger UNC. But I fell right into a routine. John Dennison and I used to have heart to hearts when we went on fields trips and during afternoon work sessions. During one of those conversations, I told him I was going to treat grad school like a job. I'd get in early, do my work, work all day, get to the gym, have dinner, work some more. But I was still going to go on dates, and see the surrounding area. Dennison laughed and said, "Cut out the dates, cut out the gym – you'll have no time."

But at graduation, he told me, "Oh my God, you did it your way. I'm so proud of you." But my secret was, the last thing I did before bed was do some geology. Always find a way to do a bit more geology each day.

Now if you understand the history of UNC and the time period, basketball was huge. Ever heard of a guy named Michael Jordan?

JR: Used to wear his shoes before I got cut from the team at age 10.

EW: I attended as many basketball games as possible. There were also football stars there. Lawrence Taylor was coming out as I was going in. There were people coming in from all over for the summer to play pickup games. People like Ralph Sampson. It was amazing to watch the talent in that place.

UNC is known as a hard rock school even though they were putting a lot of people into the industry.

ExxonMobil had coal and minerals divisions, too, not just oil and gas. In fact, my first boss had a degree in volcanology, Wendy Burgis, but she was one of the best supervisors I ever had. So, anyone can become a great manager, even with skills that aren't thought of as ideal for oil and gas. You need to follow your heart. Everything else will shine through. But what happens if you go to get an advanced degree in something like geochemistry [to get a great paying job] and when you get out, they're not hiring? You're now stuck with a degree you don't like.

If you study a broad mix of math, physics, chemistry – and especially computer science nowadays – you'll have success wherever you go.

And there are lots of places that need these skills like geology and reservoir engineering. The government has lots of branches where they study energy. Power companies. Follow your love. Do what you love to do, and the opportunities will be created for you.

JR: Make your own opportunities is a powerful way of thinking. What do you think makes exploration geologists different, for instance, from research geologists?

EW: It's not just exploration. The Research Company used to think it was Research vs. The World. But there are many different types of geologic thinking in a company like ExxonMobil. Exploration, Development, Production. You all have the same school of training, but how you think depends on where you're placed. I'll tell a story.

At the Exxon and Mobil merger, I was working for Exxon Production Company. Part of my responsibility at the time was to let employees in my new division know where they'd be at after the merger. This one guy, we were going to move him into exploration to work Eastern Europe. When I told him this, he came to tears. I thought he'd welcome it. But he replied, "You're going to move me to a place where I know nothing."

"But you're a geologist!" I replied. He had done production geology for years and was afraid that he'd be unsuccessful working exploration.

When I joined the production team, I was asking all these questions based on my experience in exploration. "Where's your source map?" I asked.

Current team members replied, "This is a producing field. We don't do that stuff here."

"Let me ask another question – what types of oil variability do you see in the field?"

"We have pressure tests and we know which wells are productive," they replied.

"How do you know the distribution of the resource?" I asked.

In my mind, I don't care if it's exploration or production or what, we need to do the basics to fully understand the field. We had a group downtown that specializes in nearfield wildcats. "Why don't we map it out and help them?" I asked.

In this way, you need to push your thinking when you change roles. It's not a different skillset. It's a different mindset. And it's different if you're a researcher vs. a production geologist vs. an explorer. In research, you're studying how to predict where there's oil and gas. You need to understand depositional environments. You're developing tools to get people better at doing their jobs. Your job in exploration is to find something new. In production, your job is to get the most oil from fewest amount of wells. You had mentioned something on lateral accretion packages....

JR: Yes, the Abreu et al. (2003) paper in Marine and Petroleum Geology.

EW: I was called to do a project in Angola. In the seismic data, there were these big clinoforms. There the main reservoirs were thought to be Cretaceous carbonates, and secondary reservoirs in submarine fans. On the cross lines, we were still on the slope, with a big canyon and interpreted submarine fans. Our analysis interpreted the "fan" to be accretionary wedges – very fine-grained sediment and mud. It was the wrong environment to drill. The scale that they were interpreting was too small. You needed regional context. From a production standpoint, that lens would have been ok. In exploration, you need to look at the whole picture to make sure you can properly interpret regional trends in sedimentation.

Now if we send that same person back to exploration, they'd return to production with a changed mindset.

JR: The ExxonMobil lab is also well known for leading field expeditions around the world to map and interpret – for one of many things – deepwater turbidite successions. When I was getting started, Carlos Dengo gave me a copy of XOM's *Field Safety in Uncontrolled Environments* by Bohacs and Oliveri. I think everyone should have a copy of this. It's indispensable. We use it for all of our field courses.

EW: Carlos was VP of research. Then Gavin Wall. Then I replaced Gavin. The big joke about ExxonMobil is that every meeting starts with a Safety Minute.

JR: A *Safety Minute*?

EW: It is the absolute truth that in our business and in the energy business more broadly, it can be very dangerous. We work in dangerous environments with dangerous materials. We need to place value on our employees and ourselves in these dangerous and often quickly changing environments.

This book came about from accidents that actually happened. For example, all geologists like to go into the field. On one field trip, I climbed up to the top of the outcrop. There was a colleague of mine trying to get to the upper ledge, so I helped pull him up. In doing so, I sat back on a cactus.

JR: Ouch!

EW: Second, on another field trip we had this great outdoorsman. He was from Norway. On his quick ascent of the hill, he was kicking loose a lot of stones. Not boulders, but surely big enough that if they hit you, you'd get hurt. At one point, we realized, "Hey we really need to put something together so have some rules out here." The office is one thing. Field trips were like the *Wild Wild West*! Some were really simple safety things, like, "If you're out working in desert conditions for four hours, have water. Don't get dehydrated."

Others included, "Who has keys in their pocket?" If that person falls off a cliff, there go your keys. We recommend having multiple sets of keys in pockets.

There was a former employee who went to work at a university who was not wearing a seat belt and lost his life when his van crashed. I don't care where you're seated – you're wearing your belt. The book was a special edition published by AAPG, which is one of those wonderful things for a company to do. Everyone had a copy. In fact, my daughter when she was at SFASU, she had two copies. I called her when she was on a field trip and asked if they were implementing the field safety information.

"Daddy they haven't opened it," she replied. I responded, "You'd better make them open up those copies and put them to good use."

JR: How did you get to become a VP at ExxonMobil? Did you grow up saying, "I want to be VP at XOM," or something to that effect?

EW: I didn't want to be a supervisor. A lot of people come in with aspirations. What we had was a global ranking system. All leaders come from high in the global ranking. I've never been the smartest guy in a room in *any* room at ExxonMobil. So, it can't be smarts. It can be how you relate to people. When I was talking to an executive in Irving, he said to me, "You have loyal followers Elijah – your people would follow you over a cliff."

There are many attributes they look for when deciding who should get leadership roles. The company has criteria. And saying you want to be a leader is not one of those criteria. Can Rex and Darren trust me to talk to the heads of state and the heads of companies? Of course, that's the communication and ethics part. I don't know how you train for those things.

At leadership courses anywhere in the world, these instructors say, "I can teach anyone to be manager. Leaders are naturally born." But also, I think it's vice versa. There are innate skills leaders have that aren't taught. You can hone, you can practice, but natural things in leaders need to be there. Oftentimes the ones leading companies are not the smartest people in a room.

Someone picked me to be a leader for the qualities I have that fit well for ExxonMobil.

JR: What was the best part of your job?

EW: The people. There was a time – before family and kids – that I really looked forward to Monday coming. I used to truly love to go to work. I'd sit down with Van Wagoner and talk sequence stratigraphy, and Bohacs on mudrocks.

JR: The authority on mudrocks.

EW: He probably thought I never believed his advanced thinking on the subject. But I was listening. He is such a great mentor, teacher, and person.

And Art – we did training together in the UK, Malaysia, Indonesia, and elsewhere. I did very little travel before ExxonMobil. The great thing about every day at ExxonMobil was that I was always learning something.

I got to meet the President of South Sudan right after it became a country in Washington, D.C. I asked him how he felt about being at the top of the political chain in the new country. He told me how he was used to wearing a cowboy hat, boots, and during the war was fighting for his life in the bush with his gun.

I met Armando Guebuza, the President of Mozambique at the time. I met him first in New York during a UN visit and then came to the

ExxonMobil campus in Spring. He asked me if we could build him a campus like ours. I punted that question to a higher paygrade.

I met Ellen Johnson Sirleaf, who was President of Liberia at the time. It was amazing to me to meet so many leaders. It was the best time, if you will, those last years as VP. I was watching and developing young and hardworking employees, helping develop them into the professionals they are now. That's the best, getting to work with so many excellent people.

What I didn't mention was all the successful wells, and the fields we discovered. We also drilled more than a few dry holes. Staying active helped me keep a job though. That was just business.

JR: What was the worst part of your job?

EW: Easy. It was the global ranking system.

In that system, for instance, if I hire 100 of the most brilliant minds, and then I tell 10 of them they're at the bottom. I had to have those conversations every year. Many of these employees had been in the top 1% at everything they'd ever done. And then they had to hear someone like me tell them that's not the case. Easily the worst part of my job. ExxonMobil promotes excellence, and that's how they pick their leaders. But not only are those 10% not going to be a leader, they might not even keep their job. The only thing that made me feel good about this process was that we put in as much effort as possible in coming up with the numbers. We worked at it really hard. It was not a flip of a coin. We worked it as hard as we could, which made me sleep a little better.

JR: What leadership trait do you value the most? What made the President hire you as VP?

EW: I was in Africa the first five years as a VP. Then I was Global Geoscience VP for Production for three, then finished in Research with three more. 11 years I had as VP. Communication is very important. Ethics and the ability to relate are certainly near the top of the list. Caring for people probably is at the top of the list.

The Explorer's Mindset

I was at a conference discussing this subject, and I liked to quote a professor from one of the Ivies on this subject. Maybe he was from Harvard or Princeton. "To be a leader, you have to serve the people." And then I realized at this conference, that's not some professor's quote.

JR: Where did servant leadership originate?

EW: Jesus Christ said that first! But that hit me in the middle of that conference presentation.

You've actually got to serve them if you want to be successful. I remember having some amazing administrative assistants. I actually had fabulous administrative assistants. Do you want to excel? You need to have people that care about you and make you succeed. They need to be interested in your success.

I was in Africa once and had a big, big issue. It was 11pm in Houston. I had to call my admin. She picked up the phone – thank goodness – and turned her light on. I think I had woken her up. She responded to my questions very quickly. She had everything I needed right beside her bed. She was obviously concerned about my trip and prepared. You need to ask yourself, "What am I going to do to endear troops to make our group succeed?"

I believe the only way to judge a leader is based on the success of their teams. But there is no magic bullet, and leadership is undoubtedly an accumulation of things.

JR: You've been around a lot of oil and gas explorers for decades…you've seen some succeed, and some fail. What is your message for oil and gas explorers today?

EW: If you have never failed, you're not a good explorer. You're not working hard enough.

Let me give you a scenario. Let's talk about Texas. It's always been a prolific oil and gas region. You could take the worst geoscientist, stick a hole in the ground and you're probably going to find oil and gas. You can take the best geologist in the world, send them to Chapel Hill and say, "Drill me a well right here." You could tell them that ten times in different areas of the campus, and if they listened to you – which they shouldn't – you're going to drill a dry hole and it will be a failure. But how do I rank these two geologists?

The successes and failures in themselves don't tell us anything about the geoscientists, just the region they're stuck in. However, you need to keep learning from your failures.

In Libya, we drilled two dry holes on my watch. We had prepared to drill two lookalikes, which isn't something you normally do in exploration, but we had inherited these prospects. What if the first one fails? Did we have a chance to change course? But there were very small windows here to drill these wells. And we had the same outcome both times.

At the after-action reviews after drilling the wells, the president at the time said, "If you didn't tell me then, don't tell me now." And his message was this, "If you know, don't tell me when it doesn't matter anymore."

And to be a good geologist, you need to get good at sharing everything with others. You need to be a good scientist, a good person, and be a geologist willing to do that. In that thinking, it's just a failed well – not a failed geologist.

If you tell me that this rank wildcat well has a less than 10% chance of finding oil, and you communicate that beforehand, our expectations are measured. But if you tell me there's a 100% chance of finding oil and you don't find it, that's a problem.

In the end, the final decision on whether or not you drill the well is not going to be yours. The decision, however, will be based on the information you give others. This brings it back to communication, ethics, and largely work ethic, so the team can really make the right assessment about the area.

Think about this: If I drill 100 wells and they each cost $1 million per well, and 1 successful well makes the drilling program a success…that scenario can happen. However, in all likelihood, what is more common such as offshore Libya the well is coming in at $100M – or even $500M – per well. That is not a recipe for success.

You need to be able to provide an accurate decision on how to spend money, and to put that money into finding new resource.

JR: What would you like the global community of geoscientists and energy professionals to know about Elijah White, Jr.?

EW: When I left ExxonMobil, I wrote a very long email. It basically said, "First and foremost I'm a Christian, a husband, a father, and a papa..." I've got grandkids now. The other family I met along the way, and it's a very important part of what I do. I get emails and phone calls all the time from colleagues. One recently said, "I retired six months ago." I'll get another email on yet another retiree next week. This is part of my community. Husbands, wives, we all get along. ExxonMobil will always be a part of my family.

People have been trying to get me to dump my ExxonMobil stock. But I can't do it. It's part of my loyalty. I have confidence in the company and its people. The executives, they say they're turning this thing around for shareholders. I happen to be one of them. I'm a proud person, not in the way that I'm too proud in that sort of way. It doesn't get in the way of my performance. I'm proud to have been able to contribute to the company's success. In my retirement, people continue to reach out. I have never met a stranger. As I mentioned, my wife says it takes us about 20 minutes longer to go anywhere because I talk to everyone.

My goal was to work hard, work long, and retire at 60. I actually had to get special permission to retire when I did. Now if I had waited four months, they would've kicked me out the door. And what else keeps me busy, I have dogs. I love my dogs, too.

JR: You're going to stay very busy with non-profit work? Not planning to go buy an oil company, start an exploration program, nothing like that?

EW: I loved my time at ExxonMobil. If I'd wanted to continue to work I would've never left.

I serve on two boards, one is called Inspiration Ranch. It's equine assisted therapy, and it's located in Tomball. I originally got involved as a volunteer, and then I stayed involved as a board member. On my retirement, they asked me to start right away. I said, "For six months following my retirement day, I plan to do absolutely nothing. So, call me back in six months." And they did, and I've been with them now two years.

JR: Six months is a short retirement.

EW: For six years, I served on the school of Arts and Sciences Board at UNC. At the end of year six, once that expired, I thought I was done. Then they listed me as "Board Emeritus" and I'm still helping out.

JR: High praise from The School or Arts and Sciences not to let you go.

EW: That keeps me quite busy. And I get calls all the time, to help out organizations including the United Negro College Fund. I've served as a co-chair with my wife of their annual gala events and have sponsored some of those. I regret I haven't been more involved in the San Antonio scene due to COVID. Though I have been active with United Way in Houston and am moving back to Houston in May.

JR: Welcome back to Houston soon, Elijah. Thank you so much.

Alex Cranberg (June 2020)

"Avoid getting 100%-itis which is a mindset in which explorers get so convinced their prospect is perfect. You need to bring partners in and go through the process of selling part of the prospect to partners, either at the equity level or asset level. You need to come to grips with the objections your partners make, that you're forced to hear even though you don't want to hear these objections. You need to deal with them, so you earn a position in that well. You need to learn to take in equity capital so you're not taking all the risk yourself. Obviously low-cost wells are easy to drill 100%. But then there are the big ones that you're sure are to be a homerun, and to make a massive discovery, so you put a substantial part of the exploration budget on it, and then you end up scratching your head with what turns out to be a dry hole. Nature has an infinite number of reasons and ways to humble you, particularly in the exploration business." – Alex Cranberg

Alex Cranberg is the President and Chairman of the Board of Aspect Management Corporation which manages the Aspect family of companies, a respected and active global enterprise focusing on oil exploration and production. Alex earned his MBA from Stanford University and recently served a term on The University of Texas System Board of Regents.

Alex is dedicated to and active in philanthropy. He is focused on diversity and innovation in education (as Chairman of ACE Scholarship Foundation) and activism in a variety of public policy areas. He was named to the Rocky Mountain Oil and Gas Hall of Fame in 2010. Alex is married to Cathy Neville Cranberg and has four children.

Anyone who knows Mr. Cranberg understands he has made numerous contributions to the energy industry around the world, and continues to inspire the next generation of oil finders to new heights. I interviewed Alex Cranberg in June 2020 to learn about leadership in the energy industry and global energy markets.

Alex Cranberg's candid description of what it takes to build a successful exploration company, with a special focus on understanding industry cycles, the importance of risk analysis, and the mindset of an explorer, will help anyone in the upstream business become a better leader. Mr. Cranberg also tells why civic duty – one of the three important parts to a well-rounded, modern life – is important for the health of a community, state, country and world. One of the early exploration leaders in Central Europe, Mr. Cranberg's company has taken regional success and inspired a global exploration program evaluating a variety of opportunities. Read the interview below.

Jon Rotzien (JR): Mr. Cranberg, I'm so thankful you had the time to visit today and share some of your company's recent achievements. Your background in petroleum engineering and business has enabled you to contribute significantly to the global energy industry – your team, CWS and other partners have invested over USD$1 billion in E&P activities since the 1990s. Could you share your background, and what led you to your current role with Aspect Holdings?

Alex Cranberg (AC): As you suggested, I've worked in the industry my entire career, both as an engineer at an operating company as well as a manager, so I have a combination of experiences relating to oil and gas. This has provided an opportunity for a broad perspective instead of working in a narrow discipline. I've always wanted to be entrepreneur. The opportunity came up in '92, when industry first was starting to use 3D seismic data at scale, and I thought we could use this as a tool to grow and to start my own company.

JR: Why is investing in global exploration and development critical today? How do companies like yours play a meaningful role in a cyclical market?

AC: I think that the industry has always been cyclical. As you've pointed out, industry has gone through a down cycle – a pretty substantial one. But it's one of many in its history. Regardless of current profitability and short term projected profitability, the need for energy is still growing. Historically, each down leg has been followed by an oil price increase, which presents an attractive investment environment. I don't see why this period of time should be any different.

JR: So, you're a Longhorn first, and then you completed an MBA at the Graduate School of Business. Why Stanford?

AC: Well, that's back there a ways in time. It's kind of a long and short story. The short one is that I saw it as a place that would give me exposure to a part of the country I hadn't really experienced before. The exposures, the network obviously. It is a tremendously reputable business school. I didn't realize it at the time how great it was, in all honesty. I'm so grateful I had the opportunity and could afford it. *Back then tuition was $5000 year!* I thought about law and business school, but I was inclined toward business. It was the best business school I could get into really.

JR: Congratulations on your drilling results in the Pannonian Basin of Hungary. There have been numerous articles in European and American news outlets following some of your discoveries with Hungarian Horizon and other companies. What was your team's inspiration for your exploration and development program in Hungary and neighboring countries?

AC: Really our inspiration was going to a country that had a relatively limited number of different companies pursing prior exploration. We started in the United States, but here you have thousands of companies, trying every combination of every idea to find oil and gas. But in Central Europe, exploration and development is restricted to essentially one government-owned company in a communist monopoly. These companies have very smart people, and they've discovered a lot of oil and gas. But there is a very important limitation that there is only one strong attitude – one philosophy – that is pursued.

And this is like the quote from Wallace Pratt, "Oil is found in the minds of men and women, first." And if those women and men are all in one company, the likelihood of them finding all the variability in exploration and development play types or prospects, is reduced. So, we thought Central Europe was the ideal place to go as a region that was dominated by state owned oil companies from the Soviet Era. I also felt like Central Europe has a great sense of "can do" and an orientation towards growth.

And if you go west from Central Europe, the environmental restrictions make it impossible to pursue oil and gas development. It's overly regulated in a certain way. And if you go east, it becomes much more difficult because the governments are more difficult to deal with. It's closed down and unfree. Central Europe is less guided by regulatory principles of the Euro, and of free and open markets. Central Europe is our Goldilocks region. Not too far east, and not too far west.

JR: It seems to me that successful companies are built with a vision, correct implementation of a strategy, adequate deal flow, deep subject matter knowledge – a lot of hard work to make smart investment decisions and probably a bit of luck – among other things. Can you describe what it has been like to grow your company to the size it is today?

AC: Certainly all of that is important. Obviously having a great team of people with expertise in their area of business is an absolutely necessary condition. Absolutely necessary. And having judgement as to where there is upside and downside to mitigate risk. Risk mitigation is absolutely the center of thinking for the successful company. We have to balance a whole series of risks – oil prices, leverage, exploration risk. Companies that manage those poorly go bankrupt. If they focus on that risk and take it on, hedge the risk that they don't know how to mitigate, those companies can withstand the test of time in our business.

That brings me to timing. With such a cyclical industry, timing is huge. And there are lots of examples of companies with success and *un-success*, having all those key elements, but they were unlucky or unskilled in working the timing. But you could also argue that learning the timing of cycles in our industry is tied to the notion of risk mitigation.

JR: If I remember correctly your original business was built upon the advantages provided by modern 3D seismic imaging technology in 1992, thereby providing Aspect a competitive edge in subsurface mapping and basin screening. Is that correct? Now, over decades, your team has assembled some of the largest 3D seismic data sets in your areas of interest (North America, Latin America, Europe, etc.). Can you tell us about more of your current and future seismic data acquisition programs? How else are you planning for the recovery in oil and gas prices?

AC: Right now, our primary focus is Central Europe. We have plans for additional data acquisition in Croatia, Hungary and Ukraine. And we're looking at other projects all the time. In the environment today when oil price is low, we also focus on reprocessing old seismic data volumes to squeeze more information out of them.

JR: Your leadership across the various roles in the industry – *as well as outside the industry* – is impressive. You serve on the Board of the Texas Medical Center and have served on the University of Texas Board of Regents. Can you share some of your key leadership and philanthropic principles?

AC: I've always believed in having a balance between family, business and civic life. These are the three legs of a stool that helps one maintain personal balance. And all three legs are important to reinforce each other. On the civic side, my primary interest is education. It is essential to prosperity and essential to the cohesion of a society. Part of the reason we have so much division is in part our education system has failed to enforce common values, and because of this failure, has promoted a lot of ignorance driving political agendas. Overall, this will be harmful.

JR: What would be your message to university students interested in making a career in the energy industry? You may have seen YouTube videos from professors that encourage students to take career paths outside of the energy industry.

AC: I think that there is a tremendous future for the energy industry. In every one of these cycles, they sound the death bell, and about 10 years later companies are bemoaning the talent gap in certain industry age groups. I understand oil and gas isn't necessarily the most fashionable industry. But if you're interested in fashion, you're probably in the wrong industry. Try fashion – or movies. But it you want to help people power their lives and achieve their way of life, you have to be able to ignore the naysayers. And I don't mean to completely ignore them, you should always be listening. But I understand a lot of people are going to be scared away, for better opportunities. For those who have the courage, it can be the right industry for you. We're going to be finding and producing a lot of oil and gas for years.

You mention energy, and in energy, there is a lot of work outside of oil and gas, or at the intersections of oil and gas and other energy forms. One thing is that these overlapping industries share a lot of common technical attributes. For instance, we're interested in geothermal, and the reservoir engineering skills required are very similar to what we apply to oil and gas. As an oil and gas company, we have some gaps compared to the geothermal companies, but also some very significant competitive advantages as well.

JR: You've been around a lot of oil and gas explorers for decades…you've seen some succeed, and some fail. What is your message for oil and gas explorers today?

AC: Let's get back to the risk pie, or the risk layer cake. If you're in the exploration business, you're in a business of taking on risk. Being able to intelligently take that risk is the most important skill set you can have. Commodity price risk and leverage risk you'd better understand, too. You can't be greedy. If you try to capture the price upside, and you leverage yourself to too great a degree, you're going to end up bankrupt, unless you're very, very lucky. You need to be able to take exploration risk while minimizing other risks and live long enough to have a diversified exploration outcome.

Avoid getting *100%-itis* which is a mindset in which explorers get so convinced their prospect is perfect. You need to bring partners in and go through the process of selling part of the prospect to partners, either at the equity level or asset level. You need to come to grips

The Explorer's Mindset

with the objections your partners make, that you're forced to hear even though you don't want to hear these objections. You need to deal with them, so you earn a position in that well. You need to learn to take in equity capital so you're not taking all the risk yourself. Obviously low-cost wells are easy to drill 100%. But then there are the big ones that you're sure are to be a homerun, and to make a massive discovery, so you put a substantial part of the exploration budget on it, and then you end up scratching your head with what turns out to be a dry hole. Nature has an infinite number of reasons and ways to humble you, particularly in the exploration business.

JR: Thank you so much Mr. Cranberg.

Above: Ventura Avenue Anticline, California, USA, home of the billion-barrel supergiant Ventura-San Miguelito-Rincon and offshore Carpinteria-Dos Cuadras oilfield trend. Center of the photo shows a key outcrop of the Plio-Pleistocene Pico Formation, one of the first formations known for production from turbidite reservoirs (mid-19th century by Josiah Stanford and others).

Benjamin Kirkland (June 2021)

"The most successful teams ...are led by empowered leadership teams who can and do trust their employees. And remember, it was the creative, crazy people who first dreamed up testing the older play, drilling below the salt, or extending the source rock map to the untested, adjacent basin!" – Benjamin Kirkland

Benjamin is currently with CNOOC International in Houston as a geologist focused on petroleum systems analysis and pore pressure prediction in North and South America. Prior to CNOOC, Benjamin spent a year as an exploration geologist with Fieldwood Energy from 2018-2019 where he worked deepwater Gulf of Mexico. He joined Fieldwood following his first professional role at Nexen Energy where he spent six years in training programs and working as a petroleum systems analyst for US GoM and international exploration. He holds a BS in geology from the University of Kentucky and a MS in geology from the University of New Orleans.

Benjamin Kirkland delivering the Kenneth E. Peters Honorary Lecture in Petroleum Geochemistry at the 72nd Annual GeoGulf Conference in Houston, Texas on April 25, 2023.

Benjamin Kirkland is one of the most knowledgeable professionals in the subjects of source rock and fluid systems in the oil and gas industry. In addition to his role in finding and assessing new petroleum accumulations around the world, he routinely is invited to share his achievements in oil and gas at industry and academic conferences, often as a keynote speaker. Kirkland teamed up with Andrew Pepper in 2020-2022 to write the definitive volume on deepwater source rocks and fluid systems for *Deepwater Sedimentary Systems: Science, Discovery and Applications*. I've seen Benjamin present numerous times at conferences, and every time Ben presents something new, interesting, impactful, and with big regional to global implications. I always enjoy learning from Benjamin, whether it is about petroleum systems in general, or more specifically dealing with deepwater exploration. Kirkland's in-depth knowledge of petroleum systems and the applications to deepwater drilling programs has inspired a new generation of oil and gas finders. I sat down with Benjamin Kirkland to learn about source rocks and petroleum systems analysis.

Jon Rotzien (JR): Benjamin, I'm so thankful you had the time to visit today and share your story. Could you share what led you to your current role?

Benjamin Kirkland (BK): Hey Jon, thanks for the invitation. I am currently in my tenth year in the industry and my seventh working full-time in petroleum systems analysis. I began my career out of graduate school with Nexen Energy in Houston in 2012, and, through my new graduate training program, I found quickly that I wanted to work with basin modeling and petroleum geochemistry. I found something so fascinating about using isotopes and biomarkers and phase behavior to let oil and gas tell us its story. I am one of a somewhat rare breed of petroleum systems folks who learned nearly everything after graduation, but it required a good three-or-so year period in which I spent *a lot* of time studying at work and at night. I am very fortunate that my managers were willing to invest in my pursuit, and I had an amazing opportunity to work one-on-one in a fit-for-purpose training program with a Weatherford OilTracers (now Stratum Reservoir) consultant for much of that time. As I began to take on more and more technical responsibility, I worked all plays in the deepwater GoM, some North Sea and West Africa evaluations, and, over the last few years, I have been working nearly every offshore petroleum province in the Americas.

JR: That's a fascinating voyage and excellent global experience. You've observed some price cycles. Energy stocks took up about~12% of the S&P 500 about a decade ago, now it's about 2%, yet oil and gas represents about 8% of the US GDP. How does the oil and gas industry navigate these difficult market conditions?

BK: Well, I am far from an expert in economics or finance, but I suspect that energy is really being punished for its perceived lack of growth potential. It seems that, in a bull market like this, investment dollars are willing to bet on large returns in emerging fields, and I think companies in the energy sector are getting a hefty discount despite their current contributions to the economy. Now, I know much more about navigating the oil and gas industry as an individual technical person than I do the markets, but our industry has some common themes all the way from the individual to the sector scale. I believe we need to focus principally on consistency and reliable delivery – exploration and production companies in particular. For the individual, that means clear goals, respected timelines, and thorough technical execution with internal/external clients, and, for companies, it means maintaining production, prospect/reserve replacement, and cost control. Because there will undoubtedly be tough economic times sooner or later, individuals, companies, and the entire sector would be smart to position themselves as lower-risk, proven, reliable options within their respective landscape. We all see that when it "hits the fan," investors rotate to value and managers go to their right-hand men. Oil and gas companies may never again see the multiples of ten years ago, but there will always be a place for reliable companies and their people that return value to stakeholders.

JR: I've seen you present several times and have learned so much every time, including the GCSSEPM Deepwater Symposium as part of GeoGulf in Houston in 2019 and the AAPG Annual Convention in 2020. What inspired you to undertake detailed studies of source rocks around the world, and in some of the most prolific Super Basins such as the Gulf of Mexico and offshore South America?

BK: To me, source rocks have an additional, fascinating facet that other rocks lack (at least in great quantity): their organic history. I fully appreciate the immense field of study in reservoir deposition and diagenesis, but there is just something about tracing source rocks back through their thermal history to deposition and organic production that draws me in. How cool is it that properties and chemical composition of petroleum we see today are a result – at least in part – of specific micro-organisms and plants in the geologic past?

JR: Very cool.

BK: As far as super basins, I just don't think things ever get much better than the Gulf of Mexico. The source rocks are prolific, the structures are astounding, and the complex migration and accumulation of hydrocarbons are downright wild at times. With that being said, the sheer size of accumulations offshore Brazil is very interesting, the new provinces in Guyana – MSGBC conjugate margin are exciting, and new ideas to extend the Upper Jurassic and OAE-associated Cretaceous source rocks are critical.

JR: Exciting opportunities brewing offshore South America and in the Gulf of Mexico today. A successful exploration team is built with a vision, strategy, deep knowledge – a lot of hard work to make smart drilling decisions and probably a bit of luck – among other things. Can you describe what you've seen in the successful exploration teams you've worked with?

BK: I have had the benefit of working in both specialist and team member roles, and I have seen quite a few teams across divisions and companies with different mandates. In my opinion, a well-rounded exploration team has personnel that can cover three key needs: creativity, experience, and execution. I would ask people to think of their teams – isn't there always one person coming up with creative, crazy ideas? And one person that has seen it all and has great perspective? And someone who works the details, knows the timelines, and helps to bring it all together? In bigger teams these could of course be several people and some people may fill multiple roles, but I believe that teams that can't cover those key needs are going to struggle. The most successful teams can cover all of these with smart, articulate people, and they are led by empowered leadership teams who can and do trust their employees. And remember, it was the creative, crazy people who first dreamed up testing the older play, drilling below the salt, or extending the source rock map to the untested, adjacent basin!

JR: You've had an opportunity to see Earth and its many resources with great perspective – early in your career. Many geoscientists can go decades without seeing the breadth and depth of basins that you have. Can you tell us more about what it takes to build "deep knowledge" in understanding sedimentary basin processes through some years of drilling, successes (as well as probably some failures)?

BK: I have indeed had the opportunity to work a number of basins in my career, but, first, I want to say that there is a huge amount of value from working one area in detail for years at a time. I have had the opportunity to work the Gulf of Mexico in at least some capacity for probably 80% of my career – both USA and Mexico, from Neogene to Jurassic, and from new ventures to operations. The work I have done in those detailed projects equipped me to approach other basins. So, to get back to your question, I can speak for myself and my methods. I always want to step back and look at some basin-scale seismic lines, because it is far too easy to fall into the trap of viewing reservoirs or source rocks as individual geologic units. By some definitions they are, but the porosity, pressure, fluid saturation, maturity, and all those other critical variables are a result on the rocks over- and underlying the unit of interest and fluids that flow through them. Development and production projects require the incredibly intimate knowledge of the reservoir architecture and its uncertainties, but exploration requires our neurons to connect with less hard data but many analogs. The burial history, onset of pressure, and basin-scale structural style are probably the key features I run through my mental algorithm, but I always want to know at least a high-level paleogeographic history and the context of the basin within key global source rock intervals.

JR: In my opinion, you're a great leader in this generation of petroleum systems analysts. You have a profoundly accurate grasp of the principles, merits and limitations of petroleum systems workflows and their value to any deepwater drilling program. Can you share some of your key leadership principles?

BK: For those of us on the younger side of the workforce working to carry the torch in our respective technical fields, we need first to be sure that we have a robust understanding of fundamentals. This ownership of the science is where leadership first comes in. It is our responsibility as the future of our fields to align ourselves and collaborate with the experienced generation that, in most cases, developed the modern concepts we take for granted. Leadership shows up next in our creativity: where does the roadmap take us next? It's ours to draw, and we need to collaborate across fields and leverage technology to ground-truth suspicions. Finally, we need to lead by the example of our execution. I use that word over and over because it is so critical. We can lead by owning the existing science and applying our novel ideas, but we have to see it through all the way until it is done. And that can be very hard. Let's think of our own projects – maybe a geoscientist can spend a month mapping seismic data for a stack of several maps. Is the work done? Maybe. But how much more effective is it when the geoscientist can deliver the maps with short documentation on the changes from previous attempts, the gross geologic inferences, and the limitations? And then stick with the maps as they go into QI workflows, rock physics models, basin models, etc? That – to me – is an example of thorough technical leadership in our field.

JR: You were a student not too long ago. What would be your message to students at universities interested in making a career in the energy industry?

BK: Times change, technologies change, the markets change, but I don't think people really change so much over generations. Young people now need to do what successful young people have always done in STEM fields: work hard to be as technically strong as possible, assert yourself but remain respectful, and create personal relationships.

JR: Great points. One more question if you still have some time. You've been around a lot of oil and gas explorers for about a decade...you've seen some succeed, and some fail. What is your message for oil and gas explorers today?

BK: We are at a time of uncertainty in our industry, and I think it's clear that the status quo for global energy supply is changing. On top of that, the way we work is shifting – decisions are augmented by artificial intelligence, data is more accessible than ever, and we can quantify our evaluations like never before. I don't believe any of this is flash-in-the-pan tech or buzzword science – this is the reality of where we are as humans. We still have the opportunity to own our future by reducing and capturing our emissions, planning to reduce cyclicity, and leveraging new technology to reduce because-I-said-so exploration. If we don't do these things, someone else will – and it probably won't be a very good deal for us. So, my message is that by remaining agile we can keep our industry relevant and responsible for a long time, and we should be prepared to show our work.

JR: Thank you so much Benjamin.

Above: Outcrops of the Cenomanian-Turonian Eagle Ford Group near Waco, Texas, USA. The Eagle Ford Group consists primarily of calcareous mudrock intervals and is divided into two formations, each comprised of two members. Of the four members, the Upper Member of the Lower Eagle Ford Formation is typically the most enriched in total organic carbon (Donovan et al., 2015), making it one of the ideal types of unconventional source rock reservoirs. The Eagle Ford Group was recently a focus of the 38th Annual GCSSEPM Foundation Perkins-Rosen Research Conference in Houston.

Ryan Weber (March 2021)

"To a geologist, time is the quintessential tool for correlation. Once a geologist knows the time, the rest of the correlation data can be calibrated. Many of our academic predecessors spent their careers researching geological events, especially sea level change, and tying them to time. Fossils and radiometric isotopes are the only geological data that is unique to time." – Ryan Weber

Ryan Weber is currently the President of Paleo-Data, Inc.; a biostratigraphic consulting firm serving the Oil & Gas sector for over 50 years. Ryan previously worked for BP as a Gulf of Mexico biostratigrapher. Ryan hails a BS and Education certificate from Minnesota State - Mankato, and an MS from the University of Nebraska - Lincoln. Ryan also served as the Earth Science Section Chair for the Nebraska Academy of Sciences. Ryan's career has applied biostratigraphy from onshore to deepwater Gulf of Mexico, the interior USA, Egypt Nile Delta, Northwest Australian shelf, offshore Mozambique, Colombia, Alaska, and the Spanish Pyrenees. Ryan's passions include Miocene and Wilcox stratigraphy, Mesozoic paleoceanography, the Minnesota Twins, nostalgic comedies, and fermentation.

Ryan Weber after presenting a deepwater reservoir workshop at the International Meeting of Applied Geoscience and Energy (IMAGE) in Houston, Texas (August 2022).

To be one of the best biostratigraphers in the world takes at least a decade of training and at least another decade of experience in basins around the world. It amazes me still that new intervals in relatively well explored basins continue to provide unusual paleontological information. With this information, however, provides some of the most influential data when it comes to determining age of the strata. The biostratigrapher's interpretation can be paramount when drilling wildcat to development wells. A relatively small price for biostratigraphic information can reduce the chances of making a stratigraphic mistake that could cost the company tens to hundreds of millions of dollars. Ryan and I were colleagues at BP years ago. Since that time, Ryan Weber has grown to become one of the most influential leaders in the field of biostratigraphy. There are few places he hasn't worked offshore. He manages a team of biostratigraphers, conducts day-to-day business as President, and still manages to find time to give back significantly to the industry and the younger generation. He has presented several times to my students at different Gulf Coast universities. It is always so interesting to listen and learn from Ryan. He is not only gifted at leading one of the top companies in the industry sector, he is talented at creating enjoyable and collaborative work environments through his friendly and genuine nature. Perhaps it's because of his many interests outside of the oil sector that make him so approachable for all of us, despite a highly technical and scientific method of interpreting nannofossils for age dating. Most industry geoscientists agree that interpreting biostratigraphic data is one of the more difficult, yet highly valuable, tasks in upstream geoscience. Ryan has a gift for translating this information to make clearer business decisions. I've been very fortunate to get to work with Ryan on several projects, most recently a course on leadership in the energy industry for the IMAGE '23 conference in Houston.

In March 2021, I sat down with Ryan Weber while he was President of Paleo-Data, Inc. to learn about biostratigraphic interpretation in deepwater petroleum fields around the world. Read the interview below.

Jon Rotzien (JR): Ryan, thank you for your time and visit today. You've had a variety of exciting roles so far in your career – from delivering technical reports on drill ships in frontier exploration plays to leading one of the world's most prominent biostratigraphy businesses.

Could you share your background and what led you to your current role?

Ryan Weber (RW): I went into the independent consultant scene right after school. Paleo-Data, the company I currently oversee, approached me while I was still in school at Nebraska. They gave me the opportunity to examine samples, go offshore, meet with their clients, and even talk with competitors. It was a whirlwind meeting everyone, seeing samples from exotic places beyond the USA; like Egypt, Mozambique and Australia. I guess BP noticed and valued the experience and approached me about a position in their GoM Development team. As a consultant and still quite green, I yearned to understand more about how my clients were using the data I was generating. It is a fulltime job just to generate and interpret this data. Then, it often felt like the data or interpretation went off into this void; never to return; because I was off to the next project or rig. I received positive feedback, for which I was grateful. As a consultant, though, the opportunity to understand the impact biostrat had to operations or development was rare. I knew it did, and I wanted to peek behind the curtain!

JR: So how did BP finally get you in the door?

RW: When BP approached me and teased the idea of an integrated team where I'd be a specialist sitting next to the geologist, geophysicist, engineers, and other specialists; I felt it was an experience too good to pass. The timing was perfect. Plus, they said I could still spend some time on analytical projects, and still generate my own data. It was great experience. I learned very quickly how the tiny little fossils affected multi-million-dollar decisions from daily drilling decisions to site facility questions; like where to put pipelines or mooring anchors. The diversity of expertise that goes into these projects is astonishing, to me. With diversity comes a diversity of personalities, which was also a valued learning experience for me. I'm very grateful to all the people who I have worked with and provided an opportunity to follow my love of learning.

Now, being back with Paleo-Data, as President, it is my turn to provide the very same opportunities for the next generation. Plus, I like to think I'm still helping majors, like BP, and independents by providing specialized data/advice and training future practitioners of the science.

JR: Energy stocks took up about~12% of the S&P 500 about a decade ago. Now it's about 2%, yet oil and gas represents about 8% of the US GDP as some CEOs have recently mentioned. Why is investing in global exploration critical today? How does your company navigate the current market?

RW: Long-term investment is the key. The barrels we produce today keep the lights on. Any profit should be reinvested to make sure we can keep the lights on tomorrow. It's pretty amazing when I came out of school, we were debating about peak oil. Operators responded with new shale technology and continued conventional exploration. Now we are debating peak demand.

JR: How does your company approach this challenge?

RW: As a small, specialized company privately owned by employees, we base our decisions on long-term trends; and just survive these short-term trends. I do worry about retaining future practitioners as there are other sectors that laborers could go in, especially in New Orleans. We are passionate about what we do, which gives us a sense of resiliency and flexibility. We understand the trends and respond as the market does. This downturn sped up many of our plans we had for the "Great Crew-Change." I have to commend our predecessors and our current staff on their resiliency and devotion to their trade.

My message to our staff has remained unchanged since becoming President in 2017: we have to market our science, not just our company. We have to upgrade or tweak our products to adjust to our clients' ever-changing needs.

JR: How are you using some new techniques or methods to achieve this goal?

RW: Currently, digitization is a hot topic. We're making old data new again just by digitizing it, and making it more accessible through the cloud or online data portals. We are consulting with operators in their (virtual) offices on grading and (de)risking their prospects as they integrate with other data. We are finding ways for our staff to be in multiple places at once with digital microscopy and photography. We are finding new ways to illustrate and analyze our data through mapping and index algorithms.

We are also partnering with other service providers like mud loggers and geochemists to provide integrated products. One that I'm particularly excited about is partnering with geochemists and running x-ray fluorescence and stable isotope stratigraphy to provide a highly resolved stratigraphy. These efforts are based on clients' feedback and experience to make their workflows simpler and more efficient.

JR: Truly fascinating how that technology has helped your company serve clients better during these challenging times.

I understand that you're teaching one of your signature short courses for Houston Geological Society in March. I remember taking one of your courses a few years ago, and I came away with a thick notebook of principles on how biostratigraphy can be applied to understand geologic risk, limit uncertainty and properly plan exploration to development wells and assess their performance. Can you explain why it is so important to understand the utility of biostratigraphic analysis in E&P drilling?

RW: Thank you for that feedback, Jon. Biostratigraphy is another tool in the toolbox. It can be designed to fit the purpose. I often refer to paleontologists and biostratigraphers as the "keepers of time." Imagine trying to get through your day without referring to a watch or calendar. I also joke that it is one of those types of data that once you have it, one thinks they do not need it. Just like how one only refers to a watch when they are not confident in their sense of time.

To a geologist, time is the quintessential tool for correlation. Once a geologist knows the time, the rest of the correlation data can be calibrated. Many of our academic predecessors spent their careers researching geological events, especially sea level change, and tying them to time. Fossils and radiometric isotopes are the only geological data that is unique to time.

JR: Absolutely, biostratigraphy underpins many of our correlation techniques in deepwater. How broad are the applications?

RW: Biostratigraphy also gives clues to the reservoir engineer as fossils are also sediment. While still alive, these organisms lived in a specific paleo-environment. It takes a bit of detective work to rationalize how the fossil we observe today got to that particular rock at depth. That detective work helps sedimentologists and engineers predict what sort of porosity and permeability (or lack thereof) they might expect based on depositional environment or style. Still, I'm a huge advocate for rock core or image logs for corroboration.

JR: That is so awesome. In fact, when you visited University of Louisiana in 2017 to give a short course and shared with the hardworking students some key tips, several of them mentioned how much they appreciated your expert advice on their way to winning another AAPG IBA world championship.

You have so many experiences to share. Can you tell us one of your favorite stories about how biostratigraphic analysis was used to provide value in a deepwater drilling program?

RW: I was ecstatic to hear about that ULL team. Congrats to them and their hard work. I have so many favorite stories that it is hard to choose. Most of them involve testing a 3-way structure against salt; and the operator does not encounter any coarse-grained material at the depth predicted from their seismic anomaly. We come in, sometimes onsite at the rig, and tell the operator that they aren't there yet, suggesting their velocity model may need adjusting; or they drilled past their chronostratigraphic target, suggesting their anomaly pinches out. In the latter case, drilling down dip usually ends up a success.

JR: How great is that thrill of discovery! And what about some of the other challenges?

RW: There are also the scenarios in development where efficiency is scrutinized more than in exploration. Biostrat is usually scrapped in an effort to reduce cost, and correlation is in high confidence. Then, there's the unexpected sub-seismic fault that messes up the plan. I never knew what a completion sump was until one of these faults shortened the geologic section a borehole experienced. The section was shortened so much that there was not enough room for a completion sump to the extent that the perforation tool couldn't be used. The operator had to re-rill the borehole. While biostrat couldn't predict the fault, we noticed it right away so they could place the redrill borehole in the correct area.

JR: There are so many ways biostrat can be used to inform business decisions.

Ryan, a successful company is built with a vision, correct implementation of a strategy, adequate deal flow, deep subject matter knowledge – and probably a bit of luck – among other things. Your company comes to mind as one of those highly successful companies. Can you describe what it takes to be a successful leader in the biostratigraphy market?

RW: Customer service is key. I quote Mark Cuban often, who says something like this, "Always be selling. To be the best, put yourself in your customers' shoes and solve their problems. Don't just pitch your product." Interestingly, I led an *ad hoc* mini-retreat with our technical staff recently.

JR: How was the retreat?

RW: The main themes that came out of that retreat were 1) *Passion:* Spending time doing what we love will get us through these economic downturns. With such a specialized skill that supports a fluid commodity, you have to love what you do in order to get through the economic slow times. 2) *Fear:* There is good fear, like the fear of touching a hot stove; and then there is the paralyzing fear of financial risk. Many Yoda quotes came up in the discussion and we identified where we wanted to go while also noting which projects were deemed too risky. That allows us to 3) *Focus* so we can be efficient with our time and capital. Lastly, we noticed the value of 4) *Networking*. We see networking more like farming than hunting. It is about planting those seeds and let them germinate rather than trying to land that big sale. Hence, we invest in these client educational opportunities.

You bring up luck. I'm a fan of research papers that feature the role of luck in geologic success in frontier exploration. In those papers, there's a side note that the "luckiest" operators are those that are involved in the most projects. This is the ol' gamblers axiom that persistence is the only way to overcome luck. Of this, I'm a firm believer, especially when it comes to networking. We plant as many seeds as we can because we don't always know which ones will germinate.

JR: And yet you somehow still find time to follow the Twins, make comedy and brew? What is brewing this season?

RW: One must have hobbies. My love of learning got me into homebrewing. There is lots of science and methodology (and some engineering) in brewing. I'm pretty boring though, usually with a pilsner or lager in the brew shop. The beverage industry seems to be moving away from alcoholic beverages, so now I'm experimenting with wort-soda or Malta. That is, no fermentation and no alcohol. The natural sugar of the malted barley and hops flavor the beverage. It tastes like Iced Tea and hop varieties now mimic any flavor imaginable. If this catches on, I may have to describe my hobby a bit differently. Although, I'm told my infatuation with homemade sauerkraut is a bit unusual.

JR: How can people purchase some of your homemade products? You mention hobbies are excellent for building rapport.

RW: I find hobbies are an excellent networking opportunity. Hobbies are another way to find common ground with someone you wouldn't otherwise suspect. I think that's why deals are made on the golf course or at the athletic club.

JR: You also like to tell jokes. Do you have any oil and gas related jokes for us today?

RW: I usually tell the old ones people heard already, like the Eiffel Tower joke. However, my wife recently pointed out that geologists are biased towards ROCK when playing Rochambeau. I guess that's why I am doing the majority of the house chores. I thought that was pretty funny.

JR: Good point. I should try paper and scissors more often. It seems a little humor can go a long way in technical committee meetings.

You also serve in other areas, such as your experience as Chair of the Earth Sciences for the Nebraska Academy of Sciences. Can you share some of your key leadership or management principles?

RW: To be honest, Jon, I have never thought of myself as a leader. I just have a hard time saying "no." To me, leadership is pretty simple: someone has to make a decision. The best leaders have a clear crystal ball or divining rod that can see the future.

Joking aside, I view leadership quite humbly. I surround myself with experienced hard-workers and a diversity of thought, which gives me numerous viewpoints and data on which to rationalize a decision. This will sound cliché: listening to this diversity of thought is important. Listening means to understand, not just hear. I often say that one doesn't truly understand a concept until one has to teach it. I try to give opportunities for myself/staff/students/family to teach or explain an important concept, because that gives me/them a listening experience.

Listening to a diversity of thought is a challenge because the viewpoints will conflict. To me, the best leaders listen to all viewpoints and decide the best route. Not everyone will agree with the decision, but they choose the best avenue with the data they had at the time. A clear crystal ball or divining rod doesn't exist, so all one can do is surround themselves with as much data as economically possible. Which brings me to the next thing: creating a safe space for people to fail.

JR: How do you do that?

RW: We learn from failure. Take walking, for example. We fall and fall until suddenly our brain and muscles learn to work together. It was so frustrating helping my daughter learn to walk. We could guide and help as much as we could, but we soon realized that we were enabling her to be dependent on us for transport. We had to keep telling ourselves, "Let her figure it out. She has to learn herself. We cannot do it for her." We created a safe environment for her to waltz and bumble around. This allowed her to experiment at her own pace. We had to put cotton in our ears when she would whine for assistance. We gave her rewards for progress. Then, seemingly out of nowhere, it happens like a miracle and the pride just emanates.

I've read many biographies and stories about successful business moguls: Gates, Allen, Jobs, Bezos, Cuban, Pickens, Moffet, Iacocca, and Perot. The common theme is that they were all passionate. Perhaps a bit obsessed. AND...they all made mistakes along the way. They picked themselves back up (i.e., persistence), learned from those mistakes, and identified how to minimize those risks in their next endeavor. Is that luck?

JR: Sounds like persistence, grit and learning from mistakes rather than luck.

What would be your message to students interested in making a career in the energy industry? You may have seen YouTube videos from professors that encourage students to take career paths outside of the energy industry.

RW: That reminds me of the scene in Ghostbusters where Ray tells Peter, who has just been sacked from professing, "You have never been in the private sector. They expect results." Likewise, several professors, outside of Nebraska, advised me as a graduate student that there was no future in paleontology and I should just become a geophysicist.

If you are passionate, flexible, and a hard-worker, there are opportunities. It is no lie that energy is a tough sector for employment now. Set your expectations realistically. I still see some entry-level positions advertised, so companies are still willing to invest in labor.

My advice is to consider the opportunity given to you. It is probably not going to be the one you want, especially right out of school. Consider what you hope to gain and learn from the experience and how that adds to your goals and aspirations. Sometimes those goals change. It certainly did for me.

To quote Gandalf or JRR Tolkien, "All we have to dec¨
do with the time given to us."

JR: You need to join our New Zealand field course if you're a Lord of the Rings fan. Have you worked some of the turbidite reservoirs in the Taranaki Basin?

RW: It's on my bucket list, Jon. Both as a geologist and as a huge fan of Middle Earth. I would love to have some 'elevenses' in Edoras while talking about turbidites.

JR: What is your message for oil and gas explorers today?

RW: That is such an interesting question, Jon. As a consultant, one sees the gambit of exploration process. I have witnessed operators who just find an amplitude and drill it. I have also witnessed operators who have a lengthy assurance process to high-grade their prospects with much scrutiny and resources. Both have about the same amount of success. I think recent research papers corroborate my observation.

During downturns, many companies re-evaluate their leases and grade their prospects. We, biostratigraphers, get pulled in to help integrate the biostratigraphy, so we have opportunities to see some of these prospects. I must say, Jon, there's lots of creativity out there. Some of these ideas are so simple, that you get that "Why didn't I think of that?" moment. As an outside consultant, I usually get excited about the simple ideas rather than the big risk, big reward ideas. Still, I am impressed about the number of these bright and ingenious prospects.

I find that what sets successful explorers apart is that they (and their middle management) know how to deal with the fear of failure. They know how to interpret their data without bias and minimize their risk. Recognizing and calling out one's bias is often contentious, which I've witnessed more than I'd like to admit. However, those contentious debates end up creating success for those explorers. So, Jon, my advice comes down to listening to multiple viewpoints and considering opportunities. Sometimes, it just comes down to persistence.

JR: Thank you so much Ryan.

Above: View from a Māori settlement known as a pā overlooking the black sands of Pukearuhe Beach and the Tasman Sea, North Island, New Zealand. Pukearuhe Beach is one of the prime outcrop locales to sample and observe biostratigraphic zonation in deepwater slope deposits of the Miocene Mount Messenger Formation and is located approximately 40 km (25 mi) northeast of New Plymouth. This channel–levee and overbank succession is comprised chiefly of turbidites and extends into the subsurface of the Taranaki Basin where it has been a producing interval in several oil and gas fields for decades. Today, the deepwater Miocene outcrops exposed along the coast of the Taranaki Basin serve as valuable analogues for other fine-grained, heterolithic, poorly indurated, litharenite petroleum reservoirs around the world.

Closing Conversations

As you've read from these explorers in the fields of applied geoscience and the greater energy industry, leadership can take many forms. Leadership adapts to the wide variety of situations requiring inspiration, vision, discipline and execution. Leadership is required in the boardroom, on the rig, in the field and in the classroom.

The Explorer's Mindset is unique in that it requires certain skills and deftness that would get one fired from another job. Technical expertise, problem solving, business acumen, tenacity and grace, and optimism are required to create future opportunities. If it has been done before, it's not exploration. Armed with these skills, explorers across the fields of geoscience and the energy industry find new resources, new scientific discoveries and new methods of analyzing and interpreting Earth.

There are many important things about leadership in the geosciences and broader energy industry. *What is the most important thing?* It depends what you want to do. If it's to maximize value, it's probably a correct assessment of the value of the natural resources in place and the business opportunity. If it's academic, it's the impact of the study. If it's government, it would probably be the greatest good for the greatest number of people. If you're a student, it would be to maximize the educational experience to prepare you for the greatest potential impact (value added) in your career.

This book interviews a small fraction of the successful leaders in the energy industry and geosciences today. There are many people who could provide sage information and demonstrate what it takes to win in industry, academia and government challenges today. Get to know them.

How will leadership differ in 10, 20, 50, 100 years versus today? Chances are most of the leadership principles will remain relevant, but they will look different in their application as the nature of human demands evolve. One thing we know: we will need energy to support a growing population.

On behalf of the entire team that made this volume possible, thank you for your interest in exploration and leadership in the geosciences. I hope these conversations provided a fresh and empowering perspective for your own leadership development to help you help teams and help humanity thrive.

Above: After a long hike at altitude, applied geologists are greeted by superb outcrops of the Eocene-Oligocene Annot Sandstone at Le Grand Coyer near Peyresq, France.

About the Interviewer/ Author

Jonathan Rotzien is President of Basin Dynamics and Adjunct Professor at University of Houston. He specializes in reservoir presence and quality forecasting in conventional and unconventional drilling programs. Prior to his present posts, he served BP and other supermajor and independent operators in a variety of basins and petroleum reservoir technical training programs. As a business owner and scientist, Rotzien has participated in oil and gas exploratory to development drilling, mapping expeditions, technical competency training and consulting and has served as lead geologist in about one-third of those ventures. He is currently Chair of the Houston Explorers Club. Rotzien received a Ph.D. in Geological Sciences from Stanford University and a B.A. degree in Geology from Colorado College.

Printed in Great Britain
by Amazon